PADDLE FORWARD

TEAMING IN THE AGE OF AI

PAT BODIN

WITH

ROBERT SCHAFFNER

LOUIS BODIN

Published by Red Queen Press

redqueenpress.com

ISBN 978-1-971173-00-9

Cover design and interior art by Jinny Seo

First edition, February 2026

Printed in the United States of America

paddleforward.com

CONTENTS

To Shiloh and Max

FOREWORD

TIM COOGAN

We've invested in AI with good tools and real capabilities, and it's not producing what we expected.

The technology works, but something isn't clicking. Teams use the tools and don't get results. Customers are frustrated. Partners are frustrated. I'm frustrated.

I've known Pat Bodin for more than twenty-five years, and Pat sees around corners the way few people do. When he told me he was writing a book about why AI-augmented teams fail, I paid attention. When he told me it was going to involve boats again, I had to laugh. Pat really likes his whitewater metaphors. But here's the thing: the image of a crew navigating rapids, reading conditions, making calls in real time actually captures what leading a team through AI adoption feels like. You can't stop the river to figure it out.

I was reading the part where Pat asks a simple question: Is the right knowledge in the loop? That's where I stopped.

My own team struggles to use AI in a way that provides real clarity for our customers and partners. We know things about them that aren't in any system, and that knowledge isn't getting into the workflow.

Naming the problem is easy. Pat shows you what to do about it.

Pat organizes the book around four moves: Read the Water, Know Your Crew, Call Your Line, Remember the Run. It's a simple framework with a lot of depth behind it. Pat did the research on how teams actually work, why they fail, what the science says, and how AI mixes everything up. Then he runs it all through a team at a logistics company figuring out the same things we are. Marcus and his crew make the dense parts stick.

What the book gave me was a reframe.

I've been treating our AI struggles as a technology problem: better tools, better prompts, better integrations. Pat's argument is different. Most AI failures aren't AI failures at all. They're team failures that AI makes visible.

That landed hard, because when I think about where we're stuck, it's not the technology. It's whether the right knowledge is getting into the workflow and whether the team can do something with what AI gives them. The tools work. The question is whether we've built the conditions to use them.

Pat built something real here. I wish I'd had it two years ago. Read it before your next AI initiative.

Tim Coogan SVP,
Global Partner Sales,
Cisco

INTRODUCTION

Eight years ago, I would have confidently declared myself a technologist who understood business. I had the credentials to prove it: CPA, CCIE, Lean Six Sigma Black Belt. I'd built companies, sold them, and helped thousands of IT professionals find relevance in their organizations. I thought I had the map figured out.

The transformation came when I realized I'd been reading that map upside down. I'm not a technologist who understands business. I'm a business leader who wields technology with purpose. This isn't semantic gymnastics. When you see yourself as a technologist first, you optimize for technical excellence: uptime, efficiency, elegant code. When you see yourself as a business leader who uses technology, you optimize for impact. You measure success by market share gained, customer satisfaction improved, competitive advantages secured.

This shift in perspective changed everything about how I approach my work. It also changed what I noticed about teams struggling to navigate a world that had shifted beneath them.

When I wrote *Get in the Boat* in 2018, I was focused on helping technologists earn their seat at the table. The framework worked. IT departments transformed from cost centers to enablers. Technologists moved from the trailing raft into the lead boat.

Then 2020 happened.

The River Disappeared

In March 2020, the river we'd been navigating didn't just change course; it seemed to evaporate entirely. One day we were perfecting our positions in the boat, the next day there was no boat to share. Conference rooms became rectangles on screens. Water cooler conversations turned into Slack threads. The informal networks that actually run organizations—the lunch invitations, the hallway observations, the ability to read a room. All of it vanished overnight.

I watched teams I'd helped unite scatter across kitchen tables and spare bedrooms. The foundations of effective teaming—trust, healthy conflict, commitment, accountability, results—had always depended on proximity in ways we'd never had to articulate. Suddenly we had to articulate them. And we discovered we didn't know how.

But here's what fascinated me: some teams didn't just survive this dissolution. They thrived. They discovered something that challenged everything I thought I knew about how teams function.

Three Transformations

Three changes had converged, and they were interacting in ways nobody had mapped.

The pandemic didn't just move work home; it deleted the infrastructure of collective intelligence: the millions of micro-interactions that transmitted knowledge and maintained cohesion. We called this remote work and argued about productivity metrics, but the real loss was harder to measure.

Meanwhile, the average enterprise had gone from a handful of software tools to well over a hundred, each promising efficiency while collectively creating fragmentation. Workers reported "tool fatigue" even as they reported feeling less productive. The tools were multiplying faster than our ability to integrate them.

Then, in November 2022, ChatGPT arrived, and suddenly everyone had access to an intelligence that could write code, analyze data, and hold conversations that felt remarkably human. The very nature of work, what humans do versus what machines do, shifted again.

These three transformations didn't politely wait their turn. They arrived together, and the frameworks we'd built weren't designed for the combination.

From Observer to Architect

In the spring of 2023, my own journey took an unexpected turn. I was recruited to serve as Global AI Architect and Evangelist for one of the world's largest tech companies. Suddenly, I wasn't just observing the AI transformation; I was helping to architect it.

This role gave me a front-row seat to how enterprises worldwide were grappling with AI integration. I worked with Fortune 500 leaders who were simultaneously excited and terrified. I guided teams through their first human-AI collaboration projects. I watched brilliant technologists become obsolete not because they lacked skills, but because they refused to evolve how they worked.

More importantly, I discovered patterns regarding which approaches worked, which failed spectacularly, and why. The successful organizations weren't the ones with the biggest AI budgets or the most sophisticated models. They were the ones that understood AI as neither a team member nor a tool, but something in between. They built frameworks for human-AI collaboration that amplified both human judgment and machine capability.

The Authenticity Paradox

But I also developed a healthy fear, one shared by many leaders I worked with. As AI becomes more sophisticated, there's a creeping inauthenticity that threatens the very essence of human collaboration.

I've watched teams delegate not just tasks, but critical thinking to AI. I've seen relationships reduced to perfectly crafted but emotionally hollow messages. I've observed "collaboration" that's really just humans serving as intermediaries between AI systems.

This fear isn't about AI taking our jobs. It's about AI taking our humanity. When every email is polished by AI, every presentation enhanced by algorithms, every decision supported by machine learning, where does authentic human connection live? When AI can simulate empathy, generate creativity, and even mimic humor, how do we maintain genuine human bonds?

The answer isn't to reject AI. The answer is to be intentional about when we use AI to amplify our humanity versus when we let it replace it. AI can help you analyze data faster, but it shouldn't be the one offering condolences to a colleague who's lost a parent. It can help draft a strategy, but it shouldn't be the sole source of vision that inspires a team.

This book wrestles with this paradox directly. How do we embrace AI's capabilities while preserving authentic human connection? How do we build teams that are both augmented and genuine?

The Team You'll Follow

The story you're about to follow is fiction, but it's built from observation.

Marcus Chen and his team at Consolidated Logistics are composites assembled from the real teams I watched navigate these changes during my time as an AI evangelist. The patterns are real. The struggles, the failures, the victories: all real. I've changed names and specifics, but the patterns should be familiar.

I've tried to be honest about what this transition requires. The teams that succeed in these pages earn it. So do the teams that fail. Some approaches work; others look promising and collapse under pressure. I've included both, because false comfort helps no one navigate real water. This isn't a book of easy wins. It's a book about a path forward. It's a path that requires more from you than the old playbooks did, but one that actually accounts for the world as it now exists.

Who This Book Is For

This book is for three types of professionals, all facing the same turbulent waters but from different positions.

If you're a technologist or STEM professional who implemented *Get in the Boat* principles, you've earned your relevance but sense the ground shifting again. You see AI not as a threat but as a force that needs orchestration. You're ready to evolve from being relevant to being essential.

If you're a business leader struggling to navigate distributed teams and AI integration, you need frameworks that go beyond traditional management theory. Your challenges aren't just about remote work policies or AI adoption. They're about maintaining team cohesion and authenticity while embracing transformation.

If you're an organizational architect, whether in HR, operations, or transformation roles, tasked with building the workplace of the future, you need more than best practices. You need principles that work whether your team is in one room or spread across continents, whether your colleagues are all human or include artificial intelligence.

The common thread: you recognize that the old maps no longer match the territory.

PADDLE FORWARD

The title of this book is a promise and a challenge.

Get in the Boat was about earning your place in the vessel: proving your relevance, learning the language of business, connecting tactical work to strategic value.

Paddle Forward acknowledges that the river itself has changed. The boat we worked so hard to board is now scattered across continents and time zones. The paddle we learned to wield is now shared with artificial intelligence; some of our fellow paddlers aren't human at all. It's not enough to just be in the boat; now you must be able to paddle in unison. Paddling forward means maintaining momentum even when you can't see the others clearly, even when the current behaves in unfamiliar ways, even when your own role in the vessel keeps shifting.

Twelve years ago, over a decent rosé in Paris, Robert Schaffner and I spent four hours discussing meaning and relevance in work. That conversation eventually led to *Get in the Boat*. Last month, we met again, him in Vienna, me in Florida, our AI assistants taking notes and suggesting connections we might have missed.

The irony wasn't lost on us. Here we were, demonstrating the very transformation we'd been studying. Distributed yet connected. Human yet augmented. The same passion for relevance and meaning but expressed through entirely new channels. And despite the AI assistance, our conversation retained its authenticity. The technology amplified our collaboration without replacing the human spark that started this journey over a decade ago.

This book asks more of you than *Get in the Boat* did. Our first book asked you to change how you communicate. This one asks you to change how you work alongside intelligence that isn't human. That book asked you to earn your individual seat; this one asks you to help build new kinds of vessels entirely.

The price is higher, but so is the promise. The professionals who master distributed teaming, AI partnership, and preserved authenticity won't just be relevant. They'll be essential. They won't just have a seat at the table. They'll be designing new tables altogether.

The river has changed. The crew has changed. The nature of paddling itself has changed.

Let's follow Marcus's team as they learn to paddle forward.

Pat Bodin

2025

PART I

READ THE WATER

1

THE RIVER HAS CHANGED

FROM CLASS 5 TO UNCHARTED WATERS

Marcus Chen had what you might call a typical Tuesday morning realization that his entire career was pointless. Not in the dramatic, throw-your-laptop-out-the-window way. More in the quiet, sip-your-coffee-and-stare-at-the-Zoom-grid way that has become the signature existential crisis of our times. He sat the way he always did in these meetings: straight-backed, still, watching.

His team meeting had been going for exactly 23 minutes. He knew this because Zoom helpfully displays a timer, presumably so you can watch your life tick away in real-time. Sarah Walsh was explaining why their latest pivot (the third this quarter) was actually a good thing, her hands moving between keyboard and trackpad even as she talked. She'd sent a pre-read document that nobody had read, scheduled this meeting across four time zones, and was now doing the work of translating between engineering's concerns, operational constraints, and leadership's expectations in real time. This was Sarah's actual job: holding context nobody else held, translating between groups that spoke different languages, making coordination look natural.

Derek Shaw was clearly playing Wordle, phone under the desk, his eyes doing that telltale up-down flutter. Lin Wei had her camera off. She'd been at Consolidated Logistics for eighteen months, since the acquisition, and Marcus still wasn't sure if this was a bandwidth issue, a preference, or a holdover from her previous company's culture, where cameras-off had been the norm. He'd never asked. She did her job well. The camera thing felt like a small battle not worth fighting.

Priya Desai wasn't on the call at all. It was 11 PM in Mumbai, and while she'd joined late-night calls before, this particular meeting had been scheduled without checking her time zone. Marcus had noticed this after the invite went out and decided not to make it awkward by pointing it out. She'd catch up from the notes. She always did.

Miles Carter, the newest addition, was the only one who looked engaged, nodding along, occasionally typing notes. He'd been hired three months ago specifically for the AI integration initiative, plucked from somewhere that had "digital transformation" in its mission statement. He was good at his job in ways that made Marcus feel old: he could produce a polished deck in an hour, synthesize a dozen reports before lunch, do things with AI tools that the rest of them were still figuring out. He was also twenty-five and had never worked anywhere without AI in the workflow. Marcus sometimes wondered what Miles saw when he looked at the rest of them.

"Maybe we need better project management software," Derek suggested, apparently having finished today's Wordle.

Sarah's response came with the weariness of someone who's had this conversation before: "We have seven project management tools. We use approximately 1.3 of them." She wasn't wrong. Marcus had personally set up accounts for Asana (used for two weeks), Monday.com (one month), Notion (still technically active but mostly for storing PDFs no one would read), Jira (which had somehow become sentient and now generated tickets on its own), Slack (494 unread messages), Teams (because IT insisted), and something called ClickUp that he was pretty sure was a fever dream.

The thing is, Marcus's team wasn't incompetent. Sarah had been featured in Forbes's "30 Under 30," though she was now 34 and hoping for "40 Under 40" to maintain the illusion of youth. Derek's code was genuinely elegant; he once reduced their API response time by 73% just to prove a point in a Slack argument. Lin had that rare combination of strategic thinking and actual execution ability that most management consultants wish they had.

They'd all found their individual relevance. They were all, by any reasonable metric, crushing it.

Except for the minor detail that their company was falling apart.

Consolidated Logistics was a $3 billion company that had never owned a truck. They were orchestrators: connecting shippers to carriers, managing warehouses, coordinating the invisible complexity that moved products from factory floors to store shelves. The company had Oakland roots going back to the 1970s containerization boom, but private equity had bought them six years ago with a different vision, one that would roll up regional players, add AI, and leapfrog the giants. Four acquisitions in three years. New leadership. A transformation mandate with teeth. Marcus had been hired nine months ago to make the AI part work. So far, the dashboards said he was succeeding.

The new routing system Marcus had championed was hitting every target. Yet, customer complaints were rising.

His phone buzzed. A text from his daughter Zoe: *dad look what i did lol*

The link opened to an operational teardown of their biggest regional competitor. Warehouse locations pieced together from job postings. Carrier partnerships inferred from LinkedIn connections and press releases. Service gaps in the Midwest where their coverage was thin. The kind of competitive intelligence that would take someone weeks to assemble from public breadcrumbs, if they knew where to look.

How long did this take? he texted back, already knowing the answer would hurt.

idk like 30 mins? claude and i just kept asking each other questions until it looked right.

Claude. Not ChatGPT, because apparently his daughter was an AI hipster.

~

There's a specific type of graph that business books love to show. You know the one: hockey stick growth, exponential curves, "disruption" represented by lines crossing dramatically. That graph won't help us. Instead, let's talk about three things that hit one after another before anyone could process the first.

Transformation One: We Accidentally Abolished the Office

On March 13, 2020, Marcus—two jobs ago, a different world—packed up his laptop and a monitor, told his team they'd "reconnect Monday," and drove home. He remembers thinking it would be like a snow day. Maybe a snow week. Two weeks to flatten the curve, they said, which in retrospect was like saying "just one more episode" when starting a Netflix series at 11 PM. Just a minor rapid to navigate.

Before 2020, remote work was what people did when they had a dentist appointment. About 5% of knowledge workers were fully remote, mostly people who wrote C++ and had strong opinions about mechanical keyboards. By 2022, depending on whose statistics you trust (and you shouldn't trust any of them completely), somewhere between 35% and 58% of knowledge workers were remote at least half the time.[1]

But here's the part nobody talks about: we didn't just move work home. We accidentally deleted the entire infrastructure of collective intelligence.

The office, it turns out, wasn't just about the free snacks. It was the millions of micro-interactions that we never noticed. The coffee line conversation where someone mentions a problem and someone else says "Oh, have you tried..." The whiteboard that accumulated ideas the way a coral reef accumulates life. The ability to see that Jeremy looks stressed and maybe we shouldn't dump more work on him today.

Anthropologist Joseph Henrich has this theory that humans aren't particularly smart individually. Raise a human in isolation and they're arguably less capable than a chimpanzee. What makes us special is our ability to accumulate and pass on cultural knowledge. We're not Homo sapiens so much as Homo copycat-iens.[2]

The office was our copying infrastructure. And we deleted it.

Transformation Two: The Great Tool Explosion

As we traded conference rooms for conference calls, something strange started happening. We deleted the office and tried to rebuild it in code.

The average enterprise reportedly went from a handful of

---

1. Pre-pandemic estimates from Gallup and the Bureau of Labor Statistics; 2022 figures vary by methodology. Gallup found roughly half of remote-capable workers were hybrid by 2022-2023; McKinsey reported 58% had work-from-home options. The range reflects genuine measurement uncertainty.
2. Joseph Henrich, *The Secret of Our Success: How Culture Is Driving Human Evolution, Domesticating Our Species, and Making Us Smarter* (Princeton University Press, 2016).

SaaS tools in 2015 to somewhere between 90 and 130 by 2023, depending on who's counting and how they define "tool."[3]

Marcus's company was actually below average with only 87. He knew this because tool #84 was specifically designed to track how many tools they were using. It had a dashboard and everything.

McKinsey called this "digital transformation." Everyone else called it "Another login to remember."

Transformation Three: The Machines Became Colleagues

November 30, 2022. ChatGPT launches. It hits 100 million users in two months, faster than any standalone application in history.[4]

Marcus's daughter was an early adopter. She talked about it like a study buddy who happened to know everything but had weird opinions about dolphins.

By 2025, the statistics were hard to ignore:

- In files where AI coding assistants were enabled, nearly half the code was AI-generated
- 47% of marketers used AI to create first drafts
- Productivity gains of 25-40% on tasks within AI's capability range, but performance *declines* on tasks outside it[5]

---

3. Okta's *Businesses at Work* reports tracked average apps per organization rising from ~88 (2019) to over 100 (2025); Productiv found organizations use 371 SaaS apps on average, with large enterprises averaging 473, though definitions vary widely.

4. UBS Research, February 2023. Threads later broke this record but leveraged Instagram's existing user base.

5. Noy and Zhang, "Experimental Evidence on the Productivity Effects of Generative Artificial Intelligence," *Science* 381 (2023): 187-192 (40% faster, 18% higher quality); Dell'Acqua et al., "Navigating the Jagged Technological Fron-

But here's what fascinated Marcus: the companies that succeeded didn't just give everyone ChatGPT licenses and call it a day. They fundamentally rethought what AI was to their organization.

The successful teams stopped thinking of AI as a search engine with personality. They started treating it as a presence with specific, complementary capabilities. They integrated it into their workflows not as a tool to consult when stuck, but as an active participant in the work itself.

Teams that used AI as a simple tool did see productivity gains, mostly from faster first drafts and automated boilerplate. Teams that learned to collaborate with AI saw something different: they started solving problems they couldn't have solved before. Not just faster solutions to the same problems. Different problems entirely.

Marcus tried to fix his team three times. This is like saying someone tried to quit smoking three times: the number itself tells you how well it went.

Attempt #1: Training

He sent everyone to workshops. LinkedIn Learning. Coursera. Sarah got certified in something called "Agile Leadership for Digital Transformation," which came with a badge she could put on her LinkedIn. Derek learned seventeen new JavaScript frameworks, sixteen of which would be obsolete by the time you read this sentence.

tier," HBS Working Paper 24-013 (2023) (25% faster, 40% higher quality inside AI's frontier; 19 percentage points worse outside it).

Result: Six individually smarter people who still couldn't ship a product on time.

Attempt #2: Tools

More software. Better software. Software to manage the software. They had integrations. They had automations. They had a Zapier setup so complex it possibly achieved consciousness.

Result: Now they could fail faster and with better dashboards.

Attempt #3: The Room

This one started with Marcus asking a different question. Instead of "How do I make my people smarter?" he asked, "How do I make the room smarter?"

He floated the idea in their next one-on-one rotation. Most of the responses were polite versions of "I don't know what that means." Derek asked if it involved more software. Sarah said it sounded like something from a management book, which was fair.

Lin was quiet for a long moment. Then she said: "We are not a team. We are six soloists who use the same Slack channel."

Marcus's pen stopped moving. He hadn't realized he'd been taking notes.

"I have been here eighteen months. I watch." She paused. "Sarah holds context nobody else holds. Derek builds things nobody else understands. Miles produces faster than anyone can review. I run operations for a region most of you have never visited." Another pause. "We are all good. But we do not work together. We work near each other."

Marcus wrote the question in his notebook: *How do I make the room smarter?*

He didn't have an answer. He had a suspicion that training wasn't it, and tools weren't it, and individual excellence clearly wasn't it. He had Lin's observation, which stung precisely because it was true.

What he didn't have was a path forward.

This is the story of finding one.

FROM GET IN THE BOAT TO PADDLE FORWARD

My previous book, *Get in the Boat*, introduced a framework for individual relevance in knowledge work. This book extends those ideas to teams navigating AI. Here's the foundation we're building on.

The RBG Framework

Get in the Boat proposed that knowledge workers operate from one of three perspectives, each with distinct priorities, concerns, and communication styles:

Red (Tactical): Internally focused on systems and infrastructure. Reds care about the technology itself: the servers, the code, the network architecture. Their core value is efficiency (doing more with less). Their primary fear is change risk (new systems, updates, replacements that might break what works). Reds are highly competent at specific technical tasks but often struggle to connect their work to business outcomes. The classic Red failure mode is working in a vacuum, prioritizing based on technical interest rather than organizational value.

Blue (Operational): Externally focused on processes and users. Blues care about how systems enable people to do their jobs. Their core value is effectiveness (getting results). Their primary concern is operational risk (are key processes working?

is the customer satisfied?). Blues serve as translators between strategy and tactics, connecting what leadership wants with what technical teams can deliver. The classic Blue failure mode is getting caught between competing demands without the authority to resolve them.

Green (Strategic): Focused on direction, growth, and customers. Greens care about organizational trajectory and competitive position. Their core value is productivity (creating value). Their primary concerns are financial risk and compliance risk. Greens operate at altitude, making decisions based on incomplete information and owning the consequences. The classic Green failure mode is dictating strategy without understanding operational or technical constraints.

The original framework helped technologists understand how to communicate across these perspectives and become relevant to their organizations. The path to relevance ran through Blue: learning to translate between technical capability and business need.

Silver: The Fourth Color

This book adds a fourth color: **Silver**, representing AI as a presence in the team.

Silver doesn't map cleanly onto the three-tier model. It's not strategic (it has no goals), not operational (it doesn't understand processes without explicit context), and not purely tactical (it can generate strategic analyses and operational plans). Silver is something else: a capability that can perform work at every level without understanding any of them.

Silver's strengths: processing speed, breadth of knowledge, availability, pattern recognition across large datasets, consistency in repetitive tasks, infinite patience.

Silver's weaknesses: no understanding of context unless explicitly provided, uniform confidence regardless of accuracy, no ability to read political dynamics or unwritten rules, tendency to hallucinate, no sense of when its output is wrong or when to stop.

How Silver Changes Each Color

The addition of Silver doesn't just add a team member. It shifts what the other colors must do to remain effective.

Red + Silver: Red's traditional value was technical competence: knowing how systems work and making them work well. Silver can now generate code, configure systems, and perform technical tasks at speed. Red's new value is verification and judgment. Can you evaluate whether AI-generated code actually does what it claims? Do you understand the system well enough to catch errors that look correct? Reds who can't verify AI output become dangerous, approving work they can't actually assess. Reds who maintain deep technical understanding become more valuable, not less, as the only check on AI-generated technical work.

Blue + Silver: Blue's traditional value was translation: connecting strategy to tactics, designing processes, coordinating across functions. Silver can now draft project plans, summarize requirements, and generate documentation. Blue's new value is workflow design and human-AI coordination. How do you structure work so AI handles what it's good at while humans retain what matters? How do you translate between AI's literalism and human ambiguity? Blues who simply insert AI into existing processes will optimize for metrics AI can measure while missing what it can't. Blues who redesign processes around human-AI collaboration create new organizational capability.

Green + Silver: Green's traditional value was strategic judgment: setting direction based on incomplete information, reading markets and politics, making decisions others couldn't make. Silver can now generate strategic analyses, market summaries, and scenario models. Green's new value is distinguishing insight from hallucination. AI can surface patterns humans miss. AI can also generate confident nonsense that sounds like insight. Greens who defer to AI analysis abdicate their core function. Greens who dismiss AI entirely miss genuine intelligence. The new skill is calibrated trust: knowing when an AI's pattern-matching is revealing something real and when it's making things up.

The Underlying Shift

In *Get in the Boat*, relevance came from understanding business context and communicating across color boundaries. That remains necessary. But Silver adds a new requirement: every color must now maintain the ability to evaluate work they didn't produce. The team's judgment is the check on AI's capability. If that judgment erodes, the check disappears.

WHAT THIS BOOK COVERS

Get in the Boat was about individual relevance: finding your place, learning to communicate across perspectives. This book is about collective navigation.

The title comes from whitewater rafting. When you're running rapids, four things determine whether you make it through: you have to *read the water* (understand the landscape before you act), *know your crew* (who can do what, where the gaps are), *call your line* (make decisions in real-time as conditions shift), and *remember the run* (learn from what happened so the next rapids go smoother).

This is the Paddle Forward framework: four modes of activity that successful teams cycle through continuously. They're sequential for learning but parallel in practice. The best teams are always reading, always knowing, always calling, always remembering. The worst teams skip steps and wonder why they keep hitting rocks.

Teams working with AI face the same challenge. The water has changed. The rapids are faster. Your crew includes a powerful new member who can paddle harder than anyone but can't see the rocks. The old playbooks don't work.

The chapters that follow explore what this means in practice.

2

THE COMPLEXITY PARADOX

WHEN EFFICIENCY BECOMES FRAGILITY

The call came at 2:47 AM, which is the hour reserved by God for phone calls that will ruin your week. Marcus Chen had been asleep for exactly ninety-three minutes. He knew this because his sleep tracker would later inform him with the clinical detachment of a device that has never experienced dread.

"Marcus, it's Derek. We have a problem."

Derek was the kind of engineer who described a server room fire as "a thermal event." If Derek said "problem," the correct mental image was "asteroid impact."

Marcus had been Director of Digital Operations at Consolidated Logistics for nine months. Long enough to feel like he understood the place. Long enough to have championed expanding the AI-powered routing system to three new regions, a decision that had looked brilliant eleven weeks ago and was looking like something else entirely now.

"Tell me," Marcus said, already pulling on pants.

In Chicago, Miles was still awake; he'd been tracking the exception reports since midnight, increasingly confused. The metrics looked fine. The system was performing within parameters. But his phone kept buzzing with Slack messages from people who sounded worried about things he couldn't see in the dashboard.

He'd messaged Derek an hour ago: *The numbers look okay to me. What am I missing?*

Derek hadn't responded. Miles would learn later that Derek had been staring at the same numbers, watching them lie, trying to find language for a failure that didn't show up in any field he knew how to query.

"It's not one thing. That's the problem. It's... everything is wrong and I can't figure out why."

Here's what Derek couldn't figure out: the routing system was performing beautifully by every metric they'd designed. Efficiency scores were up. Fuel costs were down. The algorithm was making optimal decisions at every node. And somehow, inexplicably, packages were arriving late, drivers were quitting, and three major customers had called to terminate their contracts in the past forty-eight hours.

The system wasn't broken. That was what made it so disorienting. The system was working perfectly. The world around the system had become something the system couldn't comprehend.

Six weeks earlier, the metrics had been extraordinary. Twenty-three percent improvement in route efficiency. Eighteen percent reduction in fuel costs. Customer satisfaction climbing week over week. Marcus had allowed himself to feel something dangerously close to pride.

The AI system that they orchestrated had achieved these gains through a series of optimizations that were, individually, unimpeachable. The system identified that certain drivers consistently outperformed others on specific route types, so it began assigning those drivers to those routes more frequently.

It noticed that customer delivery windows had some flexibility, so it began clustering deliveries to minimize windshield time. It discovered that certain distribution centers processed packages faster, so it began routing more volume through them.

Marcus remembered the planning meeting where they'd approved the expansion. The conference room felt different that morning: tighter, sharper, the way it gets when everyone knows their piece and thinks they know the ending. Derek walked through the technical integration, quietly proud of how cleanly the systems talked to each other. Miles, three months in and still proving himself, had pulled together the performance projections: AI-assisted, polished, compelling.

Lin had been there, sitting slightly back from the table the way she did. At one point she'd started to say something about facility capacity assumptions, something about how the Columbus numbers didn't match what she was hearing from the floor managers, but the conversation had moved on before she finished the thought. Marcus remembered noticing her pause. He hadn't circled back to ask what she'd been about to say. The data was clean. The projections were solid. What could operations tell them that the numbers didn't already show?

Priya had dialed in from Mumbai at 11 PM her time, a fact that nobody acknowledged because she never complained about it. She'd raised a question about carrier handoff timing between regions, whether the optimization would account for the coordination lag when shipments crossed from domestic to Asia-Pacific (APAC) carriers. "Good point," someone had said. "We'll make sure that's in scope." Marcus couldn't remember now if it ever had been. The meeting had moved on. There were slides to get through.

Six weeks later, he was standing in his kitchen at 3 AM, and every one of those small moments looked different in retrospect.

Each optimization made sense. Each optimization

improved the metrics. And each optimization, invisibly, changed the system it was optimizing.

The high-performing drivers, now assigned the most demanding routes, began burning out. Two of the best quit within a month. The model, noticing their departure, redistributed their routes to the next tier of drivers, who were now being pushed beyond their capacity. Driver turnover, which had been stable for years, increased forty percent in six weeks.

The delivery clustering meant customers in certain zones received packages in tight windows while customers in other zones waited longer. The customers who waited longer complained. The sales team, responding to complaints, began promising tighter windows to retain accounts. These promises became new constraints the system had to optimize around, which meant even more clustering, which meant even more customers waiting, which meant even more complaints.

The distribution centers receiving higher volume began running at capacity. Managers at those facilities, measured on throughput, started requesting earlier truck arrivals to spread the load. The AI accommodated by adjusting pickup times, which compressed driver schedules, which increased the pressure on already-strained drivers, which accelerated turnover.

The carrier relationships eroded more quietly. The system ranked carriers by cost and reliability metrics, and month by month it shifted volume toward the cheaper options. Carriers who'd been partners for years, the ones who answered calls on weekends, who found capacity during surge periods, who'd built relationships with Consolidated's facility managers over a decade, watched their volume decline. They weren't fired. They just got fewer calls. They took the hint. By October, they'd committed their capacity to shippers who still treated them like partners rather than interchangeable vendors.

The carrier relations team had seen this happening. Janet Okonkwo had flagged it in three separate reports: relationship carriers deprioritized, response rates declining, flexibility disappearing from the network. The reports had been acknowledged. The metrics showed the new carriers performing fine. Janet and two of her colleagues were let go in August, their roles "redundant" now that the system handled carrier selection.

Their institutional knowledge walked out the door with them. Nobody noticed until there was no one left to call.

None of this was visible in the dashboards. Route efficiency: up. Fuel costs: down. On-time delivery percentage: stable (because the AI was technically meeting the windows it had been given, even as those windows quietly drifted from what customers actually expected). The metrics were green. The system was dying.

By 4 AM, Marcus had the team on a call. Sarah had been awake since 2, fielding messages from three different customer contacts who'd heard something was wrong and wanted to know if their shipments were affected. She was doing what Sarah always did: translating, smoothing, buying time. "I'm telling them we're assessing the situation and will have an update by 7 AM," she said. "That gives us three hours to figure out what the situation actually is."

Lin was on from her home office, camera on for once, her glasses catching the monitor light. That alone signaled how serious this was. "Columbus closed their gates because they're at real capacity, not rated capacity," she said. "I've been saying for months that those numbers don't reflect what the facilities can actually handle. The Tuesday night shift at Columbus runs thirty percent below the day shift because that's when the experienced dock workers are off. The system doesn't know that. It just sees throughput numbers from the days when throughput is highest."

"Why didn't we know this?" Marcus asked.

"I mentioned it. In the planning meeting." Lin's voice was even. "The conversation moved on."

Derek was running diagnostics, his voice flat and precise the way it got when things were bad. "The system isn't malfunctioning. Every decision it made was correct given its inputs. But the inputs stopped reflecting reality somewhere around 8 PM, and it just kept optimizing against a world that doesn't exist anymore."

"So we turn it off." Marcus's voice was calm, the kind of calm that came from somewhere other than not caring. "Go manual."

The silence on the line lasted long enough that Marcus checked his connection.

"We can do that," Derek said slowly. "But you need to understand what we're falling back to. The carriers who would have helped us, we shifted volume away from them. They've committed elsewhere. The people who used to work the phones in a crisis, the ones who had relationships with every dispatch manager in the Midwest—"

"Janet's team."

"They're gone. We let them go in August." Derek's voice had something in it Marcus hadn't heard before. "I validated the system that made their jobs redundant. I told leadership the automation was ready. And now we need exactly the thing we decided we didn't need anymore, and it doesn't exist."

Miles had been listening, saying nothing. Finally: "What do we do?"

"We do it the hard way," Sarah said. "We get on the phone. We call every facility manager personally. We find out what's actually happening on the ground instead of what the dashboard says. We—" She stopped. "I'll start with Columbus."

It took seventy hours. It was chaos. Sarah barely slept, coordinating between operations, engineering, and increasingly angry customers. Lin worked her facility contacts, translating between what Marcus needed to know and what floor managers were willing to say at 3 AM. Derek kept the system offline and hated every minute of it.

Priya, thirteen hours ahead in Mumbai, handled the APAC coordination that nobody else had bandwidth for. Twice she flagged issues that would have become problems; both times the flags got lost in the noise of more urgent fires. She documented everything, sent summaries that got half-read, and didn't complain. This was what she always did.

Miles monitored dashboards that no longer meant anything, feeling useless in a way he'd never experienced before. The tools he was good at, the AI-assisted synthesis, the quick pattern recognition, the confident communication, none of it helped when the problem was that the tools themselves had failed. He didn't know how to contribute to a crisis that was being solved by people making phone calls.

There's a technical term for what was happening: reflexivity. The system's outputs had become its inputs, a feedback loop reshaping the very landscape it was trying to optimize. It was like trying to walk across a floor that rearranged itself with each step you took. Each step was the right step given where the tiles were. But the tiles moved because you stepped.

The routing system hadn't failed because of a bug or missing data. It had failed because it was embedded in a web of human systems (drivers with morale, customers with expectations, managers with incentives, salespeople with promises) that responded to optimization by changing. The model saw packages and routes. It couldn't see that drivers were people who got tired and demoralized. It couldn't see that customers compared their experience to neighbors. It couldn't see that its own success would change the demands placed on it.

. . .

A question kept circling in Marcus's mind, the kind of question that arrives with sharp clarity in the small hours: *How did we get this so wrong?*

The answer, he would eventually realize, was that they hadn't gotten it wrong. They'd gotten it right, perfectly right, for a problem that wasn't the problem they actually had.

They had built an expert system for a complicated challenge: given trucks, drivers, packages, and constraints, find efficient routes. The system was excellent at this. The trouble was that 'routing packages' existed inside a larger system of human behavior and organizational dynamics that didn't stay still while you optimized. The more effectively you optimized, the more you changed the thing you were optimizing. And unlike the packages, the human systems pushed back, adapted, gamed, and eventually broke.

Marcus and his team had a map. The map was accurate. It was a map of somewhere that no longer existed by the time they finished drawing it.

In the weeks that followed, Marcus developed a phrase for what they'd gotten wrong. They hadn't "read the water". They'd looked at a map and assumed the map was the river. Every metric was a measurement of the map, not the water. When the current shifted, when drivers burned out, when facilities hit real limits, when carriers stopped answering, the map didn't update. It couldn't. It was measuring the wrong thing.

Reading the water meant something different. It meant watching the actual river, not the representation of it. It meant noticing when the current felt wrong even if you couldn't say why. It meant trusting that the people in the boats, the drivers, the facility managers, the carrier contacts, knew things about the water that dashboards struggle to capture.

They hadn't read the water. They'd plotted a route on the map and called it navigation.

THE MAP WE'VE BEEN USING

For most of the twentieth century, management operated on a seductive assumption: given enough data and the right expertise, any problem could be analyzed, understood, and solved. This wasn't simply arrogance; it was a reasonable conclusion drawn from remarkable success.

Frederick Taylor's scientific management principles transformed factories. Peter Drucker's frameworks built corporations that lasted generations. Six Sigma methodologies reduced manufacturing defects to levels that would have seemed like magic to previous eras. These approaches seemed to work so well, for so long, that they became something like secular religion. Consultants preached them. Business schools taught them. Executives knelt before their altars of process optimization and root cause analysis.

The map was clear. Problems had causes. Causes could be identified. Solutions could be implemented. If something wasn't working, you analyzed harder, planned better, and executed more precisely.

This map worked beautifully for static problems. Assembly lines. Supply chains with stable suppliers. Markets with predictable demand patterns. Financial systems before high-frequency trading. The map worked because the territory it described was fundamentally orderly: complicated, perhaps, but ultimately knowable. With enough analysis, you could find the right answer.

Then the territory changed.

Digital transformation shattered stable supply chains. The pandemic reshuffled working arrangements. AI introduced capabilities that evolved faster than organizations could integrate them. Social media created feedback loops that amplified small changes into major disruptions. Climate instability disrupted assumptions about seasonal patterns.

The twenty-first century organization faces an uncomfortable reality: the old map doesn't just need updates. Large portions of it describe a landscape that no longer exists. The tools that solved twentieth-century problems can actively interfere with solving those of the twenty-first-century.

This is the context in which Marcus found himself standing in his kitchen at 3 AM, staring at metrics that were all green while his company crumbled. The routing system wasn't broken. The mental model was.

THE CYNEFIN FRAMEWORK: A BETTER MAP

Fortunately, a better map exists. David Snowden's Cynefin framework offers a way of understanding that doesn't assume everything is ultimately analyzable.[1] Instead, it proposes that problems live in fundamentally different domains that require fundamentally different approaches.

The name comes from a Welsh word meaning "habitat" or "place of multiple belongings," pronounced roughly "kuh-NEV-in".

The framework identifies five domains: Clear, Complicated, Complex, Chaotic, and Confusion. Understanding which domain your problem occupies isn't academic philosophy; it's the difference between solving problems and making them worse.

---

1. David J. Snowden and Mary E. Boone, "A Leader's Framework for Decision Making," *Harvard Business Review* 85, no. 11 (November 2007): 68-76.

The Clear Domain: Known Territory

The Clear domain (previously called Simple or Obvious) is where the relationship between cause and effect is self-evident. Best practices exist. You sense the situation, categorize it, and respond with established procedures. The challenge is execution, not analysis.

Think of a help desk ticket for a password reset. The problem is recognized. The solution is documented. A well-designed AI system can handle this faster than a human, and nobody mourns the loss of human involvement in clicking through the reset workflow. This is progress. It's also the easiest kind of progress to recognize, which is why companies love to mention it in earnings calls.

In Clear waters, AI is genuinely superior at the paddle. The patterns are established, the variations predictable, the right response codifiable. The role for humans in Clear domain work is diminishing rapidly, and that's not necessarily a tragedy. These are often tasks humans didn't want anyway.

The trap in the Clear domain is complacency. When things are running smoothly, it's tempting to assume they'll continue. But Clear domains can shift suddenly. The policy that handles routine requests fails when a genuine emergency arrives. The checklist that worked for years misses a new type of failure. Teams that forget to monitor for shifts from Clear to other domains get caught flat-footed.

The Complicated Domain: Expert Territory

The Complicated domain is where cause and effect are discoverable but not obvious. Analysis is required. Expertise matters. The problem might be difficult, but given sufficient skill and resources, the right answer can reliably be found.

Building a rocket is complicated. Designing an enterprise

software system is complicated. Diagnosing an unusual mechanical failure is complicated. In each case, the relationship between inputs and outputs follows rules that experts can identify and leverage. The solution exists; finding it requires specialized knowledge and careful analysis.

As introduced in *Get in the Boat*, this is where RBG translation becomes critical. Red technologists live here: they see complicated systems, understand how the pieces connect, and know how to manipulate those connections. The challenge is translating that expertise to Blue process thinkers and Green decision makers who see the same situation through different lenses and objectives.

This is where AI earns its keep as a teammate. Modern AI systems excel at the Complicated domain because they can process vast amounts of data, identify patterns invisible to human perception, and evaluate options against multiple criteria simultaneously. When navigating Complicated waters, AI serves as the navigator reading the map: presenting options, modeling scenarios, highlighting tradeoffs, while humans choose the route.

The trap in the Complicated domain is over-reliance on analysis. With AI providing increasingly sophisticated insights, teams can fall into "analysis paralysis": endless optimization seeking a perfect solution that doesn't exist, or worse, one that becomes obsolete while they're still calculating. Military strategist John Boyd's OODA Loop framework (Observe-Orient-Decide-Act) offers a useful corrective.[2] Boyd's key insight was that speed through the loop matters more than perfection at any single stage. AI has dramatically shortened the Observe and Orient phases. The bottleneck in modern teams is often

2. Robert Coram, *Boyd: The Fighter Pilot Who Changed the Art of War* (New York: Little, Brown and Company, 2002). Boyd developed the OODA loop during the 1970s; his key insight was that the key to victory lies in operating at a faster tempo than the adversary.

the Decide phase, where humans understandably hesitate to commit. Deciding means being wrong in a way that has your name on it, while analyzing forever means being wrong in a way that's everyone's fault.

The Complex Domain: Emergent Territory

Now we enter the domain that defines much of modern organizational life: Complexity. In the Complex domain, cause-and-effect relationships exist but can only be perceived in retrospect. You cannot predict what will work. You can only discover it through experimentation and adaptation. This is the domain of innovation, culture change, market disruption, and, critically, any situation where human behavior plays a significant role.

It's where Marcus's routing problem actually lived, though his team didn't recognize it. The system wasn't just routing packages. It was operating within an ecosystem of human decisions, weather patterns, infrastructure dependencies, and market conditions that interact in ways no algorithm can fully anticipate. Each package route is a simple problem. Eight hundred packages interacting with driver morale, customer expectations, facility capacity limits, and human shift schedules? That's complex.

The approach in Complexity is fundamentally different: Probe first through safe-to-fail experiments, Sense what emerges, and then Respond by amplifying what works and dampening what doesn't. Unlike Complicated problems, where sufficient analysis can predict outcomes reliably, Complex systems adapt as you act on them. The very interventions you make reshape the landscape you're navigating. There is no best practice here: only emergent practice discovered through iteration. Anyone who tells you they have a "best practice" for navigating complexity is either lying to you or lying to themselves.

For AI-integrated teams, the Complex domain requires a crucial handoff. AI can serve as lookout, spotting patterns and anomalies that human perception might miss. But the human must hold the paddle. Not because humans reason better (in many analytical tasks, they don't) but because humans are *inside* the system being navigated. They feel when something's off before they can articulate why. They hear what's said in hallways that never makes it to dashboards. They bear the consequences of being wrong.

AI excels at pattern recognition: given what has happened before, what is statistically likely next? But Complex problems are precisely those where cause and effect are entangled in ways that only become visible in retrospect. Historical patterns may mislead because the system you're analyzing isn't the system you're acting on. In this territory, someone must decide which experiments to run, interpret ambiguous results, and commit to action despite irreducible uncertainty. That someone must be accountable for being wrong. AI can inform these decisions. It cannot own them.

The Chaotic Domain: Crisis Territory

The Chaotic domain is mercifully rare but unmistakable when it arrives. Here, cause and effect cannot be discerned in time to matter. The building is on fire. The market is crashing. The crisis is unfolding faster than anyone can analyze. You know you're in Chaos when nobody can even agree on what's happening, let alone what to do about it.

The approach is urgent and counterintuitive: Act first to establish some stability, Sense what emerges from your action, and Respond to shift the situation toward a more manageable domain. Analysis is a luxury you cannot afford. Decisive action, any action that creates a foothold, is what matters. The goal isn't to solve the problem but to make the problem solvable.

In Chaotic conditions, AI should not be making decisions. This isn't because technology can't help: it can, by providing rapid information access or executing clearly defined emergency protocols. But the moment is too fluid, the stakes too high, and the need for human judgment too acute to filter through algorithmic intermediaries. Chaos demands human presence, human decision-making, and human accountability. Nobody wants to explain to the board that the company-ending crisis was handled by a language model.

The Fifth Domain: Confusion

At the center of the Cynefin framework lies a domain of Confusion (sometimes called Aporia or Disorder). This is the state of not knowing which domain you're in, and it may be the most dangerous territory of all.

When teams operate in Confusion, they default to whatever approach feels most comfortable: usually the one that's worked for them before. Analytical teams analyze. Action-oriented teams act. Engineering teams build something. None of these responses are wrong in the right context, but all can be catastrophic in the wrong one.

This is where AI introduces a particularly insidious trap. AI systems can present Complicated or even Complex problems as if they were Clear. The interface is clean, the output confident, the recommendations specific. Unless you know to question it, an AI hallucination can masquerade as established fact. A pattern identified from historical data can look like a reliable rule even when circumstances have fundamentally changed.

It's not uncommon to see teams take AI recommendations and treat them as gospel, not because they were lazy or careless, but because the AI presented information with identical confidence whether it was drawing from an explicit source or just making an educated guess. LLM models sound exactly as confident when right as when completely wrong. Humans must do the work of distinguishing between those cases.

Your team's first job in any significant situation is not to solve, it's to locate. Which domain are we in? What approach does this context demand? Get that wrong, and brilliant execution will still fail.

THE NEW RISKS: WHAT AI CHANGES

Understanding Cynefin is essential, but applying it in an AI-integrated world requires grappling with some uncomfortable emerging realities. The framework is solid. The terrain it maps has shifted.

Cognitive Atrophy: The Use-It-or-Lose-It Problem

There's reason to believe that when humans offload cognitive work to AI systems, they don't just free up mental capacity: they may actually lose capability over time.[3] Call it cognitive atrophy: the mental equivalent of muscle wasting from disuse. You stop doing math by hand, and eventually you can't do math by hand, and then you can't recognize when the calculator gives you an obviously wrong answer.

Consider what this means for teams. If your AI handles all the Complicated domain work (analysis, pattern recognition, optimization) how do junior team members ever develop the expertise to know when the AI is wrong? This creates what we might call the Junior Developer Paradox: if AI writes all the code, how do junior developers ever learn enough to become senior developers who can review the AI's work? The pattern

3. Shannon Vallor, "Moral Deskilling and Upskilling in a New Machine Age," *Philosophy & Technology* 28, no. 1 (2015): 107-124. Vallor's analysis focuses on moral skills within a virtue ethics framework; the extension to cognitive capabilities more broadly is the author's.

repeats across industries. If AI drafts all the legal briefs, how do new lawyers develop judgment about what makes a good argument? If AI reads all the radiology scans, how do residents learn to see what they're looking at?

The solution isn't to avoid AI: that ship has sailed and wasn't seaworthy anyway. The solution is intentional friction: deliberately preserving opportunities for humans to do cognitive work manually, even when AI could do it faster, specifically to maintain the judgment capacity needed to oversee AI in high-stakes situations. Just as athletes do strength training they'll never use in competition to build the underlying capacity their sport requires, teams need cognitive exercises that maintain human expertise even when that expertise isn't strictly "necessary" for the immediate task.

The Liminal Drift: Your Skills Are Expiring

The boundaries between Cynefin domains aren't static. AI is actively pushing tasks from Complicated toward Clear, democratizing capabilities that once required years of expertise. What was a high-value human skill last year (writing basic SQL queries, creating passable graphic designs, drafting routine legal documents) is now firmly in AI territory. Last year's expertise is this year's commodity. If your primary value proposition is "I'm the person who knows how to use the complicated tool," you should be nervous. Complicated tools are getting simpler faster than you're getting smarter.

This creates what we might call skills expiration dates. The half-life of professional capabilities is shrinking. Teams that anchor their value proposition in Complicated domain expertise will find that anchor dragging as AI claims more of that territory. "I'm really good at analysis" is less of a competitive advantage when everyone has access to AI that's pretty good at analysis.

The survival strategy is clear: continuously migrate up the Cynefin framework toward Complexity. The human competitive advantage lies not in analysis but in synthesis, not in optimization but in innovation, not in processing information but in making meaning from it. These Complex domain capabilities are, for now, distinctly human territory.

The Interface Problem

Here's what chess taught us after Deep Blue: raw capability isn't the bottleneck. Kasparov observed that teams with modest AI and modest human skill but excellent processes consistently beat teams with superior components but poor coordination.[4] The lesson isn't "humans plus AI wins"; recent research suggests that's not reliably true.[5] The lesson is that *how* you combine matters more than *what* you combine.

This is why the frameworks in this book matter. Without a shared language for complexity, teams default to implicit assumptions about when AI should lead and when humans should. Those assumptions are often wrong. And unlike most wrong assumptions, these generate confident-sounding reports right up until the moment everything falls apart.

---

4. Garry Kasparov, *Deep Thinking: Where Machine Intelligence Ends and Human Creativity Begins* (New York: PublicAffairs, 2017). The insight that "a weak human player plus machine plus a better process is superior" first appeared in Kasparov's essay "The Chess Master and the Computer," *New York Review of Books*, February 11, 2010.

5. Michelle Vaccaro et al., "When Combinations of Humans and AI Are Useful: A Systematic Review and Meta-Analysis," *Nature Human Behaviour* 8 (2024): 2293–2303. Meta-analysis of 106 studies found human-AI combinations performed worse than the best of humans or AI alone on average, with gains appearing only in content creation tasks.

THE DOMAIN DRAFT

Theory is useful, tools are better. Theory that you have to look up is close to useless. Here's a simple decision framework your team can use to determine who should hold the paddle in any given situation. I call it the Domain Draft, and it should take less time to apply than it took you to read this sentence.

If the problem is REPETITIVE (Clear Domain):

AI holds the paddle. Humans steer from the back. The work is automation, scheduling, and execution against known parameters. Human intervention should focus on exception handling and ensuring the problem remains in the Clear domain.

If the problem is ANALYTICAL (Complicated Domain):

AI navigates the map; humans choose the route. Let AI process data, model scenarios, and surface options. Reserve human judgment for weighing tradeoffs, selecting among good-enough solutions, and deciding when analysis has reached the point of diminishing returns.

If the problem is NOVEL (Complex Domain):

Humans hold the paddle. AI serves as lookout. The work is experimentation, sensing, and adaptation. AI can help spot patterns and anomalies, but the judgment calls (which experiments to run, what the results mean, when to commit) must be human-driven.

If the problem is HUMAN (Requires Agreement, Not Just Solution):

AI stays on the shore. Some challenges aren't about finding the right answer but about building the alignment and commitment to act on any answer. Negotiation, conflict resolution, culture change, stakeholder management: these require human presence and human relationship. No algorithm can substitute for actually talking to people.

The key practice: before diving into any significant problem, pause to draft your domain. Ask explicitly: "Which domain does this problem live in? Based on that answer, who holds the paddle?"

Make this a ritual. In stand-ups. In project kickoffs. In incident reviews. The few seconds it takes to consciously locate your problem will save hours, or worse, spent applying the wrong approach. It feels pedantic until the day it saves you from a 3 AM phone call.

Warning Signs: When Domains Shift

Problems don't announce when they're migrating from one domain to another. But they leave clues. Here are the warning signs that your problem may have moved:

From Clear to Complicated: The "best practice" stops working. Exceptions multiply. The checklist needs more branches. What was automatic now requires judgment calls. The procedure that worked fine for sixteen months suddenly doesn't.

From Complicated to Complex: Expert analysis becomes circular: more data doesn't clarify, it confuses. Stakeholders disagree not just on solutions but on problem definition. The system behaves differently each time you probe it. People keep saying "But that doesn't make sense."

From Complex to Chaotic: Events outpace your ability to make sense of them. Every action generates unexpected consequences. The situation deteriorates faster than you can respond. Your chat channel looks like a live feed of panic.

Into Confusion: Team members disagree on what kind of problem they're facing. The same data supports multiple contradictory interpretations. The conversation loops without progress. Someone says "I don't even know what question we're trying to answer anymore."

When you notice these warning signs, stop working on the problem and start working on the domain assessment. A problem that has shifted domains without recognition is a problem that's about to get a lot worse.

WHY MARCUS'S TEAM GOT IT WRONG, AND WHAT THEY LEARNED

Let's return to Marcus and his 3 AM disaster. What actually happened, viewed through the Cynefin lens?

The routing system was designed for a Complicated problem: given these constraints, optimize these routes. The system was good at this. Excellent, even. The metrics proved it, and Marcus had the slide deck to show anyone who asked.

But the actual problem lived in Complexity, and nobody had asked the slide deck about that. The routing system existed inside an ecosystem of human systems that responded to optimization by changing. Drivers weren't just packages that happened to have legs. They had morale, preferences, social networks, and the option to quit. Customers weren't just delivery endpoints. They compared experiences, complained to sales, and made decisions based on factors no algorithm captured. Managers weren't just efficiency nodes. They had incentives, pressures, and workarounds that created ripple effects the system couldn't see.

The team's error wasn't in the system design. The error was in domain diagnosis. They treated a Complex problem as Complicated, and the system executed brilliantly against the wrong understanding. Every metric confirmed they were winning, right up until they'd already lost.

If they'd recognized the true domain, they would have approached differently. Instead of optimizing against fixed metrics, they would have probed: tried changes in limited scope, sensed the system's response including human responses, adjusted based on what they learned. They would have designed feedback loops that captured not just route efficiency but driver satisfaction, customer perception, and facility manager behavior. They would have expected the landscape to shift and built monitoring for shifts rather than just outcomes.

They didn't do any of this because nobody asked the domain question. The routing problem felt Complicated. It looked Complicated. Every individual piece of it was Complicated. But the whole was Complex, and treating it otherwise meant the system's very success was creating its failure.

Marcus's team is learning to ask, "What domain is this really in?" before applying any solution. To watch for feedback loops that cross human systems. To be suspicious of clean metrics and confident recommendations.

"The system recommends X" has become "The system recommends X, and here's what it can't see."

It works. It also costs something.

Marcus sometimes misses the six weeks when he believed they'd solved the problem and could just trust the dashboard. That belief was wrong, but it was peaceful.

Janet's LinkedIn says "logistics consultant" now. Derek

knows because he looked her up once, drafted an apology, but closed the tab.

~

The 3 AM calls have stopped. Marcus's sleep tracker has noticed, and it would like him to know that his patterns have "improved." It's proud of him, in the way that software is proud of things, which is not at all.

What bothers him now is something else. In the post-mortems, tracing back through Slack threads and email chains, he kept finding the same shape: someone had information that would have helped, and it sat there. The signals existed. They didn't propagate.

He's started noticing this everywhere. A question in a Slack channel. Fourteen people see it. Someone answers confidently. Everyone moves on.

The routing system sent him an automated report last Tuesday. "Route efficiency up 2.3% month-over-month." He forwarded it to Derek without comment. Derek replied with a single emoji: the one that's laughing so hard it's crying, or possibly crying so hard it looks like laughing. Marcus still isn't sure which one Derek meant. He suspects Derek isn't either.

He's learning to read the water. But he's starting to see another problem.

3

WHAT DISTANCE DOES

WORKING ACROSS TIME AND SPACE

The message was fine. That's the thing nobody could get past in the postmortem. Sarah had written a perfectly reasonable message.

It arrived in the #logistics-api channel at 3:50 PM Pacific on a Thursday. Sarah was at her desk in Oakland. Technically, though "at her desk" meant she was also on a video call with the Phoenix distribution center, also monitoring a Slack thread about a carrier integration that was going sideways, also half-reading an email from the client she was getting ready to ask about. The message took her eleven seconds to write:

Heads up - Meridian is asking about timeline for the API changes. Greg called me directly which is unusual. Can someone confirm we're still on track for the 15th?

She hit enter and switched back to the Phoenix call, where someone was explaining that the new scanning system worked fine, except when it didn't.

Here is everything that happened next, in the order it happened:

3:50 PM Pacific. The message appeared. Slack dutifully sent notifications to fourteen people, nine of whom had notifications muted because they were in meetings or had learned that constant pings made them want to throw their laptops into the Bay.

3:55 PM. Derek, thirty feet from Sarah's desk, saw the notification. He was debugging a slow query that had been causing timeouts for two days, and he'd finally isolated the problematic join. The words "API changes" registered, but those API changes were Miles's thing, mostly, or at least Miles had been the one presenting about them in the last all-hands. Derek made a mental note to check back once he'd committed his fix. The mental note went where mental notes go.

3:57 PM. Lin saw the message. She was also in Oakland, in the office she'd been assigned when Consolidated acquired her company a year and a half ago. It was a nice office—good light, a door that closed, a window facing the courtyard where people sometimes ate lunch. She still felt like a guest in it. The family photos on the desk were hers. The mug was hers. The thin-framed glasses she took off now, cleaning them with the cloth she kept in her desk drawer, were hers. But the space itself still felt borrowed, nineteen months in.

Lin knew the answer to Sarah's question. The API changes were not on track for the 15th. They weren't disastrously behind, but the dependency on the warehouse management system update meant they were looking at the 22nd, realistically, and that assumed the WMS team didn't hit any more surprises. Lin knew this because the WMS update affected her distribution center workflows, and she'd been in a planning meeting about it that morning.

She put her glasses back on and started typing a response. Then she stopped.

Sarah's message was addressed to the channel, not to her. The question was "can someone confirm." Lin wasn't the someone. She was operations, not engineering. The API changes weren't her project. She'd been in a meeting where the timeline was discussed, but that meeting had been a sidebar, not a formal review, and maybe the timeline had changed since then. Maybe engineering knew something she didn't. If she posted incorrect information to a channel with fourteen people, including Marcus, she'd look like she was overstepping, or worse, like she didn't know the boundaries of her own role.

In her previous company, you answered questions when you were asked. You volunteered information upward through your manager. You didn't broadcast into cross-functional channels unless someone specifically requested your input. She'd been at Consolidated for nineteen months and she still wasn't sure if those rules applied here or not. Everyone seemed to talk to everyone about everything, except when they didn't, and she hadn't figured out the pattern.

She deleted the three words she'd typed and went back to the capacity planning spreadsheet—the one she updated every Friday, the one that tracked actual facility capacity against rated capacity, the one nobody had ever asked to see.

4:18 PM. Miles saw the message. Miles was in Chicago, two hours ahead, which meant it was 6:18 PM and he was technically done for the day but still online because he was new enough to worry about looking like he wasn't committed.

Miles knew about the API changes. He'd been working on the integration documentation and had sat in on several of the engineering syncs. He didn't know the timeline was slipping, because he hadn't been in Lin's sidebar meeting that morning, but he knew what the original timeline was and he'd seen the project tracker, which still showed the 15th.

He also knew that Meridian was a big account. He'd read the account summary when he was onboarding. Greg calling Sarah directly seemed like a thing that should get a fast response.

Miles asked an AI to help him draft a reply that synthesized what he knew about the project status. He was good at this. It was, honestly, one of the things that made him useful: he could pull together context quickly and communicate it clearly. The AI helped him structure the response, and he edited it to sound more like him and less like a corporate FAQ.

He posted:

Hey Sarah - we're tracking for the 15th based on the last sync. The core endpoint work is done, and QA is in progress. Main dependency is the auth token migration, which eng has been working through. Happy to set up a call with Meridian if they want a direct update from the technical side.

It was a good message. Confident, specific, proactive. It directly addressed Sarah's question. It offered a next step.

It was also, in ways Miles had no way of knowing, wrong.

4:26 PM. Sarah saw Miles's response, felt a small wave of relief, and replied with a thumbs-up emoji. She forwarded Miles's summary to Greg at Meridian with a note that said "Confirming we're on track - let me know if you'd like to schedule a technical deep-dive." Then she went back to the Phoenix call, where the scanning system had developed a new symptom.

7:50 PM Pacific / 8:20 AM Mumbai, Friday. Priya started her day and worked through the overnight Slack backlog. Forty-three messages across twelve channels. The logistics-api thread was message thirty-one. She read Miles's response, noted that it seemed handled, and moved on.

Except.

Something nagged at her. She'd been on a call with the WMS team in Bangalore the previous week, and they'd mentioned the warehouse management system update, and there had been something about dependencies. She couldn't remember the details. The thread looked resolved. Miles had answered confidently. Sarah had accepted the answer. Priya wasn't even sure the WMS thing she was remembering was related to the API changes, or if she was conflating two different projects.

She moved on to message thirty-two.

9:15 AM Pacific, Friday. Greg from Meridian called Consolidated's CEO directly. This was unusual. Greg and the CEO had met at a conference two years ago and exchanged numbers in the way that executives do, but Greg had never actually used the number. He was using it now because he'd received Sarah's "confirming we're on track" email, and then he'd received a separate email from his own technical team saying that Consolidated's WMS contact had mentioned the 22nd in a call that morning, and he wanted to know which date was real.

The CEO, who did not know which date was real, said he would find out immediately.

9:23 AM. Marcus's morning became significantly worse.

The postmortem took two hours and solved nothing.

This is not a criticism of the postmortem. Some problems don't have solutions, only accommodations. The postmortem correctly identified what had happened. It could not identify what should have happened instead, because every individual decision in the chain was defensible.

Sarah's message was clear and appropriately scoped. She asked a direct question to the relevant channel. She followed up when she got an answer. She communicated with the client promptly. If you were evaluating Sarah's performance that day, you would give her full marks.

Derek's non-response was normal. He was working on something else. The question wasn't addressed to him. Someone else answered. Engineers who drop everything for every Slack message don't ship code, and Derek shipped code. The query fix he committed that afternoon saved the company approximately $5,400 per month in cloud computing costs, which nobody mentioned in the postmortem because it wasn't relevant but which Derek thought about frequently in the days afterward.

Miles's response was proactive and professional. He synthesized available information, communicated it clearly, and offered to help further. The information he had access to was simply incomplete. He didn't know what he didn't know; this is not a character flaw but the default human condition.

Lin's silence was invisible. Nobody knew she'd started typing a response. Nobody knew she had relevant information. In the postmortem, when Marcus asked if anyone had known about the timeline slip before Greg's call, Lin said "I'd heard something in a sidebar but I wasn't sure if it was current." This was true. It was also, Marcus thought, exactly the kind of information that would have helped. He didn't say this. He wasn't sure how to say it without it sounding like he was blaming her, and he didn't think he was blaming her, and he also wasn't sure he wasn't blaming her.

Priya's decision not to pursue her nagging feeling was reasonable. She was thirty-one items into a forty-three-item backlog. The thread was marked resolved. She had a half-remembered fragment from a tangentially related call. Escalating that would have felt like making noise.

The CEO's annoyance was understandable. The client relationship recovered, eventually. The API changes shipped on the 22nd.

What Marcus couldn't stop thinking about was this: they had fourteen people in that channel. At least three of them, it turned out, had partial information that, combined, would have surfaced the problem. None of them combined it. The system had no mechanism for combination. It had only individuals, making individual decisions, in sequence, without visibility into each other's context.

In an office, some of this would have happened differently.

Sarah might have asked the question out loud, and Lin, overhearing, might have said "Actually, I heard something about that this morning." Derek might have seen Sarah's expression after reading Greg's email and asked what was wrong. The fragments that existed in different people's heads had natural collision points: the coffee machine, the hallway, the overheard conversation.

They didn't have those collision points anymore. They had Slack channels, and Slack channels are not conversations. They're depositions. You say something, it enters the record, someone responds to the record, the record grows. What you don't say doesn't exist.

Marcus wrote in his notes: *Nobody did anything wrong. The system is wrong. What system?*

He stared at the question for a while. He didn't have an answer yet.

Marcus kept returning to the Slack thread in the days that followed. Not to relitigate it, that was done, but because something about it nagged at him. Fourteen people in the channel. At least three with relevant information. A clear question, clearly asked. And still the signal had failed to propagate.

The RBG model he'd learned years ago—Red builders, Blue orchestrators, Green decision-makers, each speaking a different language—had assumed you could see your audience. Watch their eyes narrow. Hear the "wait, say that again?" The feedback was immediate. The adjustment was real-time.

What happens when the only audience is a text field?

THE RBG TRANSLATION PROBLEM, AMPLIFIED

In synchronous settings, RBG translation happens through continuous micro-adjustments. A Red engineer starts explaining why the authentication system needs to be rebuilt. *The current implementation uses session tokens with a 24-hour TTL, but we're storing them in a distributed cache without proper invalidation, so when users—* The executive's eyes narrow. The engineer notices, recalibrates. *We're replacing the locks on all the doors. Same doors, same keys for users, but locks that actually work. Two weeks, no customer-facing changes.* The executive nods. Translation accomplished.

This happens dozens of times in any substantive conversation. We read facial expressions, body language, and tone of voice. We notice when someone checks their phone or shifts in their chair. We pick up on the slight hesitation before a response that signals uncertainty. Most of this processing is unconscious. We don't think of it as translation; it just feels like talking.

Strip that away and you're left with text on a screen. The same Red engineer writes a Slack message about the authentication architecture. The same Green executive reads it six hours later, between other messages, with no access to the context in which it was written. The confusion that would have been visible on the executive's face now happens invisibly. The executive makes an assumption about what the engineer meant, possibly wrong, and either acts on that assumption or files the message away as something to deal with later. The correction that would have happened in real time doesn't happen at all.

Each color has characteristic communication patterns that interact differently with async:

Red communication tends toward precision and

completeness. In synchronous conversation, this can be exhausting for Blue and Green listeners, but at least they can interrupt and ask for the executive summary. In async, Red's thoroughness becomes a wall of text that other colors skim or skip entirely.

There are bug reports that read like doctoral dissertations. The summary says "Login button unresponsive." Paragraph four, after extensive discussion of race conditions and event loop behavior, mentions that this only happens in Safari, only on the first Tuesday after a full moon, only for users whose email contains a hyphen.

Derek's non-response to Sarah's message was a quieter version of this same pattern. He saw "API changes," filed it as technical, and assumed it was Miles's domain. He wasn't wrong, exactly. But his categorization meant he stopped reading before he got to "Greg called me directly which is unusual", the six words that signaled this wasn't routine. Red's instinct to sort by technical ownership meant the relational signal got filtered out.

Written communication rewards clarity and specificity. But precision about the wrong things, precision without awareness of the audience, becomes its own form of miscommunication.

Blue communication tends toward process and coordination. Orchestrators think in terms of dependencies, timelines, stakeholder management. Their messages often assume shared context about project status and team dynamics. Can you check with Sarah about the timeline concerns? Which Sarah? Which timeline? What concerns? The Blue sender knows there's only one Sarah currently worried about a timeline, but the Red recipient, heads-down in code for three days, may know four Sarahs and zero timelines.

In synchronous settings, Blue can quickly fill in gaps when someone looks confused. In async, those gaps remain gaps.

Blue also tends toward frequent check-ins, which can become problematic in async. The instinct to "stay aligned" translates into a stream of messages that fragments everyone's attention. The coordination that feels essential to Blue feels like interruption to Red and unnecessary overhead to Green. Sarah's message was the quieter version: context that lived in her head, reduced to a Slack message that was just the visible tip of it.

Green communication tends toward strategic ambiguity. Executives often speak in directions rather than destinations, in principles rather than specifics. This is partly because strategy genuinely requires flexibility, and partly because precision creates accountability that executives prefer to preserve. In synchronous settings, this ambiguity gets resolved through follow-up questions, through reading between the lines, through the shared context of being in the same room when the direction was set.

In async, strategic ambiguity is dangerous. "Let's revisit our timeline" could mean "I'm mildly curious about the timeline," or "Move the deadline," or "I'm concerned but don't want to create panic," or "Someone important asked me about this and I need cover." Without real-time access to tone and context, recipients guess at meaning and often guess wrong. They also hesitate to ask for clarification, because asking a senior person "What do you mean?" feels more fraught in writing than in conversation.

The CEO's message to Marcus after the Meridian incident was a masterclass in Green async failure. It said: "Let's discuss the client communication process when you have a chance." This could have meant "I'm disappointed but willing to help you fix it," or "This is a formal warning," or "I'm checking a box so legal is covered," or "I want to understand what happened before I decide how angry to be." Marcus spent a day and a half catastrophizing before the conversation, which turned out to be genuinely collaborative. The ambiguity cost him sleep and focus for no reason except that Green's natural communication style combines badly with async's lack of context.

DOMAIN MISMATCH: THE CYNEFIN COMPLICATION

RBG translation assumes you're solving the right kind of problem the right way. Often you're not, and async makes it worse.

Clear domain work is async-native.

Routine decisions, status updates, straightforward requests: these translate well because context is stable and vocabulary is shared. "The deployment is scheduled for Thursday at 2 PM Pacific" means exactly what it says. Nobody needs a meeting about it. For Clear work, async isn't a compromise; it's an advantage.

Complicated domain work is async-possible but fragile.

Analysis and design can happen async if the team invests in explicit context translation. The danger is that Complicated work often requires back-and-forth: "Wait, did you consider X?" "Yes, but then Y." "Hmm, what about Z?" Synchronously, this takes minutes. Async, it takes days, by which point decisions have been made on incomplete analysis and the Slack thread has forked into seven sub-conversations that nobody has the will to reconcile.

Complex domain work fights async at every step.

Probe-sense-respond requires tight feedback loops. You try something, watch what happens, adjust. The "watch what happens" part is hard when half the team won't see results for twelve hours, by which point "what happens" has become "what happened, and also three other things." The Meridian incident was Complex: multiple stakeholders, incomplete information, interdependencies invisible from any single vantage point. Trying to resolve it through async messages was like steering through rapids by sending letters to the paddle holders.

Chaotic work is synchronous or nothing.

Async chaos management is an oxymoron. But teams sometimes don't recognize they've entered Chaos until the async messages have already made things worse. Until the confident wrong answer has reached the client and the reply-all has begun.

CONTEXT TRANSLATION: THE ESSENTIAL ASYNC SKILL

There's a pattern in async failures: someone sends a message that makes sense to them, and a recipient interprets it in a way that makes sense to the recipient, and those two senses don't match.

Sarah's message: "Meridian is asking about timeline."

In her head: major account, strained relationship, escalation signal. In Miles's head: routine status inquiry, exactly the kind of thing he could answer quickly and look responsive.

The mismatch isn't about intelligence or effort. It's about context. Sarah was operating in a context dense with client history and relationship signals. Miles was operating in a context shaped by project documentation and role clarity. Neither context was wrong. They were just different, and the message didn't carry enough information to bridge the gap.

Consider the spectrum:

Version 1: *"Can someone confirm we're on track for the 15th?"*

Version 2: *"Heads up: I just got off a call with Meridian Corp—they're our biggest prospect for Q1. Their CTO wants to see the API integration working before he'll sign, and he's presenting to his board January 15th. I think we need to revisit our timeline. Not saying we definitely need to accelerate, but if there's any flexibility, this is the deal to flex for. Can you look at dependencies and let me know what would break if we pulled the deadline from February 1st to January 10th? Specifically worried about the auth work Vikram's doing."*

Sarah's actual message fell somewhere in between. She flagged that Greg's direct call was unusual, which was a signal. But signals only work if recipients are calibrated to read them. Derek stopped reading before he got there. Miles wasn't looking for relationship signals; he was looking for a question he could answer.

Most people write closer to Version 1 because it feels efficient. Also professional. Like the kind of message a busy, important person would send. The efficiency calculation is wrong in a way that's invisible until someone counts the total cost. But the deeper problem isn't individual message quality. It's that async has no mechanism to detect when context was inadequate until after the damage is done.

TRUST WITHOUT EYE CONTACT

Trust tends to be more fragile than resilient, and async makes that asymmetry worse.

Synchronous teams build trust through accumulated small moments. The coffee conversation where you learn someone's kid just started chemo. The look on their face when the demo crashes and you both know the client saw it. These moments create a texture of relationship that makes collaboration feel safe.

Async teams don't get most of these moments. Trust must be established through different mechanisms: consistency of follow-through, clarity of communication, reliability over time. These are slower trust-builders, which means async teams often operate with thinner trust reserves than they realize.

The problem compounds because damage is harder to detect. In synchronous settings, you can usually tell when someone is offended. You address it in the moment, clarify intent, repair before damage accumulates. In async, you might not know your message landed badly until someone's behavior changes weeks later. A silence that means "I'm thinking" is indistinguishable from a silence that means "I'm furious."

Lin's silence in the Meridian thread was a trust problem, though it didn't look like one. She had relevant information. She started typing, then stopped. Not because she didn't care, but because she wasn't sure it was safe to volunteer information outside her lane. She'd been at Consolidated nineteen months and still couldn't read the unwritten rules: who spoke, when, about what. None of it was explicit. The ambiguity was itself a trust failure: the team had never made explicit what kind of contribution was welcome from whom.

Written communication makes this worse. Tone is difficult to convey. A message intended as neutral reads as curt. A joke reads as criticism. Sarcasm is almost always a mistake; the message you thought was obviously playful reads as hostility to someone in a different mood, a different time zone, a different level of caffeination.

What researchers call the "flexibility paradox" is largely a trust problem. Remote workers report better work-life balance but also higher rates of stress and loneliness.[1] The mechanism is broken trust in boundaries. The flexibility that async promises—work when it works for you—curdles into anxiety that you're never really off. This happens when teams haven't established trusted norms around availability, when the implicit expectation is always-on even if the explicit policy says otherwise.

The policy says you can unplug at 6 PM. Your manager's last message arrived at 9 PM. Your colleague responded at 10 PM. The policy is clear; the signal is clearer. Every organization says work-life balance matters. The actual culture is revealed in when the messages arrive.

Psychological safety, a key enabler of team learning, appears harder to establish in async settings. When you can't see how people react to your contributions, you can't calibrate what's safe to say. When feedback arrives hours later in written form, it feels more like judgment than conversation. We'll return to this in Chapter 7.

THE TEAMMATE WHO NEVER SLEEPS (AND WHAT THAT ACTUALLY MEANS)

There's an obvious question: if async communication is hard because humans aren't always available, what happens when one of your teammates is always available?

AI systems are inherently async. They don't sleep, they don't have time zones, they process information whenever it's submitted. A team that has mastered async communication is better positioned to integrate AI than a team still depending on real-time correction.

---

1. Buffer, *State of Remote Work 2020* (2020). Twenty percent of remote workers cited loneliness as their biggest struggle—tied with collaboration difficulties—while 18 percent reported difficulty unplugging after work. Survey of 3,521 remote workers, data collected November 2019.

AI can serve as translation layer, context provider, and documentation generator: three roles that address exactly where async breaks down.

Consider translation. A Red engineer posts: *"Implemented the caching layer with LRU eviction, 5-minute TTL, 10k entry limit. Should reduce p99 latency to <50ms under normal load."* The AI offers: *"Want me to translate this for the stakeholder update? Something like: 'The system will now respond faster for most users, even during busy periods.'"* The engineer can accept, modify, or ignore. The translation cost, previously invisible and often unpaid, becomes visible and optional.

Context provision is harder and more dangerous. If Miles had asked an AI to highlight context about the account before responding—the relationship history, the previous miss, the stakeholders involved—he might have recognized that "confirming we're on track" was higher-stakes than it appeared. It could have flagged: *This client has had delivery issues before. Sarah's note that "Greg called directly" suggests urgency. Consider confirming timeline with operations before responding.*

But that's not what happened. Miles used AI to draft a confident, well-structured response based on the information he already had. The AI helped him sound more authoritative about his incomplete picture. It didn't prompt him to question whether his picture was complete. It didn't know to.

This is the thing about AI as a communication tool: it amplifies whatever dynamic is already present. If you're using it to synthesize context you wouldn't otherwise access, it expands your awareness. If you're using it to polish a message you were already going to send, it just makes you sound more confident about whatever you already believed. The tool doesn't know which one you need. Often, neither does the human.

Documentation is where AI helps most reliably. The discipline of async work depends on writing things down, and writing things down takes time, which means it often doesn't happen. Call it the Documentation Prisoner's Dilemma: everyone benefits from good documentation, nobody wants to write it. AI shifts the equilibrium. Meeting recordings become transcripts, summaries become searchable artifacts. Documentation happens as a byproduct rather than an additional burden.

Teams that master async communication will find AI integration more natural. The discipline of explicit context, clear documentation, structured handoffs: these are exactly what AI needs to be useful. Teams that struggle with async will struggle with AI for the same reasons: they're depending on implicit coordination that neither async nor AI can provide.

Marcus understood this now in a way he hadn't before Meridian. He could name it: async strips away the correction mechanisms that make translation work. He could even see the direction.

What he couldn't see was how to get there. His team wasn't going to become co-located. The time zones weren't going to rearrange themselves. Sarah wasn't going to magically have fewer channels to monitor or more hours in the day.

He wrote in his notebook: *We know what's broken. We don't know how to fix it yet.*

The call from James Whitford—VP Operations, Marcus's boss—came Thursday afternoon. Not a calendar invite through his EA. Whitford himself, direct line.

"I'm going to need your team for something," Whitford said. "Can't say what yet. But it's the kind of thing that could matter. For the company, and for you."

Marcus waited.

"Get them ready," Whitford said. "I'll know more soon."

The call lasted less than two minutes. Marcus sat with it for the rest of the day. Whitford didn't make calls like that casually. Something was taking shape in rooms Marcus wasn't in, and his team was being considered for it.

Get them ready.

They weren't ready now. He didn't know how to make them ready for more.

MARCUS'S WHITEBOARD: READ THE WATER

See Concept Reference: Read the Water for key frameworks and definitions.

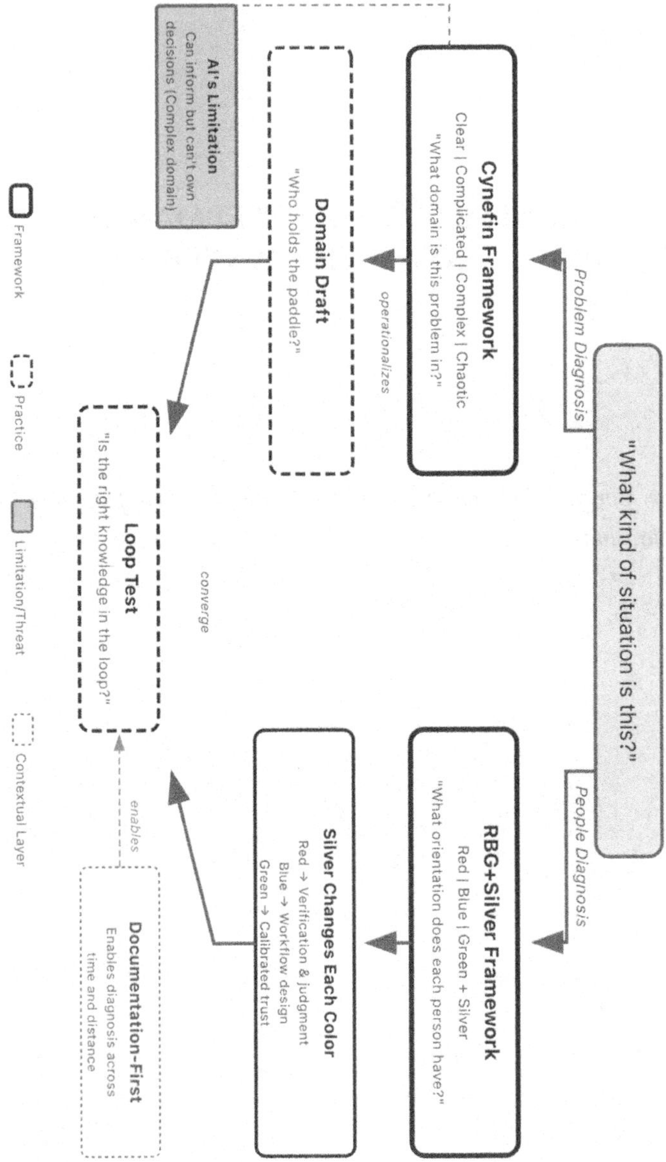
"What kind of situation is this?"
Problem Diagnosis
People Diagnosis
Cynefin Framework
Clear | Complicated | Complex | Chaotic
"What domain is this problem in?"
RBG+Silver Framework
Red | Blue | Green + Silver
"What orientation does each person have?"
operationalizes
Domain Draft
"Who holds the paddle?"
Silver Changes Each Color
Red → Verification & judgment
Blue → Workflow design
Green → Calibrated trust
AI's Limitation
Can inform but can't own decisions (Complex domain)
converge
Loop Test
"Is the right knowledge in the loop?"
enables
Documentation-First
Enables diagnosis across time and distance
Framework
Practice
Limitation/Threat
Contextual Layer

PART II

KNOW YOUR CREW

4

NEITHER TOOL NOR TEAMMATE

THE THIRD THING

Derek solved the memory leak late on a Thursday afternoon, which shouldn't have bothered him. The office had mostly emptied out; across the floor, a few monitors still glowed, but the nearest occupied desk was several rows away.

The problem had been haunting them for two weeks. One of the legacy routing modules was bleeding memory under specific conditions, accumulating quietly until the system slowed to a crawl and needed to be restarted. Derek had spent hours tracing the issue through code he'd written four years ago, back when the system was simpler and certain shortcuts seemed reasonable.

He'd been describing the problem to ChatGPT, not expecting much, just thinking out loud in the way that sometimes helped him see things differently. He'd explained the data structures involved, the conditions that triggered the leak, the approaches he'd already tried.

The AI suggested something he hadn't considered. A lazy evaluation pattern borrowed from functional programming, combined with a pooling strategy that would contain the memory growth rather than trying to eliminate it at the source. Derek had used pooling before, but not in this configuration. The approach was elegant in a way that felt slightly foreign.

He implemented it. Not blindly. He caught two issues the AI couldn't have known about: an edge case involving the legacy database connector, and a timing constraint related to how the system handled peak load. The AI's solution assumed a cleaner architecture than actually existed. Derek adapted it to the architecture he actually had.

The fix worked. Memory usage flattened. The restarts stopped. Three weeks of frustration resolved in an afternoon.

The next morning, Derek mentioned the fix in standup. Memory leak resolved, here's the ticket, moving on. Nobody asked how he'd solved it. Nobody asked if he'd used AI. It wasn't the kind of thing people asked about yet, the same way nobody asked if you'd used Google to look something up. The tools were just part of the environment.

He thought about mentioning it anyway. Thought about saying "ChatGPT suggested an approach I wouldn't have tried." But what would that accomplish? The problem was fixed. His name was on the commit. If he announced that the clever part came from somewhere else, what was he actually saying about himself? That he was honest? That he was replaceable? These felt like the same admission.

He moved on to the next ticket without adding anything.

Marcus, watching the standup from the corner of the conference room, noticed that Derek seemed quieter than usual. He made a note to check in later, then forgot. There were seven other things demanding attention, and Derek had just fixed a problem that had been causing headaches for weeks.

A PRESENCE ON THE TEAM

Derek's fix worked. The AI contributed something genuinely useful; Derek contributed something the AI couldn't provide. This is what good collaboration looks like. The uncomfortable question Derek didn't ask in standup is the one this chapter needs to address: what exactly had he collaborated with?

Is AI a teammate or a tool?

The honest answer is that it's neither, and the question is probably wrong.

The "tool" framing gets something right. AI has no genuine agency. It doesn't want anything. It doesn't care about outcomes. Gary Klein and colleagues, studying human-AI teaming challenges, call it the "Basic Compact": the understanding that participants share goal alignment and will work to maintain common ground.[1] Your colleague double-checks the numbers before the client meeting without being asked. The nurse mentions something that's probably nothing but feels off. AI cannot participate in this compact any more than your spreadsheet can.

But the tool framing misses something. A hammer doesn't change how you communicate with your colleagues. A calculator doesn't radically alter the distribution of cognitive labor on your team. AI does both. It generates outputs that look like contributions. It creates coordination challenges that feel like managing a human collaborator.

The "teammate" framing gets that part right. But it misses the absence of genuine understanding, the lack of stake in outcomes, the fact that your human colleagues know what you

---

1. Gary Klein et al., "Ten Challenges for Making Automation a 'Team Player' in Joint Human-Agent Activity," *IEEE Intelligent Systems* 19, no. 6 (2004): 91–95. The Basic Compact involves commitment to goal alignment and detecting any loss of common ground that might disrupt joint activity.

meant even when you said something different. AI cannot do this.

So here's the formulation I find most useful: AI is a presence in the team that changes how the team functions, even though it cannot truly join the team. This is what makes Silver different from the other colors in the RBG framework. Red, Blue, and Green describe orientations that humans can adopt and shift between. Silver describes a capability that humans must work alongside without ever fully integrating.

This is deliberately imprecise. It has to be. The concept is genuinely new, and forcing it into familiar categories is exactly what leads teams to misuse AI by treating it as something it isn't.

If this feels unsatisfying, good. We're in genuinely new territory. Some bushwhacking is required.

THE MEMORIZED HOSPITAL

AI doesn't think. You know this. You forget it the moment the output sounds intelligent.

What AI does is predict. It predicts what words should come next in a sequence, based on patterns learned from astronomical quantities of text. It has seen so much human writing that it can convincingly mimic human reasoning without actually performing it.

Consider an analogy. Imagine you memorized every conversation that had ever occurred in a hospital. Every diagnosis, consultation, interaction between doctors and patients. You memorized them so thoroughly that given the first half of any medical conversation, you could reliably predict what words would come next.

You would sound exactly like a doctor. A patient might not be able to tell the difference. But you wouldn't understand what any of it meant. You'd just know that when humans say X, they tend to follow it with Y. An extraordinary impression of medical reasoning, with no actual medical reasoning taking place.

This is AI. The impression is so good that it fools us constantly. Systems that produce the shape of analysis without the substance of analysis.

Here's why this matters: the specific ways AI fails follow directly from this architecture.

Humans make intuitive leaps, connect unrelated fields, recognize when something doesn't fit even if we can't articulate why. We sense when a deal is going bad or a colleague is upset or a plan won't survive contact with reality. AI extrapolates patterns. It cannot make genuine leaps, only statistically likely next steps.

Derek's fix worked because he could evaluate the AI's suggestion against his own experience. He could recognize "this won't work with our legacy connector" because he understood both the suggestion and the system. The AI understood neither. It just produced text that looked like a solution.

CONFIDENT EMPTINESS

Here's where this gets teams into trouble.

AI sounds equally certain whether it's correct or hallucinating. The system that suggests an elegant solution to a query optimization problem delivers that suggestion with the same authoritative tone it uses to fabricate statistics or invent research that doesn't exist. We're wired to treat confidence as a credibility signal because, among humans, it's a decent-enough predictor. Not great, maybe 20% better than random, but enough that the instinct stuck. AI broke that instinct in about three years. It will tell you the wrong thing with exactly the same tone it uses to tell you the right thing. The confidence feels like it means something. It never does. Confident emptiness.

AI also identifies patterns it cannot explain. It sees that X co-occurs with Y in training data and concludes a relationship exists. Sometimes this finds something real. Sometimes it surfaces noise. And sometimes it locates patterns that were true historically but no longer apply. Somewhere in the training data, fax machines are still relevant. The AI cannot distinguish between these cases because distinguishing requires understanding what the patterns mean.

AI lacks tacit knowledge entirely.[2] Humans swim in oceans of unspoken context. You know that when the CFO says "that's interesting" she means "over my dead body." You know that the quarterly deadline isn't really the deadline; it's two days before. You know which rules are rules and which rules are suggestions everyone ignores. You know who actually makes decisions regardless of what the org chart says. You know the real org chart—the one nobody printed.

AI knows none of this unless you explicitly provide it. And even then, it knows the words without understanding the significance. The AI's outputs don't have a blank space labeled "tacit knowledge would go here." They just proceed as if that context doesn't exist, because from the AI's perspective, it doesn't.

INSTITUTIONAL MEMORY

The following week, the AI helped Miles put together a vendor comparison for a contract renewal. Three carriers, side by side, performance metrics and pricing and capacity projections.

---

2. Michael Polanyi, *The Tacit Dimension* (Chicago: University of Chicago Press, 2009). Polanyi's central thesis: "We can know more than we can tell."

Clean analysis. One carrier came out clearly ahead on the numbers.

The recommendation came up in the Thursday operations sync. Miles walked through it. The numbers were straightforward. Consolidated was paying more for equivalent service. Switching made sense.

"Any concerns?" Marcus asked.

Sarah didn't have any. Derek wasn't paying attention; this wasn't his domain. Lin was reviewing the comparison on her screen. The carrier Miles was recommending, Pacific Northwest Freight, had been on the preferred vendor list at her old company before the acquisition. She remembered why they'd eventually moved away from them. It wasn't in any database. It was a pattern of small problems: late pickups that were always someone else's fault, damage claims that took months to resolve, a sales team that promised things their operations couldn't deliver. Nothing dramatic. Nothing that would show up in the performance metrics Miles was presenting, which only covered the past eighteen months. Just an institutional memory that the numbers looked better than the experience.

Lin scrolled back through the comparison on her screen. She thought about mentioning it. But what would she say? "I have a bad feeling about this carrier based on something that happened at a company that no longer exists"? The data in front of them was clear. Her information was old, anecdotal, possibly no longer relevant. Pacific Northwest might have improved. Companies do improve.

The conversation moved on. Marcus approved the recommendation. Lin stayed quiet.

Two months later, Sarah mentioned in passing that Pacific Northwest was becoming a headache. Late pickups. Damage claims taking forever. Their sales team kept promising things that didn't happen.

"Weren't they highly rated?" Marcus asked.

"On paper," Sarah said. "The metrics looked great. The reality is different."

Lin, sitting in the same meeting, didn't say that she'd known this. What would be the point? The decision was made. Mentioning it now would sound like "I told you so" for something she hadn't actually told anyone.

The vendor issue wasn't a crisis. They'd manage the contract, push Pacific Northwest on the service issues, maybe switch again at the next renewal. It was a small thing. Small things are how most organizational knowledge gets lost. Not in dramatic failures that prompt postmortems, but in quiet moments where someone knows something, doesn't mention it, and the organization proceeds slightly worse than it needed to.

The AI had done its job. It had analyzed the data it had access to. It couldn't know about Lin's experience at a company Consolidated had absorbed a year and a half ago. It couldn't access institutional memory that existed only in someone's head. It had produced a confident recommendation based on the information available, and the information available was incomplete in ways that were invisible to everyone except the person who didn't speak.

IGNORANCE AUDITS

A phrase that should set off alarm bells: "The AI should have known."

AI systems have no access to what you didn't tell them. If your organizational context wasn't explicitly provided, it doesn't exist. If your institutional memory wasn't stated, it cannot be accounted for. If there's a gap between what the data shows and what someone learned the hard way, the AI lives on the data side, unaware that the other side exists.

This produces outputs that are genuinely good within the scope of what the AI was given, and genuinely blind to everything outside that scope. The vendor analysis was correct for the data Miles provided. It was useless for the decision that actually needed to be made. There's no seam showing. The analysis didn't have a section labeled "things I don't know about your company's history with these vendors." It didn't have a section labeled "questions you should ask your colleagues before trusting this." It just presented itself as finished, because from its perspective, it was. Confident incompleteness. The most dangerous kind of wrong: wrong in ways that look complete.

After the routing system disaster, Marcus started requiring what he called "ignorance audits." Before accepting any significant AI output, someone had to list three things the AI couldn't possibly know about the situation. It felt silly at first. It slowed things down. People rolled their eyes. But it caught some problems. The context about which stakeholders had history with which decisions. The informal constraints that existed in people's heads but not in any database.

It didn't catch the issue with Pacific Northwest. The ignorance audit could prompt the question "does anyone have history with these vendors?" But prompting the question isn't the same as making it safe to answer with "I have a vague bad feeling from a company that no longer exists." That required something Marcus's team didn't have yet.

A few weeks after the vendor decision, Marcus booked Conference Room C for 4pm on a Thursday. No agenda. Just "AI debrief—informal."

Conference Room C was the small one, the one with the window that didn't open and the whiteboard nobody had erased since July. Someone had written "*Q3 PRIORITIES*" in blue marker and underlined it twice. The priorities themselves had been wiped away, leaving the heading presiding over nothing.

Derek arrived first, laptop open, half-watching a deployment that didn't need watching. His coffee cup said *SUDO MAKE ME COFFEE*. Lin came in with tea, taking her usual seat slightly back from the table. Sarah was on her phone in the hallway, finishing something, one finger raised in the universal sign for "one minute." Miles was a rectangle on the wall monitor, slightly pixelated, his home office bookshelf carefully arranged behind him.

"We're just talking," Marcus said, once everyone had settled. "I want to know what you're noticing. About working with AI. What's working, what's not."

No one spoke.

Miles unmuted first. "I'll start: The vendor analysis I put together last week. AI pulled together three years of performance data in about an hour. Found patterns I wouldn't have spotted manually. That felt like collaboration. Like having another competent research analyst on the team."

"But the vendor thing," Derek said. He stopped. Started again. "A colleague would have asked questions. Would have said 'Does anyone know these carriers?' The AI just... produced."

"It can't know what it doesn't know," Sarah said, looking up from her phone. "That's what I keep running into."

Miles said something about spreadsheets. His audio cut out on the key word. Derek looked at the monitor, decided it wasn't worth asking him to repeat it, and responded to what he thought Miles meant: "A spreadsheet doesn't make you feel like you're thinking with someone. When the AI suggested that fix, it felt like a conversation. Then I have to remind myself there's no one on the other end."

Marcus turned to Lin. "You've been quiet."

This was not a surprise. Lin was usually quiet. Marcus

asking her directly was also not a surprise; he'd been doing this more since Meridian, making space for people who didn't grab it themselves.

"The vendor analysis was correct," Lin said. "The numbers. The logic. It just didn't know enough about Pacific Northwest."

"Your experience with them."

"But I did not say anything. Because what I had was not data. It was a feeling. Old problems at a different company." She looked at her tea. "The AI had a clean analysis. I had a sense that something was wrong. In that room, the analysis felt more real."

Miles's video froze for a second, then caught up. "That's just how evidence works, though. Data beats anecdotes."

"Except when the anecdotes are right," Sarah said.

"Sure, but how do you know which—"

"We tried 'the AI says it's fine' with routing," Derek said. "Remember how that went?"

The room got quiet. On the monitor, Miles looked like he wanted to respond but thought better of it.

Derek leaned back, eyes on the ceiling. "I don't think we're going to figure out what AI *is*. The metaphors all break. Maybe we just watch what actually happens. The query thing worked because I stayed in the loop. I checked the solution against what I knew. The vendor thing failed because Lin's knowledge never got into the loop."

He shrugged. "Not 'is AI good or bad.' Just 'is the right knowledge in the loop or not.'"

Marcus thought of the Basic Compact, the thing he'd been reading about: teammates who instinctively checked whether the loop was complete. AI couldn't do that. It didn't know there was a loop.

Lin nodded. Small, but visible. Marcus noticed.

"That's not a framework," Miles said.

"No," Marcus said. "But it's a start."

The meeting ended ten minutes later. No action items. No follow-up scheduled. No one suggested putting it on the calendar as a recurring meeting, which was how you knew it had actually been useful. Just five people who understood something slightly better than they had an hour before.

Derek walked back to his desk. The commit notification was still on his screen, his name at the top. Good work. The AI had helped. Together they'd solved a problem faster than either would have alone.

But that wasn't what stayed with him. What stayed with him was his standup brief, the morning after. He'd mentioned the fix. Ticket closed, moving on. He hadn't mentioned how the solution came together. The clever part, the part that made the fix elegant instead of just functional, had come from somewhere else. His name was on the commit.

Nobody had asked. It wasn't the kind of thing people asked about, not yet. The tools were just part of the environment, like Google, like Stack Overflow. You didn't cite your sources in standup.

Still. He'd thought about mentioning it. And then he hadn't.

He wasn't sure what that silence meant. He wasn't sure what any of this meant yet.

That uncertainty, at least, was something the AI couldn't help with.

5

RIGGING THE BOAT

STRUCTURE AS STRATEGY

The conversation with Sarah went fine. That was the problem.

Marcus had prepared for it carefully. He'd reviewed the Meridian situation, identified specific moments where different choices might have changed the outcome, and thought about how to frame feedback that was honest without being demoralizing. He was, by his own assessment, pretty good at these conversations. Twenty years of management had taught him how to deliver hard truths in ways people could hear.

Sarah listened. She nodded in the right places. She agreed that her message to the channel had assumed too much shared context. She acknowledged that, saying "Greg called me directly, which is unusual" was doing a lot of work that she hadn't made explicit. She committed to being more deliberate about flagging urgency, providing background, making the implicit explicit.

"That's helpful," she said. "Thanks for taking the time."

Marcus left the conversation feeling like he'd accomplished something. She'd heard the feedback. Things would improve.

A week later, a client named Parsons sent an email to James Whitford, Marcus's VP, asking why Consolidated seemed unable to maintain continuity on their account.

The details were mundane in the way that structural failures always are. Sarah had been preparing for a site visit to Phoenix. Before she left, she'd handed off a follow-up conversation with Parsons to Derek. Simple enough: confirm the integration timeline, answer any technical questions, keep the relationship warm until she returned.

She'd explained the situation clearly. Derek had executed exactly what she'd asked.

The problem was a conversation Sarah had two days earlier. Parsons had called with concerns about a scope change, and Sarah had talked them through it. The call ended well. Parsons felt heard. But the call had also surfaced that Parsons was nervous about a specific technical dependency, something they'd been burned on before with a different vendor. Sarah had mentioned this to Marcus in the hallway outside a meeting. "Parsons is skittish about the authentication integration. We should make sure Derek knows to handle that carefully." Marcus had nodded. He was late to the meeting. The information entered his mind and then, apparently, exited.

Derek's follow-up email was technically perfect. Professional, accurate, responsive to the questions Parsons had asked. It also walked directly into the authentication topic with the cheerful confidence of someone who had no idea there was a history there. From Parsons's perspective, it was confirmation that Consolidated didn't actually listen to them, that concerns raised in one conversation evaporated by the next.

The postmortem was brief and unsatisfying. Sarah had communicated the handoff. Derek had executed it. Marcus had heard the context that would have mattered but hadn't connected it to Derek's task. The information existed. It just hadn't traveled to where it needed to be.

"I thought you'd tell Derek," Sarah said to Marcus.

"I didn't know Derek was handling Parsons," Marcus said.

"I sent an email."

"I get three hundred emails a day."

They looked at each other. There was nothing to say. Nobody had done anything wrong.

Marcus thought about Whitford's call. *Get them ready. I'll know more soon.* That had been two weeks ago. Whatever Whitford was planning—something to do with Lindquist Logistics, the Midwest operation they'd acquired earlier that year—the decision was getting closer. And now Whitford had a client email asking why Consolidated couldn't maintain continuity on a routine handoff.

Marcus thought about Pacific Northwest too. The vendor situation that was still being managed, the knowledge Lin had that nobody knew to ask for. That hadn't reached Whitford. Probably. But he could see the shape of something now: failures that weren't dramatic enough to trigger alarms, just persistent enough to form a pattern. The kind of pattern that answered the question *is this team ready* without anyone having to say it out loud.

That night, Marcus sat in his home office at eleven-thirty, not quite ready to sleep. The desk lamp made a small circle of light; beyond it, the room was dark, the window giving back only his own reflection. He'd had a beer, Sierra Nevada Pale Ale, his usual. He was doing the thing he did when something was bothering him, which was to search for answers in the way that modern people search for answers: typing half-formed questions into the void and hoping something useful came back.

"Why do teams fail when the people are good"

The results were what you'd expect. Listicles about communication. Articles about trust. The kind of advice that sounds wise and means nothing: *leverage diverse perspectives, break down silos, empower your people*. Management writing has a particular genius for producing sentences that everyone agrees with and no one can act on. Marcus had read versions of this for twenty years. He'd *given* versions of this advice, standing in front of whiteboards, using words like "alignment" with a straight face. Sarah had nodded and agreed and committed to doing better. So had a hundred other people he'd coached. The nodding wasn't the problem. The nodding was easy. Something else was the problem, and the listicles weren't going to tell him what.

He refined the search. Added "research." Added "evidence." He was tired and irritated and not in the mood for someone's thought leadership.

Somewhere in the second page of results, he found a reference to a researcher named Richard Hackman. The preview text mentioned a statistic: team design is nearly forty times as powerful as coaching in affecting team performance.

He clicked through. Read.

Kept reading.

Forty times. The number lodged in his brain. He thought about his conversation with Sarah. The careful preparation. The specific feedback. The commitments she'd made. He had coached her perfectly. She had received the coaching perfectly. And then a week later, information failed to flow from a hallway conversation to an email because the structure didn't carry it.

The structure was forty times more important than the coaching.

He'd spent an hour preparing to coach Sarah. He'd spent zero hours examining whether the structure of his team made success possible.

Marcus closed his laptop, then opened it again. He wasn't going to sleep anyway.

THE 40X MULTIPLIER

Richard Hackman spent thirty years studying teams that actually exist.

This might sound like an obvious thing for a researcher to do. It wasn't. Most team research happens in laboratories, with undergraduate psychology students assembled for an hour to solve puzzles that don't matter. The students get course credit. The researchers get publications. Nobody learns anything about teams that have to show up again tomorrow and work with the same people they disappointed today. Hackman studied airline cockpit crews making life-or-death decisions, symphony orchestras navigating forty competing egos, and later, intelligence analysts piecing together threats from scattered evidence.

His teams had stakes. They had history. They had the kinds of interpersonal dynamics that develop when people work together for years rather than forty-five minutes in a psychology building. The research was messier because reality is messy. It was also more useful for the same reason.

The finding that stopped Marcus at midnight was this: Hackman's 60-30-10 rule. Sixty percent of a team's effectiveness is determined at setup—boundaries, composition, direction—before the work begins. Another thirty percent is determined at launch, during the first meeting when norms are established. Only ten percent is influenced by ongoing interventions once the team is running.[1]

---

1. The 60-30-10 rule appears in J. Richard Hackman, *Collaborative Intelligence: Using Teams to Solve Hard Problems* (San Francisco: Berrett-Koehler, 2011), drawing on his research with intelligence analysts. Hackman's foundational work on team conditions appears in *Leading Teams: Setting the Stage for Great Performances* (Boston: Harvard Business School Press, 2002), with the essentials/enablers framework developed in Ruth Wageman, Debra A. Nunes, James A. Burruss, and J. Richard Hackman, *Senior Leadership Teams: What It Takes to Make Them Great* (Boston: Harvard Business School Press, 2008). The "40x"

Read that again. Ninety percent of whether your team succeeds or fails is baked in before the work is underway. The conditions you set up, the boundaries you draw, the composition you choose, the norms you establish at launch. These aren't preliminary activities you rush through to get to the real work. They are the work.

The 40x number comes from a comparison. Researchers looked at what happened when teams got better coaching versus what happened when teams got better design. Coaching helped. Design helped forty times more.

This doesn't mean you shouldn't coach. It means coaching a poorly structured team is like teaching someone to swim better while they're drowning in a riptide. The technique might be excellent. The conditions make it irrelevant.

Marcus had coached Sarah. Sarah had improved, probably. It hadn't mattered because the structure didn't carry information from hallway conversations to the people who needed it. No amount of coaching would fix that. Sarah could become the greatest communicator in the history of logistics companies and the structure would still drop context at transition points. She'd just drop it more eloquently.

The uncomfortable implication: most managers spend most of their time on things that matter less than the things they're not spending time on. They coach, motivate, align, inspire. They have one-on-ones. They give feedback. They rally the troops. These activities feel like leadership because they look like leadership. They're also not where the leverage is.

The leverage is in the boring work that happens before anyone feels led. Boundaries. Composition. Protocols. Who's on the team and who isn't. What information flows where. Which decisions require consultation and which don't. This is the stuff

---

comparison of team design versus coaching is cited in J. Richard Hackman, "What Makes for a Great Team?" *APA Science Briefs*, June 2004.

that gets skipped because everyone's eager to start the real work, not realizing they've already done the work that will determine whether the real work succeeds.

Hackman called this "setting the stage." The performance matters. The conditions for performance matter more.

THE SIX CONDITIONS

Hackman identified six conditions that predict team effectiveness. Three are essential—without them, teams cannot function. Three are enabling—they amplify what's possible when the essentials are in place.

A Real Team

The first essential is having a real team. This means boundaries that are actually clear: everyone knows who's in and who's out. It means stability, so membership isn't churning constantly. And it means genuine interdependence—a shared fate, not just shared Slack channels. This sounds obvious until you test it. Most teams fail. Membership is ambiguous. People drift in and out of meetings without anyone being sure if they're participants or observers. "The team" becomes a label attached to whoever happens to be working on something this week.

A Compelling Direction

The second essential is a compelling direction. Clear enough that every member, asked separately, would describe it the same way. Challenging enough to engage genuine effort. Consequential enough that someone outside the team actually cares. Try the test: ask each member of your team, in separate conversations, what the team is trying to accomplish. If you get the same answer, you're ahead of most.

The Right People

The third essential is having the right people. This means complementary capabilities—but capabilities include more than technical skills. The ability to work as part of a team is a capability too, and it's the one that gets neglected. Teams select for domain expertise and assume collaboration will work itself out. It often doesn't. Someone can be brilliant at their specialty and corrosive to every team they join. Technical skills can be developed; collaborative behavior is harder to change.

These three are the essentials. Without them, nothing else matters. The enablers build on top.

Sound Structure.

Sound structure is the invisible architecture—how decisions get made, how information flows, where handoffs happen, who knows what. Meridian had good people with good intentions passing information through a structure that kept losing it.

Supportive Context

Supportive context means the organization provides what the team needs: information, resources, rewards that don't punish collaboration, air cover when things go wrong. Teams exist inside organizations, and organizations can starve them without meaning to. The team that gets penalized for missing individual metrics while hitting collective goals learns quickly what actually matters.

Expert Coaching

Expert coaching means someone who can help the team improve how it works together, available at key moments like beginnings, midpoints, and when teams are stuck, not as constant oversight. The wrong kind of attention, micromanagement disguised as support, makes things worse.

None of these conditions emerge automatically. Not from proximity. Not from good intentions. Not from hiring smart people and assuming they'll figure it out. The time you skip here, you pay back later at punishing interest rates.

Marcus, reading this at midnight, thought about his team. They had never discussed boundaries. He wasn't certain who was on the team and who was adjacent to it. They had a direction in the sense that they had a project name. They had the right people in the sense that everyone was individually competent. They had structure in the sense that meetings appeared on calendars.

By Hackman's criteria, he wasn't sure they were a team at all.

THE MAP OF EXPERTISE

Hackman's research didn't address distribution, because in his era it wasn't yet a defining feature of work. Now it is.

Your team is probably not entirely in the same room. Some members may be in different time zones. Some may be fully remote, their physical location irrelevant except for the timestamp on their messages. You may have contributors who've never met in person and never will.

This changes nothing about whether the six conditions matter. It changes everything about how much precision they demand.

Picture a gradient. On one end: a fully co-located team, same room, same hours, coordinating through presence and conversation. On the other end: a fully distributed team across many time zones, primarily asynchronous, with AI handling parts of the workflow. Most teams sit somewhere in between, and the spot keeps shifting, often mid-project, often without anyone noticing until something breaks.

Co-location is forgiving. When your boundaries are ambiguous, you notice quickly because the wrong person shows up to a meeting. When direction drifts, you hear it in hallway conversations. When a handoff is incomplete, the receiver taps the sender on the shoulder. The feedback loops are fast. Mistakes get caught early. You can tolerate slop in the design because the environment corrects errors cheaply.

Distribution is unforgiving. Someone misses a meeting and nobody notices for a week. Each location drifts in its own direction. A handoff is incomplete and the receiver either waits twelve hours for clarification or proceeds with assumptions. The feedback loops are slow. Mistakes compound. The environment punishes imprecision ruthlessly.

The more distributed your team, the more deliberate your structural design must be. Not because distribution changes the requirements, but because it raises the cost of getting them wrong.

There's a concept from cognitive psychology that becomes critical here: transactive memory.[2] The technical term for "who knows what."

Teams don't just accumulate knowledge. They develop a map of where knowledge lives. Derek knows the legacy systems. Lin knows operations. Sarah knows the client relationships. The map lets team members access expertise they don't personally hold. You don't need to know everything if you know who knows what. Teams with well-developed transactive memory outperform teams with more total knowledge but

2. Daniel M. Wegner, "Transactive Memory: A Contemporary Analysis of the Group Mind," in *Theories of Group Behavior*, ed. Brian Mullen and George R. Goethals (New York: Springer-Verlag, 1987), 185–208. Wegner introduced the concept to describe how groups develop shared systems for encoding, storing, and retrieving information—knowing "who knows what" in a group.

weaker maps.[3] It's not enough for expertise to exist. Everyone needs to know where it lives.

The Parsons failure was a transactive memory failure. The expertise existed. The map didn't route to it.

Co-located teams build transactive memory through ambient exposure. They overhear conversations. They see who people go to with questions. They absorb who knows what by being present while knowledge gets used. The map builds itself —imperfectly, but automatically, like learning the layout of a building they work in every day.

Distributed teams don't get this. They're not overhearing anything. They don't see who gets consulted because consultations happen in DMs and video calls they're not on. The map has to be built deliberately, maintained deliberately, and consulted deliberately. Most teams skip all three and wonder why information doesn't flow.

Marcus's team had five people, or maybe six depending on how Priya was counted. They had been working together for months. He realized he could not confidently describe what each of them knew.

He knew Derek was technical and Lin was operations and Sarah was client-facing. Beyond those broad labels, the map was blank.

The map wasn't just incomplete. In some areas, it was blank in ways he hadn't noticed were blank until right now.

---

3. Leslie A. DeChurch and Jessica R. Mesmer-Magnus, "The Cognitive Underpinnings of Effective Teamwork: A Meta-Analysis," *Journal of Applied Psychology* 95, no. 1 (2010): 32–53. Their meta-analysis found that compilational team cognition—where knowledge is distributed across members, exemplified by transactive memory systems—showed stronger effects on team performance ($\rho = .44$) than compositional team cognition such as shared mental models ($\rho = .32$).

Marcus spent the weekend reading. By Monday he had a notebook full of notes and the uncomfortable feeling of someone who has just learned that the thing he's been doing for twenty years has a name, a literature, and a body of evidence suggesting he's been doing it wrong.

He scheduled a meeting for Thursday afternoon, Oakland time, which meant it was plausible for Chicago but impossible for Mumbai. He noted this fact and then didn't know what to do with it. Priya couldn't attend a 3 PM Pacific meeting without being online at 3:30 AM. Earlier meant conflicting with Sarah's client calls. Later meant conflicting with Derek's kid's soccer practice. The earth's rotation, which had seemed like a solved problem, turned out to be incompatible with collaborative work.

He scheduled it for 3 PM and sent Priya a message saying he'd follow up with her separately. This felt like exactly the kind of structural problem he was trying to address. He was about to hold a meeting on team structure that exemplified poor team structure. There was probably a lesson in that. He decided not to learn it yet.

Thursday came. Derek was already in the Oakland conference room, folded into a chair that looked too small for someone his height. The window faced the parking structure; you could see the bay from the floor above, but not from here. Lin and Sarah arrived together. Miles was a rectangle on the screen. Marcus had printed copies of Hackman's six conditions, one for each person, which felt slightly embarrassing, like he was about to run a workshop.

"I want to try something," he said. "It might be a waste of time. I'm not sure yet."

Derek looked at the printout. "What's this?"

"A framework for thinking about team structure. I found it over the weekend."

"You found it?"

"I was up late. I was trying to figure out why Parsons happened. And Meridian before that." Marcus stood at the whiteboard, fountain pen still in his hand from the notes he'd been taking. Derek's expression was unreadable. Lin was watching, quiet as always. Sarah had her phone face-down on the table—a small concession. "I kept coming back to the same thing. Everyone did their jobs. Nothing worked."

Sarah nodded. She'd been on the receiving end of the Parsons fallout, apologizing to a client for a failure that wasn't exactly her fault but also wasn't exactly not her fault.

"So I started reading about teams and why they fail. There's a researcher named Hackman who studied this for thirty years. Airline crews, orchestras, intelligence teams. Real teams with real stakes." Marcus gestured at the printout. "He found that sixty percent of team effectiveness is determined at setup, another thirty percent at launch. Only ten percent once the team is running. Ninety percent is baked in before the work starts. Not effort. Not skill. Structure."

Derek was scanning the page. "Six conditions for team effectiveness."

"Right. And I want to see how we measure up. Not as a performance review. As a diagnostic. Figure out what's broken before we try to fix it."

There was a pause. On the screen, Miles leaned forward slightly, interested. In the room, Derek's expression was harder to read.

"I've seen a lot of these," Derek said. "Frameworks. They come and go."

"I know."

"Usually someone from HR brings them. We do a half-day offsite. Fill out worksheets. Someone writes action items on a flip chart. The flip chart goes into a closet. Nothing changes."

Derek wasn't being hostile. He was being accurate. Marcus had been to those offsites. He'd facilitated some of them. The flip charts were probably still in closets somewhere, their action items perfectly preserved and perfectly ignored.

"I know," Marcus said again. "I've run some of those offsites. They didn't work because we were trying to fix people. Coaching them. Aligning them. This is different. This is about whether we're set up in a way where good work is even possible."

He paused, trying to find the right words. "I've been thinking about what happened with the routing disaster. And Meridian—the handoff that fell apart. And Parsons—the expertise we had but didn't use. They're all different failures, but there's a pattern. We keep optimizing pieces without understanding the whole river."

"River?" Sarah asked.

"Sorry. It's a framework I've been building in my head. Marcus paused, aware of how it sounded. "Whitewater rafting. When you're running rapids, four things matter. You have to read the water—understand the landscape before you act. You have to know your crew, who can do what, where the gaps are. You have to call your line, make decisions in real time as conditions shift. And you have to remember the run, learn from what happened so the next one goes better."

Derek's expression suggested he was calculating how many more metaphors he'd have to endure before retirement. The answer, whatever it was, seemed to disappoint him.

"Hackman's research is about the second one," Marcus continued. "Knowing your crew. Are we actually a team, or just people in the same meetings? Do we know what each other knows? That's what I want us to figure out today."

Derek didn't say anything. He also didn't check his phone, which Marcus took as a small victory.

"Let's start with the first one," Marcus said. "Real Team. Bounded, stable, interdependent." He looked around the room. "Who's on this team?"

Silence.

"That's not a rhetorical question. I actually don't know the answer, and I'm the one supposedly leading the team."

Sarah spoke first. "Well, the five of us in this meeting. Plus Priya."

"Six people," Marcus said. "Okay. Is Priya on the team, or is she a stakeholder we work with?"

"She's on the team," Sarah said, but there was uncertainty in her voice.

"She runs regional ops in Mumbai," Derek said. "She has her own team. Her own priorities. She helps us when we need stuff from APAC, but is that the same as being on *this* team?"

"I talk to her almost every day," Sarah said.

"You talk to lots of people every day."

Marcus wrote on the whiteboard: *Priya - team member or stakeholder?*

"What about Miles?"

On screen, Miles looked surprised to be singled out. "What about me?"

"You were hired for the AI transformation initiative. Are you on this team, or are you a resource we're borrowing?"

"I..." Miles paused. "I'm on the team. I think. I report to you."

"You report to me for this project. But the AI transformation initiative touches three other teams too. If they need you, do they get you? Do I get a vote?"

"I don't know," Miles said. "That hasn't come up."

"It will."

Marcus wrote: *Miles - dedicated or shared resource?*

"This is the boundary problem," he said. "We've been operating for months without agreeing on who's actually in the group. That might seem like a technicality, but it's not. When boundaries are unclear, accountability is unclear. Is Priya responsible for making sure APAC context reaches us, or is she a helpful outsider we can't rely on? Are we competing with other teams for Miles's time, or is he ours?"

"Does it matter?" Derek asked. "We've been getting work done."

"We lost Meridian. We almost lost Parsons. We've been getting work done the way a car with a slow leak gets you to work. It's fine until it isn't."

The direction conversation was worse.

Marcus asked what the team was trying to accomplish. He expected some divergence. He did not expect what he got.

Derek: "Modernize the infrastructure. Get off the legacy systems before they become a liability."

Sarah: "Improve client response times. Most of our complaints come from slow turnaround."

Miles: "Prove that AI can add value at scale. That's why I was hired, right? To show what's possible?"

Lin didn't say anything. Marcus waited. The silence stretched.

"Lin?"

She looked at the table. "We're trying not to be the team that caused the next routing disaster."

The room went quiet in a different way than before.

"That's not..." Sarah started, then stopped.

"It's true, though," Derek said. "After the routing thing, everything else felt like damage control. Like we were trying to prove we weren't incompetent."

"That's not a direction," Marcus said. "That's fear. A direction tells you what to do. Fear only tells you what to avoid."

"Fear has been working," Lin said quietly. "We've been very careful since the routing failure."

"Careful isn't a strategy. And it's not working. Parsons happened because we were so busy being careful about the technical stuff that we dropped context on the relationship stuff. We can't be careful about everything all the time."

Marcus looked at the whiteboard where he'd written the four different answers. Infrastructure modernization. Client response times. AI value proof. Avoiding disaster.

"These aren't the same goal," he said. "They're not even compatible. If Miles is optimizing for proving AI value and Sarah is optimizing for client response times, what happens when those conflict?"

"They haven't conflicted," Miles said.

"They will. And when they do, how do we decide? Right now we don't have an answer. Everyone optimizes for their own version and hopes it works out."

Derek was looking at Lin. "When you said the thing about the routing disaster. Did you mean that?"

"Yes."

"That's what you think about? When you're working?"

"It's what everyone thinks about. Nobody says it."

Marcus had worked with Lin for months. He'd had exactly zero conversations with her about what she thought the team's purpose was. He'd assumed she understood the direction because she did her job. She did her job very well. But the direction she was serving was one she'd inferred from trauma, not one anyone had spelled out.

He wrote on the whiteboard: *Direction - unclear, possibly contradictory. Revisit.*

"We're not going to solve this today," he said. "But we need to solve it. A team without a clear direction is just people in the same meetings."

They were an hour in. The energy was flagging. Marcus could see Derek glancing at the clock. Miles had turned his camera off briefly, then back on, which probably meant he was checking something else.

"Got somewhere to be?" Sarah asked, noticing.

"Running thing this weekend," Derek said. "Need to get some miles in before dark."

"What is it, a 5K?"

"Fifty miles." Derek's voice was flat, matter-of-fact. "Up and over Shasta."

Sarah stared at him. "You're joking."

"He does this," Lin said quietly. "Every few months."

Derek shrugged. "It's not a race. Just a run." He was lean, wiry—it made sense.

"One more thing," Marcus said. "Then we can stop."

He drew a rough grid on the whiteboard. Names on one axis, knowledge areas on the other.

"Transactive memory. Who knows what. This is the map of where expertise lives on the team." He looked at the blank grid. "I'm going to admit something. I don't know what most of you know. I know your job titles. I know roughly what you work on. I don't know what you actually *know*."

"What do you mean?" Sarah asked.

"Derek. What does Lin know?"

Derek turned to look at Lin, then back at Marcus. "Operations. Supply chain. The APAC distribution network."

"What specifically? If I have a question about warehouse capacity in Singapore, does Lin know that?"

"I... don't know."

"Lin, do you know that?"

"Some of it. Priya knows more."

"What do you know that Priya doesn't?"

Lin thought for a moment. "Historical context. How the acquisition companies did things before Consolidated bought them. What we tried that didn't work. The reasons behind some of the processes that seem arbitrary." She paused. "Also how those acquisitions went. What got lost in the integration. Patterns that repeat."

Marcus hadn't known Lin came from one of the acquired

companies. He'd known she'd been at Consolidated for almost two years. He hadn't connected that she had years of context from before the acquisition—context about what happens when Consolidated absorbs a company.

"Derek, did you know that?"

"I knew she came from..." Derek paused. "Actually, I don't know which acquisition. There were three, right?"

"Four," Lin said. "And counting."

Marcus wrote on the grid: *Lin - historical context, pre-acquisition processes, APAC operations.* It felt pathetically incomplete.

"Your turn," he said to Derek. "What do you know?"

"The routing system. The legacy infrastructure. Where the technical debt is buried."

"What about the client-facing systems?"

"Some. Sarah knows those better."

"What about AI integration?"

Derek hesitated. "I know how to use the tools. Miles knows more about what's possible."

"Miles, what do you know?"

"AI capabilities. Prompt engineering. How to get the tools to do what you want." Miles paused. "I know what the AI can do. I'm less sure about what our specific systems can do."

"So if you needed to understand a technical constraint, who would you ask?"

"Derek, I guess."

"Have you?"

"Not really. I usually just ask the AI to help me understand the documentation."

Derek made a sound that wasn't quite a laugh. "The documentation I wrote?"

"I don't know who wrote it."

"So you're using AI to interpret my documentation instead of asking me."

"It's faster." Miles said this the way you'd explain that cars are faster than walking. He wasn't wrong. He also wasn't seeing Derek's face, which was doing something complicated.

Derek looked like he wanted to say something else but didn't. This was, Marcus realized, a tiny preview of a much larger problem. The person who knew the thing was sitting ten feet away. The person who needed to know the thing had trained himself to ask a machine instead. It was faster. It was also building a team where nobody needed each other, which wasn't a team at all.

Marcus captured it on the grid: *Miles - AI capabilities. Unclear boundary between personal knowledge and AI-mediated knowledge.*

The map was mostly blank. Miles didn't know what Derek knew. Derek didn't know what Lin knew. Everyone knew what Sarah knew because Sarah talked to everyone, but that meant Sarah was the de facto routing system for information, which explained why she was exhausted and why things fell through the cracks when she was traveling.

"This is bad," Sarah said, looking at the grid.

"It's honest," Marcus said. "Bad would be if we kept operating like the map exists when it doesn't."

They met again the following Thursday. And the Thursday after that. The conversations got slightly less awkward. Slightly.

Marcus had been warned, by Hackman's research and his own experience, that structural change was slow. Knowing this intellectually didn't make it less frustrating to live through.

Some things moved.

The boundary question got an answer, or at least a working hypothesis. Priya was a team member, not a stakeholder. This meant she needed to be in the loop on decisions, not just consulted when they needed APAC context. It also meant they needed to solve the time zone problem rather than routing around it. They established an async standup that Priya could contribute to during her morning, which their afternoon would inherit. It wasn't perfect. It was explicit.

Miles was dedicated to the team for the current quarter. After that, they'd revisit. The other teams that wanted him could request time through Marcus rather than pulling him directly. This created some friction with Marcus's peers. He decided to live with it.

The direction question was harder. They didn't arrive at a single inspiring sentence. What they got was closer to a priority stack. First: don't break things that are working. Second: improve client experience, measured by response time and satisfaction scores. Third: build infrastructure that would enable future capability. Fourth: demonstrate AI value where it served the first three goals.

It wasn't poetry. Lin pointed out that "don't break things" was still reactive, still rooted in fear. Marcus acknowledged this. He didn't have something better. The stack at least gave them a way to settle conflicts: client experience beat infrastructure investment, which beat AI demonstration projects. When Miles proposed something that would showcase AI capability but introduced risk to a stable system, they could say no and explain why.

The transactive memory work was ongoing. They'd started documenting who knew what, not exhaustively but enough to route questions. Derek knew the technical architecture, the legacy system quirks, the history of what had been tried and abandoned. Lin knew operations, APAC logistics, and the institutional knowledge from the acquisition. Sarah knew client relationships, stakeholder politics, and the unstated rules about how decisions actually got made. Miles knew AI tooling and prompt engineering, with an asterisk that his knowledge was entangled with the AI's in ways nobody fully understood.

Marcus found himself thinking in colors. Derek was Red: internally focused on systems and infrastructure, caring about the technology itself, wary of changes that might break what worked. Lin and Sarah were Blue: focused on processes and how systems enabled people to do their jobs, though Lin's Blue was internal operations while Sarah's was client relationships. Marcus himself was Green: strategic direction, organizational trajectory, the altitude where decisions got made with incomplete information. And Miles was something new: fluent with Silver, able to work with AI in ways the others couldn't, but without the years of independent practice that would let him catch what the AI missed. The team had all the colors, but no reliable translation between them.

The grid lived in a shared document. It was updated sporadically. It was better than nothing.

Handoffs got a template. Five fields: current state, intent, next actions, open questions, landmines. The template was ignored about half the time. When it was used, it helped. When Sarah went to Phoenix, she handed off Parsons with explicit notes about the authentication sensitivity. The handoff worked. Whether it worked because of the template or because everyone was now paranoid about repeating the Parsons failure, Marcus couldn't say.

Some things didn't move.

Lin participated more in the Thursday meetings but remained largely silent in Slack. The pattern of waiting to be asked was deep. Marcus tried to create explicit invitations: "Lin, what's your read on this?" Sometimes she answered. Sometimes she said she didn't have anything to add. He couldn't tell if she actually didn't have anything to add or if she was defaulting to the habit.

After one meeting, he asked her directly. "You see things other people don't see. The routing disaster thing. The 'six soloists' comment. But you don't volunteer it. Why?"

Lin was quiet for a long moment. "Where I worked before, you didn't speak unless you had something definite. You didn't speculate in meetings. You didn't raise problems unless you had solutions. That was the culture."

"That's not the culture here."

"I know. But the habit is..." She gestured vaguely. "It's not something I can just decide to change."

"What would help?"

"Being asked." She paused. "You asking. That helps."

Marcus nodded. It was an answer, but it wasn't a solution. He couldn't be in every conversation, asking Lin specifically what she thought. The structure needed to invite her participation without depending on him to do the inviting. He didn't know how to build that.

By the end of the month, they were better. Marcus could feel it. The meetings had more signal, less noise. The handoffs had fewer gaps. The map of who knew what was thin but it existed. They had a direction that wasn't inspiring but was at least shared.

The Friday before Christmas, Miles sent a message to the team channel. He'd been working on the quarterly planning analysis that Sarah needed for a client presentation. "Done early," he wrote. "Let me know if you need anything else."

Marcus looked at the attached document. Twenty pages of projections, market analysis, competitive positioning. It was thorough. It was well-structured. The formatting was clean.

He noticed that Miles hadn't asked anyone to review it before sending. He'd produced it, declared it done, and moved on. The template for handoffs included an "open questions" field. Miles's message had no open questions. He was confident.

Marcus thought about saying something. He wasn't sure what to say. Miles had done what was asked. He'd done it quickly and well. The fact that Marcus felt uneasy about the confidence was maybe just Marcus being paranoid. Or maybe it was the thing Hackman couldn't account for: the structural conditions were better, but something about how Miles worked with AI hadn't changed. Hackman's research was from an era when teammates couldn't be replaced by typing a question into a box. The framework didn't have a condition for that.

He made a note to revisit it after the holiday. The note said "Miles - confidence - check." It was the kind of note that makes perfect sense when you write it and means nothing three weeks later. He closed his laptop and didn't think about it again until it became a problem.

6

THE DUAL COMPETENCY

USING IT AND NOT USING IT

The presentation was Tuesday, January 7th. Sarah had blocked two hours for prep on Monday, which became ninety minutes after a client emergency, which became forty-five minutes after Marcus needed her input on something urgent. Nobody had stolen her time. It had just been redistributed by people who wanted it more than she did, or at least more loudly.

She spent those forty-five minutes reviewing Miles's analysis. It was good. The formatting was clean, the logic was clear, the projections were supported by data. She made a few wording changes, adjusted a chart that felt cluttered, and moved on. She had seven other things to do before end of day.

The client was Calloway Industrial, a regional manufacturing company that had been with Consolidated for three years. Not the biggest account, but a relationship Sarah had worked hard to build. They'd had bumps. Every long-term client relationship has bumps. The goal of this presentation was to show them the path forward: here's what we can deliver in the coming year, here's why it's going to be better than last year.

The presentation went fine until it didn't.

Sarah stood at the screen, clicking through the Q2 projections with practiced ease, when the client's operations director, a woman named Deborah who took notes during presentations in a way that felt like evidence collection, interrupted.

"These capacity numbers. Where do they come from?"

"They're based on our distribution network modeling. We looked at historical throughput, seasonal patterns, current infrastructure—"

"I've seen numbers like these before. From you. Last year." Deborah's tone wasn't hostile. It was tired. "You projected twenty percent improvement in regional turnaround. We got eight."

"That was a different situation. We've made infrastructure investments since then—"

"The numbers looked just as confident last time."

Sarah didn't have a good answer. She had the analysis in front of her. The analysis said the numbers were achievable. But Deborah wasn't asking about the analysis. She was asking whether Sarah, personally, believed Consolidated could deliver what it was promising.

Sarah realized she didn't know.

She'd reviewed the work. She'd adjusted the formatting. She'd approved the projections. But she hadn't built her own view of whether those projections were realistic. She'd trusted the analysis because the analysis was thorough and Miles was good at his job and the AI tools he used were sophisticated. She'd evaluated the document. She hadn't evaluated the claims.

"Let me get back to you on the capacity assumptions," Sarah said. "I want to make sure we're giving you numbers we can stand behind."

It was the right thing to say. It was also an admission that she'd walked into the room without having done that already.

After the meeting, Sarah called Marcus from her car.

"Calloway pushed back on the Q2 projections. Capacity numbers. Deborah thinks we're overpromising again."

"Are we?"

"I don't know. That's the problem. The analysis says we can hit them. But I don't have an independent read."

"Where did the capacity assumptions come from?"

"Miles pulled them from the distribution modeling. System-reported numbers."

Marcus was quiet for a moment. "Have we checked those against what ops actually thinks is achievable?"

"I... no. The numbers came from the system."

"Get Lin on a call. Ask her if those Q2 numbers are real."

Lin answered on the third ring. Sarah explained the situation: Q2 capacity projections, Calloway's skepticism, the need for a sanity check.

There was a pause. Then Lin said: "Which distribution centers are we talking about?"

Sarah pulled up the analysis. "Phoenix, Chicago, and the Southeast regional hub."

"The Southeast numbers are wrong."

"Wrong how?"

"The system reports theoretical capacity. Maximum throughput if everything runs perfectly. It never runs perfectly. Charlotte has had equipment issues for two years, ever since the expansion. They built out the facility to hit growth targets but cut the maintenance budget to make the numbers work. The database shows what we could do if we fixed the problems, not what we can actually do."

"How far off are we?"

"For Q2? Maybe fifteen percent below what you're projecting. Could be more if the maintenance issues get worse."

Sarah closed her eyes. "Why didn't this come up when Miles was building the analysis?"

"He didn't ask me. He pulled the system data."

"The system data is wrong?"

"The system data is optimistic. It's always been optimistic. Everyone in operations knows that. We adjust for it when we do our own planning."

Everyone except the people making decisions.

Sarah thanked Lin and hung up. She sat in her car in the Calloway parking lot, looking at the analysis on her laptop. Twenty pages. Clean formatting. Confident projections. A fifteen percent gap nobody caught because nobody asked the person who would know.

She called Marcus back.

"The Southeast numbers are wrong. Fifteen percent optimistic, maybe more."

"What's Deborah going to do?"

"Put the expansion on hold until Q3. At minimum." She paused. "This isn't like Parsons. That was a handoff problem. This is us being wrong about something we should have checked."

"Lin."

"Lin. She explained it in the diagnostic: her old company's rules about not speaking without certainty. We heard her. We invited her to speak up. Here we are anyway."

Knowing the problem hadn't fixed it.

THE CONTAMINATION PROBLEM

There's a reassuring diagram that shows up in every AI governance presentation: human in the loop, catching errors, adding judgment. The arrows are clean. The boxes are labeled. Nobody ever comes back a year later to check whether the diagram was true.

A 2024 meta-analysis of 106 experiments found a troubling

pattern: human-AI combinations performed better than humans alone, but not reliably better than AI alone.[1] Across tasks from detecting fake reviews to screening baggage to forecasting demand, the pattern held. The researchers distinguished between "augmentation"—beating humans alone—and "synergy"—beating both humans and AI alone. Augmentation was common. Synergy was rare. The human in the loop often made things worse.

The effect was strongest for tasks requiring judgment about ambiguous inputs. Capacity projections that depend on operational realities the database doesn't capture. Analyses where the question of "are these assumptions correct" has no algorithmic answer. Exactly the kind of work Sarah was reviewing.

The obvious explanation is wrong. It's not that humans are stupider than AI. Humans working independently outperform AI on plenty of tasks requiring judgment, context, or novel situations. The problem is what happens to human capability when it's positioned as AI's reviewer rather than AI's peer.

Sarah reviewed Miles's analysis. She read through the projections, checked that the logic held together and made some wording changes. The document looked professional. The reasoning was clear. The numbers were internally consistent.

What Sarah did not do was build her own view of whether Q2 capacity projections were realistic. She didn't pull up the operational data and ask "Does this match what I know about our facilities?" She evaluated the document that existed. She didn't generate the document that should have existed.

This is the contamination mechanism. Once you've seen

---

1. Michelle Vaccaro, Abdullah Almaatouq, and Thomas Malone, "When Combinations of Humans and AI Are Useful: A Systematic Review and Meta-Analysis," *Nature Human Behaviour* 8 (2024): 2293–2303. The meta-analysis found an effect size of Hedges' g = -0.23 for human-AI teams compared to AI alone.

the AI's output, your attention has already been directed. You can examine it more carefully. You can decide specific claims are wrong. What you cannot do is pretend you don't know what frame the AI used, what questions it asked, what structure it imposed. If the AI missed something entirely, if it framed the analysis in a way that excluded relevant considerations, you inherit that blind spot. You're looking for mistakes in what exists. You cannot find what isn't there.

Sarah's forty-five minutes of review were spent inside the world Miles's analysis had created. The Southeast hub's equipment issues weren't in that world. The gap between system-reported capacity and operational reality wasn't in that world. Lin's knowledge from the pre-acquisition days wasn't in that world. Sarah evaluated competently within a frame that was missing something important, and her evaluation couldn't surface what the frame excluded.

Call this sequential review: seeing the AI's output before forming an independent view. It feels like oversight. It's actually inheritance.

For straightforward tasks with obvious failure modes, sequential review is often fine: formatting a presentation, summarizing meeting notes, the kind of work where being wrong is immediately visible and easily corrected. Capacity projections for a skeptical client aren't that. The stakes are different. The question of whether your assumptions are correct is genuinely difficult, not trivially checkable.

Sarah didn't make a process error. She applied a process suited to simple tasks to a task that wasn't simple.

PARALLEL INVESTIGATION

One response is parallel investigation: committing to your own view before seeing what the AI produced. Same task, same information, independent analysis. Only after you've documented your own assessment do you compare it to the AI's output.

Research on sequential review is sobering: humans are less likely to intervene with the least accurate AI recommendations —the larger the error, the less likely the correction.[2] The frame contaminates the review. Parallel investigation—committing to your own view before exposure—breaks that pattern. Humans who form independent views first catch errors that sequential reviewers miss. They also catch errors of omission: things the AI didn't consider, frames that excluded relevant factors.

When you build your own view first, you create something to compare against. The AI's output lands on prepared ground. Discrepancies become visible because you have a map that differs from the AI's map.

Sarah, working in parallel, would have started with a question: what do I think we can actually deliver in Q2? She would have built a view independent of Miles's analysis. When she looked at the projections, the Southeast hub numbers would have felt wrong. Not because she caught a calculation error, but because her map said something different.

She didn't do this, because nobody asked her to.

Parallel investigation is expensive. It requires the reviewer to do real work, not just evaluate someone else's work. And people resist it. Research on cognitive forcing interventions—designs that make users form judgments before seeing AI output—found that the designs most effective at reducing overreliance received the worst user ratings.[3] People don't want to

---

2. Daniela Sele and Marina Chugunova, "Putting a Human in the Loop: Increasing Uptake, but Decreasing Accuracy of Automated Decision-Making," *PLOS ONE* 19, no. 2 (2024): e0298037. In a study of 292 participants, human-in-the-loop review increased uptake of AI recommendations but decreased overall accuracy.

3. Zana Buçinca, Maja Barbara Malaya, and Krzysztof Z. Gajos, "To Trust or to Think: Cognitive Forcing Functions Can Reduce Overreliance on AI in AI-

do the extra work. They trust their ability to catch errors in review, even when the evidence says they can't.

An alternative that may matter more: task decomposition. Instead of having humans review AI output, divide the work so AI owns certain subtasks entirely while humans own others with uncontaminated judgment. The question isn't "Did the AI get this right?" but "Which parts of this problem require human judgment that AI output would contaminate?"

For the Calloway analysis, this might have meant: AI handles data assembly and formatting. Human judgment—Sarah's, informed by conversations with Lin—handles the question of whether projected capacity matches operational reality. Not review after the fact, but division before the work begins.

The Cynefin framework helps here. In the Clear domain, sequential review works fine; errors are visible by inspection. In the Complicated domain, whether the output is correct depends on assumptions and analysis that can be wrong in ways invisible from the output itself. This is where parallel investigation starts to justify its cost. The Calloway analysis was a Complicated problem. Whether Q2 projections were realistic depended on operational realities the database didn't capture. It required external knowledge. It required Lin.

Miles treated it like a Clear problem. So did Sarah. The workflow didn't prompt them to ask which domain they were in.

Here's the structural trap: sequential review is faster. It's also worse. Organizations default to the faster approach because the costs of "worse" are diffuse and delayed while the costs of "slower" are immediate and visible. Sarah's forty-five minutes of review felt productive. The meeting where the client lost confi-

---

Assisted Decision-Making," *Proceedings of the ACM on Human-Computer Interaction* 5, CSCW1 (2021): 1–21.

dence happened a week later. By then, the connection between process and outcome was obscured by a dozen intervening events.

The obvious response is to assign reviews to your most experienced people. If you've tried this, you may have noticed it doesn't work as well as it should. The research reveals a paradox: novices benefit most from AI assistance but are most vulnerable to over-reliance, while experts may dismiss AI recommendations including correct ones.[4] A study of management consultants found that lower performers improved by 43% with AI help, versus 17% for top performers.[5] The people who gain the most are also the people least equipped to catch what AI gets wrong.

The Sarah/Miles dynamic maps to this pattern. Sarah, more experienced, trusted professional-looking output but lacked the specific operational knowledge to catch the gap. Miles, the novice, got the most productivity gain from AI—and was most blind to what he was missing. Neither the expert's wariness nor the novice's trust produced the right outcome.

There's a version of this story where Miles is the problem. He's young, he's overconfident, he relies too heavily on AI. The solution is training, or supervision, or replacing him with someone more seasoned.

---

4. Susanne Gaube et al., "Do as AI Say: Susceptibility in Deployment of Clinical Decision-Aids," *npj Digital Medicine* 4 (2021). The study found susceptibility to bad advice was source-independent—participants followed incorrect recommendations at similar rates whether attributed to human experts or AI systems.

5. Fabrizio Dell'Acqua et al., "Navigating the Jagged Technological Frontier: Field Experimental Evidence of the Effects of AI on Knowledge Worker Productivity and Quality," Harvard Business School Working Paper 24-013 (2023). When tasks fell within AI's capability frontier, consultants achieved 40% higher quality; outside that frontier, they were 19-24 percentage points less accurate than control groups.

That version is incomplete.

Miles did what he was trained to do. He used the tools available to him. He produced work that looked professional and was internally consistent. The gap between system-reported capacity and operational reality wasn't something he knew to ask about. He didn't know what he didn't know.

This is the condition of everyone who works with AI. The tools are confident. They produce outputs that have the shape of expertise. They don't flag their own limitations. They don't say "By the way, you should probably check this with someone who knows the operational history of your Southeast hub." They just produce.

The human who uses these tools inherits their blind spots. Not through carelessness, but through the structure of the interaction. The AI sets the frame. The human works within the frame. What's outside the frame is invisible.

Sarah, reviewing Miles's work, inherited the same blind spots. She worked within the frame Miles's analysis created. The frame excluded Lin's knowledge. Neither Miles nor Sarah knew to include it, because the frame didn't have a hole labeled "operational context from acquired companies goes here." It just presented itself as complete.

~

Marcus asked Miles to come to Oakland for a conversation. Not a disciplinary meeting. Something harder: a reckoning with what Miles actually knew.

They sat in Marcus's office, door closed. A leather notebook sat on the desk between them, worn soft at the corners.

"Walk me through how you built the capacity projections," Marcus said.

Miles explained. He'd pulled data from the distribution modeling system. He'd asked Claude to help him structure the analysis. He'd cross-referenced with historical throughput numbers. He'd validated that the projections were consistent with seasonal patterns.

"At any point, did you form your own view of whether those numbers were achievable?"

Miles paused. "I validated them against the data."

"That's not what I asked. Did you have an independent sense, before the AI produced the analysis, of what realistic Q2 capacity would look like?"

"I… no. I don't know our facilities well enough to have that kind of intuition."

"So who did you check with?"

"The data came from the system. The system is supposed to reflect reality."

"The system reflects what's in the database. Lin could have told you that Southeast has been running below theoretical capacity for two years. Derek could have told you about the equipment issues. Sarah could have told you that Calloway has been burned before on optimistic projections. Any of them would have helped. But you didn't ask."

Miles looked at the table.

"I'm not blaming you," Marcus said. "The analysis you produced was good. The AI helped you make something polished and professional. But polished isn't the same as right. And professional isn't the same as informed."

"I thought I was being thorough."

"You were thorough within the data you had. The problem is what you didn't have."

THE EROSION TRAP

The sales pitch for AI is augmentation: the tools make you more capable. The research suggests they also make you less capable, in precisely the ways that matter for oversight. A survey of 319 knowledge workers found that higher confidence in AI correlated with less critical thinking enacted.[6] The mechanism isn't carelessness. It's that the tools make care feel unnecessary. Skills that aren't practiced decay. You become a better editor and a worse author. But editing AI output is precisely the skill that doesn't work.

How fast does erosion happen? Faster than you'd expect. A study of physicians using AI-assisted colonoscopy found that adenoma detection rates in non-AI-assisted procedures dropped from 28.4% to 22.4% after just three months of AI exposure.[7] Six percentage points. In a skill that catches cancer. On a three-month timeline.

There's a second capability that erodes: context management. Knowing what data matters. Knowing what the database doesn't capture. Knowing who holds relevant knowledge that won't appear in any system query. Context management erodes through abstraction (you stop tracking where data comes from, what it excludes, whose knowledge isn't in the system). When AI tools handle data retrieval and assembly, they present outputs as complete. The question "what's missing from this frame?" stops feeling necessary. You lose the habit of asking before you lose the capability to answer. The augmentation is immediate and visible. The erosion is gradual and invisible.

And there's a third problem: maintaining capability without AI feels worse once you've experienced the alternative. Research on AI collaboration found that transitioning from AI-assisted to solo work decreased intrinsic motivation and

---

6. Hao-Ping Lee et al., "The Impact of Generative AI on Critical Thinking: Self-Reported Reductions in Cognitive Effort and Confidence Effects From a Survey of Knowledge Workers," in *Proceedings of the 2025 CHI Conference on Human Factors in Computing Systems* (ACM, 2025). See also Shannon Vallor on "moral deskilling" and Parasuraman & Manzey on automation complacency.

7. Krzysztof Budzyń et al., "Endoscopist deskilling risk after exposure to artificial intelligence in colonoscopy: a multicentre, observational study," *Lancet Gastroenterology & Hepatology* (2025).

increased feelings of boredom.[8] AI takes over the analyzing and crafting processes that make tasks engaging. Once you've experienced AI assistance, working without it feels like a downgrade. The "dual competency" isn't just hard to maintain because of time pressure. It's hard because the alternative has become tedious.

Miles had never worked without AI assistance. He'd entered the workforce after the tools were ubiquitous. He was excellent at using them: prompting effectively, structuring complex requests, iterating toward good outputs. These are real skills. In the color framework, Miles was fluent with Silver but underdeveloped in Red and Blue. He could make AI do things, but he lacked Derek's Red orientation—the internal focus on how systems actually worked, the wariness about changes that might break things. He lacked Lin's Blue orientation—the concern with how processes enabled people to do their jobs, the awareness of operational realities that never made it into databases. Silver fluency without Red or Blue grounding meant he could produce impressive outputs he couldn't fully evaluate.

What Miles lacked was the independent judgment that comes from doing the work yourself, repeatedly, over years. The intuition that says "these numbers feel wrong" before you can articulate why. He couldn't develop this by using AI more skillfully. The judgment comes from building your own analyses, getting them wrong, and learning why. This is the bind: the tools are genuinely useful, but using them erodes the capability that makes human oversight valuable.

---

8. Suqing Wu et al., "Human-generative AI collaboration enhances task performance but undermines human's intrinsic motivation," *Scientific Reports* 15 (April 2025). The study also found that performance gains from AI collaboration did not transfer to subsequent solo work.

CRYSTALLIZED THINKING

There's a consultant I know who writes three-page prompts. They always start the same way: two paragraphs of context the AI would never ask for. Project background. Client history. What had gone wrong on similar analyses before. Then a section she calls "You will be tempted to," listing the confident-sounding mistakes the AI would make if she didn't head them off. *You will be tempted to treat all regulatory environments as stable. They are not. Flag any assumption about future policy as uncertain. You will be tempted to average historical capacity figures. Averages hide the variance that kills you.* Finally, explicit instructions about what to do when it doesn't know something: say so, don't fill in the blanks, don't guess.

Her colleagues find this excessive. The tools are good now. Why treat them like unreliable interns?

It's because the three pages aren't instructions to the AI. They're crystallized pre-AI thinking. Before the AI runs, she has documented what she expects to see, what she's uncertain about, what would concern her if absent. The AI output lands on prepared ground.

She's not reviewing the AI's work. She's comparing maps. Hers, made first, and then the AI's.

The discipline feels redundant when the AI is producing good work. That feeling is the trap. The work seems unnecessary right up until you discover the AI built its confident analysis on assumptions you should have questioned.

Miles could have done this for the Calloway analysis. Before asking the AI to structure projections, he could have spent thirty minutes writing what he knew, what he was uncertain about, who might have relevant knowledge. He could have flagged that capacity projections depend on assumptions about facilities he'd never visited.

He didn't because nobody asked him to. The workflow was

to produce the analysis, not to document your view, produce the analysis, then compare. The second version takes longer, but it's also the only one that catches what Miles missed.

THE DUAL COMPETENCY

You need to be good at using AI, and you need to be good at not using AI.

The first skill is increasingly table stakes. Prompting well, understanding capabilities, knowing how to access what the tools can do. People who can't use AI effectively will be at a disadvantage in most knowledge work.

The second skill is what makes the first skill safe. Generating your own views. Preserving the cognitive muscles that atrophy with disuse. Knowing what you think before you ask.

These skills are in tension. Every hour practicing one is an hour not practicing the other. This is not a problem you can solve by being careful. Careful is a feeling. Feelings don't prevent atrophy. Only practice prevents atrophy. You have to actually do the work without AI sometimes, not because it's more efficient, but because it's the only way to maintain the judgment that makes your oversight worth anything.

And you can't trust how it feels. A study of sixteen experienced software developers working in their own repositories (codebases they'd maintained for years) found they predicted AI assistance would make them 24% faster. Afterward, they believed they'd achieved a 20% speedup. They'd actually taken 19% longer.[9] A forty-point gap between perception and reality. Miles thought he was being thorough. He validated against the data. He felt like he'd done good work.

9. METR, "Measuring the Impact of Early-2025 AI on Experienced Open-Source Developer Productivity" (2025). The study used Cursor Pro with Claude 3.5/3.7 Sonnet. Developers' subjective experience of productivity gain did not match objective task completion time.

Marcus, sitting with Miles in the Oakland office, tried to articulate this.

"You're good at using the tools," he said. "The analysis you produced was well-structured, professionally presented."

"But wrong."

"Missing something. Which is different from wrong, and in some ways harder to catch." Marcus paused. "Here's what I want you to think about. If the AI disappeared tomorrow, what would you be able to do?"

Miles didn't answer immediately.

"I don't mean what would take longer. I mean what do you actually know, independent of what the tools can access? What judgment do you bring that isn't dependent on asking Claude to structure your thinking?"

"I don't know," Miles said. "I've never worked without it."

"That's not a criticism. It's the situation you're in. But it means you need to be deliberate about building capability outside the tools. Not because the tools are bad. Because you need to catch what they miss. And you can't catch what they miss if you can't think without them."

Miles didn't respond.

"You're not going to stop using AI. But you need to know which mode the situation calls for. The AI can't tell you. That judgment has to come from you."

Two weeks later, Marcus got an email from Miles.

"I tried something different with the Henderson analysis. Before I used any AI tools, I spent an hour writing down what I thought I knew and who I should talk to. Then I called Lin. Then Derek. Then I did the analysis."

Marcus read on.

"It took longer. The first draft was rougher. But when I compared my notes to what the AI helped me build, I caught two assumptions that were wrong. I wouldn't have caught them otherwise."

There was more.

"I thought about what you asked. About what I do that doesn't depend on the tools. I do film photography sometimes. Weekends. Manual everything—no autofocus, no digital preview. You have to think before you shoot because you can't fix it later. I never connected that to work before."

There was a final line.

"AIs are good at building things. They aren't so good at knowing what to check. That part has to be me."

Marcus forwarded the email to Sarah without comment. She wrote back: "Progress."

It wasn't a transformation. Miles would slip back into old patterns. The pressure to produce quickly would reassert itself. The work without AI would feel tedious in ways it hadn't before—that's the motivation trap, and knowing about it doesn't make it go away. The structural forces pushing toward AI dependency are stronger than individual discipline can reliably overcome.

But there was a twenty-five-year-old analyst in Chicago who had, for the first time, checked his work against someone else's knowledge instead of just the database. Who had noticed the gap between what he could produce and what he could evaluate. Who was starting to ask which mode the situation called for.

He'd remember to do it again. Sometimes. That's not nothing.

MARCUS'S WHITEBOARD: KNOW YOUR CREW

See Concept Reference: Know Your Crew for key frameworks and definitions.

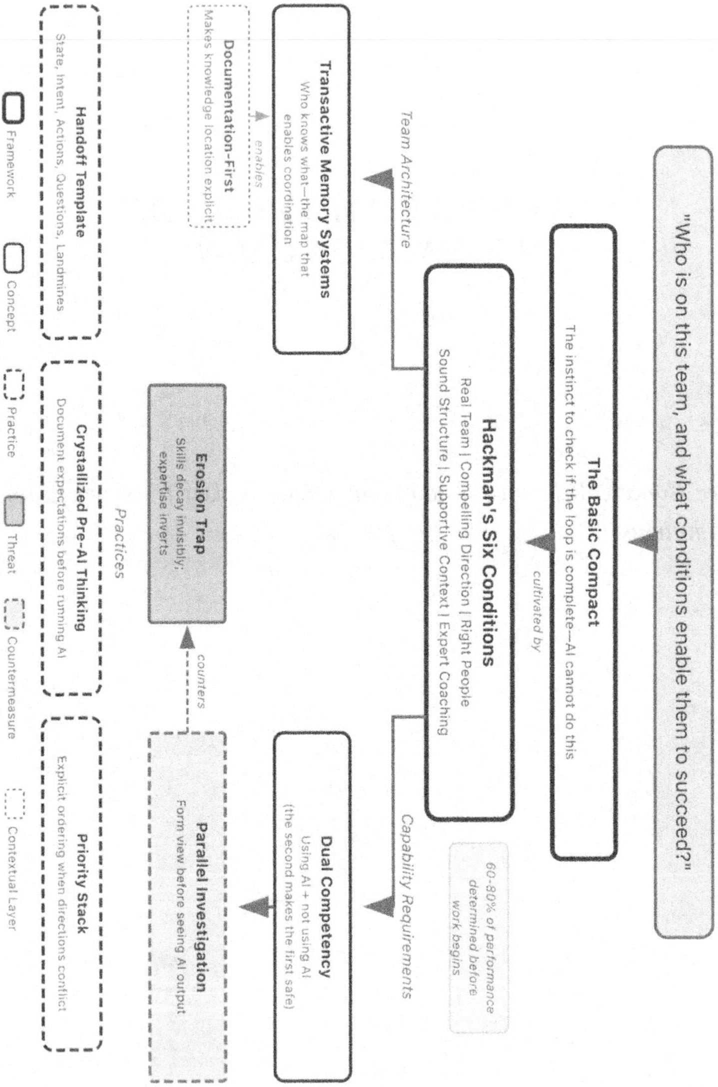
"Who is on this team, and what conditions enable them to succeed?"
The Basic Compact
The instinct to check if the loop is complete—AI cannot do this
cultivated by
Hackman's Six Conditions
Real Team | Compelling Direction | Right People
Sound Structure | Supportive Context | Expert Coaching
60-80% of performance determined before work begins
Team Architecture
Capability Requirements
Transactive Memory Systems
Who knows what—the map that enables coordination
Dual Competency
Using AI + not using AI
(the second makes the first safe)
Documentation-First
Makes knowledge location explicit
enables
Erosion Trap
Skills decay invisibly; expertise inverts
counters
Parallel Investigation
Form view before seeing AI output
Practices
Handoff Template
State, Intent, Actions, Questions, Landmines
Crystallized Pre-AI Thinking
Document expectations before running AI
Priority Stack
Explicit ordering when directions conflict
Framework
Concept
Practice
Threat
Countermeasure
Contextual Layer

PART III

CALL YOUR LINE

7

TRUST FALLS AND WATERFALLS

THE NEW FOUNDATIONS OF SAFETY

The promotional surge hit the Northeast corridor in late April, three weeks after they'd reduced the capacity buffer and Consolidated's operations team discovered the difference between "rarely used" and "not needed."

The buffer had been insurance: reserved capacity with backup carriers. It cost money to hold. Analysis showed they'd used it meaningfully twice in eighteen months. The proposal to reduce it by forty percent had clean math and a professional slide deck.

The math was still clean. The slide deck was still professional. And Sarah had just spent twenty-nine hours coordinating emergency capacity across three time zones while premium spot rates ate into next month's variance report.

Marcus's mouth was dry. He hadn't thought to get coffee yet, and he was only now noticing. What concerned him, sitting in his office the following Monday, was simpler: someone should have seen this coming. The promotional calendar was visible. The carrier constraints were predictable. This wasn't a black swan; it was a gray one, the kind of crisis that is as foreseeable in foresight as it is obvious in hindsight.

Someone on his team should have raised a flag. No one had. He needed to understand why.

After Parsons, after the structural changes, after the transactive memory grid and the handoff templates—Marcus had wanted something to show. Evidence that they'd heard the question and had an answer. So three weeks before the buffer decision, they'd started documenting how they actually worked. And they'd started using CommTrack.

CommTrack was a communication analytics tool with a name so functional it had clearly survived from an era before marketing got involved. It tracked communications. It did this very well. Whether this was entirely good remained to be seen.

Now Marcus was going to use it to understand what had happened.

He pulled up the transcript for the buffer decision meeting.

The discussion lasted twenty-two minutes. Finance had presented the analysis. Miles had asked two clarifying questions. Sarah had raised a process point about notification timing. Lin had been silent.

Derek had spoken six words. CommTrack helpfully provided the exact quote: "Sounds reasonable to me. Good analysis."

This wasn't a status update. This was a technical decision about the carrier allocation system, which Derek maintained. Derek had opinions about his systems. Strong ones. The idea that Derek would have nothing to say about changing parameters in a system he'd built was like suggesting a chef had no views on the seasoning.

Four of Derek's six words were "sounds reasonable to me."

That wasn't Derek being checked out. That was Derek actively declining to engage.

Marcus pulled the data wider: Derek's participation across six weeks of meetings.

In routine meetings, Derek was Derek: present, occasionally sardonic, contributing when he had something to add. But in meetings where technical judgment was required, the profile changed. Shorter contributions. Fewer questions. More deference. His average contribution length dropped by sixty percent in technical discussions compared to administrative ones.

Marcus thought about the memory leak fix from two months ago. Derek had been animated, precise, confident. Walking through the architecture, explaining why the obvious solutions wouldn't work. That was Derek operating at full capacity.

The Derek in the CommTrack data was someone else.

It started six months ago, last October. Right after the routing disaster.

Later, piecing together what had happened, Marcus would learn what those twenty-two minutes had looked like from Derek's side.

The week before, Derek had run the buffer utilization data through an AI model. Not "How often did we use the buffer?" but "Under what conditions did we need it?"

The pattern had surfaced within minutes. The buffer was specifically needed when regional volume spikes coincided with primary carrier constraints. Promotional windows. Weather disruptions. The promotional calendar showed a major retail push in late October. If primary carriers were constrained, they'd need the buffer.

Derek saw the flaw immediately. The correct action was obvious: speak up.

He could even frame it as a question rather than a claim. "Have we cross-referenced this against the promotional calendar?" Simple. Low-risk. The kind of thing Derek would have said without hesitation six months earlier.

But back in October, Derek had been the voice that said the routing system was sound. He'd validated the logic. He'd told Marcus the approach was solid. He'd been confident, and his confidence had helped carry the decision.

The system had been catastrophically wrong. Drivers quit. Customers left. Janet Okonkwo and two others lost their jobs.

Derek hadn't been wrong about the code. The code was fine. He'd been wrong about something harder to define: whether the system's logic would survive contact with the world it was meant to operate in. He'd vouched for something he understood technically and missed something he should have seen.

The postmortem had been fair. Nobody blamed Derek specifically. The failure was systemic, emergent, the kind of thing that happens when complex systems interact with human systems in unpredictable ways. Marcus had said as much.

But Derek remembered being the confident voice. He remembered saying "this works." He remembered being wrong in a room full of people who'd trusted his judgment.

Now he was going to be the voice again. Question the finance analysis. Flag a risk nobody else was flagging. Put himself on record.

And if he was wrong this time? If the promotional surge didn't materialize, or the carriers held, or the buffer reduction worked fine? He'd be the engineer who cried wolf. The one who'd already been wrong once, expensively, and was now raising false alarms.

If he was right, nobody would remember. Avoided problems don't get postmortems. If he was wrong, everyone would remember. That asymmetry had always existed. It just hadn't mattered to Derek before.

It mattered now.

"Any concerns with the methodology?" the finance analyst asked.

Derek thought about saying something. He thought about the promotional calendar, the historical pattern, the questions he could ask.

"Sounds reasonable to me," Derek said. "Good analysis."

Six words. The meeting moved on.

Marcus messaged Derek privately: "Got time for a call this afternoon?"

The response came eleven minutes later. Derek's average Slack response time was three minutes.

"Sure. 3 work?"

Three would work.

Marcus sat with the data longer than he needed to.

After the routing disaster, he'd spent weeks on the technical postmortem. System architecture, data flows, feedback loops. The system had optimized itself into a corner, chasing metrics that looked right while the reality underneath shifted. A reasonable mistake. An expensive one, but understandable.

He'd thought he understood what had broken.

Now, looking at six weeks of CommTrack data, he was less sure. The routing system's failure had been technical. But the failure he was looking at now was something else. Something about what people felt safe saying, and why they'd stopped.

Derek had been willing to tell Marcus when something was wrong. That was what made him valuable. Not just the technical skill, but the willingness to be the voice that said "I don't think this works" when everyone else was nodding along.

Somewhere in the past three months, that willingness had disappeared. CommTrack could show Marcus exactly when. It couldn't show him why.

The old contract between professionals and their teams had quietly stopped holding. The one that said your expertise is what makes you valuable here.

Once that contract breaks, everything that depends on it starts to break too.

THE OLD FOUNDATION

What Marcus was looking at in the CommTrack data had a name, though he didn't know it yet.

Psychologists call it psychological safety, and it turns out to predict team performance better than almost anything else researchers have measured. The term originated with Edgar Schein and Warren Bennis in 1965, but Amy Edmondson made it practical for work teams and brought it into mainstream research.

She defined it as a shared belief that the team is safe for interpersonal risk-taking. This sounds obvious until you watch teams that don't have it. People sit in meetings knowing something is wrong and say nothing. They have questions they don't ask, objections they don't raise, information they don't share. Not because they're lazy or disengaged, but because the perceived cost of speaking up exceeds the perceived benefit.

Her research showed that psychological safety strongly predicted team learning behavior: the willingness to seek feedback, discuss errors, experiment. Google's Project Aristotle later studied 180 teams and found psychological safety was the most important factor in team effectiveness, more important than individual talent or resources. Teams with high psychological safety learn faster, innovate more, talk about errors more openly. Teams without it accumulate the kind of silent risks that surface at 2:47 AM when Derek calls to say "we have a problem."

But here's what the research assumed without quite stating: the foundation on which people felt safe taking risks was stable expertise. The contract looked like this: I am valuable because of what I know and can do, and this team recognizes that value. From that foundation, I can take interpersonal risks.

This made sense because knowledge used to be durable. What you learned stayed valuable. The hierarchy of competence was clear: junior people deferred to senior people on domain questions because senior people genuinely knew more, and everyone could see that they did.

Edmondson's foundational 1999 research studied manufacturing teams; her earlier work on hospitals examined medication error reporting. These were environments where a senior worker's thirty years of experience couldn't be replicated by a machine in thirty seconds. The question of what happens to psychological safety when expertise itself becomes unstable wasn't on anyone's radar then. It needs to be now.

Three Disruptions

Three things have happened roughly simultaneously. Each one erodes the old contract. Together, they break it.

The first two we've already encountered: distance dissolves visibility, and digital mediation strips repair signals. These made the old contract harder to maintain. The third one challenges whether the contract's terms still apply.

AI disrupts the competence hierarchy directly.

When researchers study how people respond to AI integration, they tend to find a pattern: some enthusiasts who see opportunity, some resisters who actively avoid or undermine adoption, and a larger group in the middle. The middle group is ambivalent. They use the tools. They find them valuable. And they feel vaguely worse about themselves for needing them.

This ambivalence has a specific structure. It's not generic anxiety about job loss, the kind of worry that's haunted workers since the Luddites. It's something more personal: I needed a machine to do what I'm supposed to be good at. The tools help and the help stings.

When your professional identity rests on competence, and a tool can replicate aspects of that competence in seconds, the identity wobbles even if your job is secure. The expertise that used to be solid ground starts to feel like a ledge.

And here's where it connects: Edmondson's framework covers admitting mistakes and asking for help. Those are interpersonal risks people have always faced. But AI introduces a vulnerability that the research never anticipated: admitting you used AI assistance. Admitting you needed it. Admitting you're not sure, anymore, which parts of your work are really yours.

Teams without explicit norms around this treat AI use as vaguely shameful. Something to obscure rather than discuss. The senior engineer doesn't mention that the elegant solution came from his third prompt. The analyst presents findings without noting where her thinking ended and the model's began. Everyone is doing this. Nobody is talking about it.

Derek's silence wasn't about fear of looking stupid. It was about fear of looking replaceable. Not replaceable by another engineer. He could handle that competition, he had been handling it for fifteen years. Replaceable by a system that didn't even know it was competing.

THE NEW FOUNDATION

If the old contract is broken, what replaces it?

One answer is "nothing, we're all doomed, enjoy the apocalypse." This has the advantage of requiring no effort but the disadvantage of probably being wrong. The less dramatic answer is that the source of value has shifted, and teams that recognize the shift can build something stable on the new ground.

The new foundation is judgment. Not what you know, but what judgments you can make that AI cannot.

This is what people always say when machines start doing what humans do: "ah, but the really human stuff, they can't touch that." Usually this is followed by machines touching exactly that, and the goalposts moving again. So let's be specific about the meaning and you can judge whether this is actual solid ground or just the next ledge.

Consider what used to constitute expertise in technical work. Writing correct code. Designing efficient algorithms. Architecting scalable systems. Leading technical teams. AI increasingly handles the first two. What remains is the senior stuff: knowing which problems are worth solving, understanding why we're building something rather than just what, recognizing when the technically correct solution is organizationally wrong.

The hierarchy didn't disappear. It flipped. The entry-level skills became automatable. The things that looked like "soft skills" or "experience" or "gut feel" turned out to be the hard ones to replicate.

The economist David Autor calls this Polanyi's Paradox: we know more than we can tell, and therefore more than we can program.[1] A senior engineer senses that an architecture will create problems six months out but can't reduce that intuition to a checklist. A master craftsman knows when the wood "feels right" in ways that resist explicit description. This knowledge can't be written down, but it can be acted on. AI systems, however sophisticated, operate on what can be made explicit. This layer of tacit knowledge remains inaccessible to them, at least for long enough to plan around.

This leads to the core insight: the thing AI cannot do is know when to trust AI. That judgment is irreducibly human. It requires understanding context, stakes, failure modes, organizational dynamics: human factors that AI cannot perceive.

The new contract: I am valuable because of the judgments I can make that AI cannot, and this team recognizes and develops that capacity.

This is what Derek had been providing without knowing it, and withholding because he couldn't see its value.

~

Three o'clock. Derek's face appeared in the video call with the muted wariness of someone who knows they've been summoned, but not why.

Marcus had thought about how to open this. He'd considered showing the CommTrack data immediately. He'd considered asking about the buffer decision directly. Both felt like ambushes.

"I've been looking at how the buffer decision happened," Marcus said. "Trying to understand what we missed."

---

1. David Autor, "Polanyi's Paradox and the Shape of Employment Growth," NBER Working Paper No. 20485 (September 2014). Autor named the paradox after Polanyi's observation in *The Tacit Dimension* (1966) that "we can know more than we can tell."

Derek's expression didn't change. "The analysis looked solid. Finance did their homework."

"It did look solid. But you maintain that system. You know how it behaves under stress. And in twenty-two minutes of discussion, you said six words."

A pause. Derek's eyes moved slightly, the tell of someone calculating how much trouble they're in.

"It was a finance presentation. They had the data."

"You had more data. Or you could have." Marcus let that sit. "You changed six months ago, last October. Right after the routing disaster. Before that, you talked plenty in technical reviews. After, you went quiet. I need to know what happened."

"The routing disaster happened." Derek's voice was flat. "I was part of that. I validated the approach. I said it looked good. And then it broke everything."

"So, you stopped weighing in on technical decisions because you were wrong once?"

"I was wrong in a way that cost people their jobs." The words came out harder than Derek probably intended. "Three people in carrier relations. Because I said the system looked sound."

"The system did look sound. The failure mode wasn't predictable from—"

"I should have seen it." Derek cut him off. "That's the point. I've been doing this for fifteen years. I should have known that optimizing a complex system would create feedback loops. I should have asked different questions. I didn't."

Marcus interrupted, "Can I tell you something I haven't figured out how to think about yet?"

Derek's wariness shifted. This wasn't the preamble to a performance review.

"Two months ago I used AI to summarize the market analysis reports for Q3 planning. Forty pages down to two. Saved me probably four hours."

"That seems reasonable."

"The summary was wrong. Or not wrong exactly. The trends were real. But there was a footnote in the original about European regulatory changes, and the model either missed it or didn't think it was significant. I didn't catch it because I never read the original. I presented projections to Whitford based on a timeline we couldn't meet. He presented them to the board. Two weeks later, legal caught it and Whitford had to revise everything."

"I didn't hear about that."

"No. Because I told everyone it was 'new information coming to light.' Which was technically true and the exact kind of technically true that makes you hate yourself a little."

Marcus paused. This was the part he'd been circling.

"Here's what I still can't figure out. I'm still doing it. Used it this morning. I tell myself I'm more careful now, but I don't actually know if that's true. I read the originals sometimes. Not always. I'm not sure I've learned anything except to be more anxious about something I'm going to keep doing anyway."

Derek was quiet, processing.

"Why are you telling me this?"

"Because I think we're stuck on the same thing. And because I've been looking for someone to say this to who might actually understand it."

"The buffer decision. I had analysis."

"I thought you might."

"I asked a different question than finance did. Not 'how

often did we use it' but 'under what conditions.' The pattern came back in two minutes. Promotional windows plus carrier constraints. The October surge was on the calendar. It was obvious once you saw it."

"So you knew."

"The machine knew. I looked at the output and thought 'yes, that seems right.'" The flatness in Derek's voice was the sound of something he'd been carrying for weeks. "Which is exactly what I thought about the routing system. The analysis seems right. Validate and proceed. And then it breaks everything and three people lose their jobs."

"So you didn't trust—"

"It's worse than that." Derek cut him off. "The routing disaster, I keep thinking about it as one mistake. One time I validated something wrong. But I've been using these tools for everything for the past year. Hundreds of decisions. And I have no idea which of those were actually good calls and which were mistakes that just haven't exploded yet. The routing system wasn't a failure. It was a sample. One revealed sample from a distribution I can't see."

Marcus sat with that.

"I don't know how to make that less true," he finally said. "I can't tell you your judgment is reliable. I don't know if mine is."

"That's not actually comforting."

"It's not meant to be. It's meant to be shared." Marcus paused, searching for the right way to say this. "You've been carrying this like it's yours alone. But everyone using these tools is making the same bet. Most of them don't even know they're making it."

"Still not comforting."

"No. But your silence isn't protecting you from anything. It's just guaranteeing your judgment isn't in the room when we make decisions." He stopped. "Whatever the odds are that you're wrong, they're better than the certainty that you're absent."

Derek almost smiled. "You're saying my unreliable judgment is still better than nothing."

"I'm saying the alternative to imperfect isn't perfect. It's zero."

Two weeks later. Not a formal presentation. Marcus had framed it as "documenting our AI practices for the Whitford review," which was true enough and provided cover for what was actually happening.

Derek walked through how he'd approached the memory leak problem. The real version. He'd described the symptoms to the model, got back three hypotheses, rejected two immediately because they misunderstood the caching architecture, spent an hour figuring out why the third was subtly wrong, then reprompted with what he'd learned. The fourth attempt identified the actual issue.

"So, the fix came from AI," Miles said.

"The fix came from the fourth prompt. After I spent hours crafting the right context for the model. And rejected three wrong answers." Derek paused. "The system generates plausible outputs. It doesn't know which ones are good. That's still my job."

He showed them a failure case too. A suggested fix from the previous month that would have corrupted the carrier database. Syntactically correct. Logically coherent. It would have destroyed six months of allocation history.

"How did you catch it?"

"I've been writing systems like this for fifteen years. The pattern didn't feel right."

Miles leaned forward. "But can you articulate what felt wrong? If we could document that—"

"No." Derek said it flatly, then softened slightly. "I mean, I've tried. The short answer is I can't fully explain how I knew. Fifteen years of pattern recognition that I can't reduce to a checklist."

The room was quiet for a moment.

Lin said nothing during the session.

An hour later, Derek's Slack showed a message from her: "The fourth prompt thing. I do the same with vendor data. Never told anyone."

He stared at it for a moment. Then typed back: "Apparently we're not supposed to keep that secret anymore."

"Apparently."

A pause. Then: "It's easier when it's not just you."

Derek sent back a thumbs up emoji, which was inadequate but true.

CommTrack would show the shift in Derek's participation patterns over the following weeks. More words in technical discussions. More questions. A willingness to say "I ran this through and here's what I think" that had been absent for three months.

The tool hadn't changed. Derek's relationship to being measured had.

Other patterns were visible in the data if you knew how to look. Sarah appeared in nearly every communication channel, threading conversations together that wouldn't otherwise connect. Lin's meeting silence contrasted sharply with her detailed async contributions, which arrived at odd hours and often contained the most useful observations. Marcus flagged these for later. They weren't problems yet. They were shapes in the water, worth watching.

Miles had produced his framework by the end of the week. It was thorough, well-structured, and useful mostly as an exercise. The part that actually mattered resisted documentation.

The documentation effort continued. The team was getting better at describing how they actually worked, which meant confronting how much of it was messier than any process document would suggest.

Derek still played Wordle during status meetings. Some patterns weren't problems.

The pattern where a senior engineer silently withdrew his judgment for three months: that one had been worth seeing. CommTrack couldn't tell you why someone went quiet. It could tell you when.

What you did with that information was still a human problem.

Spring was turning toward summer, the sun reaching his desk by six now, warm on his hands. Whitford's deadline, whatever it was for, kept approaching.

8

THE CULTURAL COLLISION

WHAT LIES BENEATH THE SURFACE

By early June, the documentation effort had been going well, which should have been a warning sign.

Six weeks of capturing how work actually happened across Consolidated's operations. Process maps. Decision trees. Escalation protocols. Regional inputs from Mumbai, Phoenix, a recently acquired operation. The AI had synthesized forty-six pages of documentation into twelve pages of clean analysis: "How Carrier Relationships Work Across Consolidated Operations."

Miles had structured the prompts, iterated on the outputs, refined until the synthesis felt comprehensive. Whitford wanted to understand their operations before whatever was coming. This would give him that.

Marcus scheduled a cross-team working session to validate the synthesis before it went upstairs. Core team plus regional leads. Final review before submission.

The calendar invite said: "Please review the synthesis and come prepared to discuss."

Different people read that differently.

. . .

The meeting opened with eight rectangles on screen, which was progress. Three months ago it would have been eight rectangles pretending to be a team. Now it was eight rectangles that had learned, painfully, to function as one.

Marcus facilitated from Oakland. Miles would present remotely; it was his work. Derek and Sarah flanked Marcus in the conference room, Lin slightly apart, camera on for once. On video: Carmen from Phoenix operations, crisp and direct, already annotating her copy. David Lindquist from the Midwest acquisition, present but watchful—he'd been sitting in on their documentation sessions for weeks, reporting back to his own leadership.

And Priya, from Mumbai. 10:30 PM her time, which the meeting analytics would log as engagement. Small gold earrings caught the light from her desk lamp. What the analytics couldn't capture: her husband reading alone in the next room, the familiar guilt of being pulled between worlds.

Priya had read the synthesis twice. The section on Mumbai operations described processes she didn't recognize. Carrier selection criteria that existed in documentation but not in practice. Escalation paths that were formally correct and practically useless. The relationships that actually made her region work weren't there.

In Mumbai, Priya was known for getting things done when formal channels failed. She navigated carrier relationships, client demands, her own team's dynamics with a fluency that came from fifteen years in logistics. She could read a room, find the right person, know when to push and when to wait. Her Rolodex—she still thought of it that way, though it was really a spreadsheet with personal details about every key contact—was the operational infrastructure that made the formal infrastructure function.

None of that transferred to a video call with Americans she barely knew.

. . .

Miles walked through the synthesis. Section by section. Carrier selection logic. Escalation protocols. Regional variations.

The synthesis was an artifact: comprehensive, well-organized, professionally presented. But responses to artifacts are driven by assumptions that vary in ways no one can see.

Miles saw validation. He'd built this. Challenge would feel like challenge to his work, which it partly was.

Derek saw incompleteness. "This captures what the documentation says. Is it what actually happens?" His skepticism was useful, if predictable.

Carmen engaged directly. Questions about Phoenix operations, clarifications about carrier relationships in the Southwest corridor. She had concerns, she raised them, she got answers. The format worked for her.

Priya was silent.

Her camera showed her attentive, watching, present. In thirty minutes of discussion, she'd contributed nothing.

What it actually meant was more complicated.

In high power distance contexts, authority is natural and appropriate. Senior people speak; junior people listen. Challenging authority, especially publicly, feels inappropriate regardless of whether the challenge has merit.

The synthesis had been presented by Miles, endorsed implicitly by Marcus, wrapped in the authority of AI-generated analysis. For Priya, disagreeing in this setting—synchronous, public, with people she didn't know well—meant challenging a structure she hadn't been invited to challenge. Her silence wasn't absence of opinion. It was a culturally coherent response to a situation where her opinion hadn't been explicitly requested by someone with standing to request it.

The meeting format said "everyone's input is welcome." The format's structure said something else. Direct questions to the room. Rapid exchange. Confidence rewarded, hesitation read as absence. Everything that made Priya effective in Mumbai didn't function here.

So she waited. For a direct question. For explicit invitation. For some signal that her perspective was actually wanted, not just formally welcomed.

The signal didn't come.

Sarah noticed something off.

She'd developed a sense for it, these past months. The rectangle that was too still. The person who should have opinions but wasn't voicing them. She'd learned, sometimes painfully, that silence in distributed teams rarely meant agreement.

"Priya, do you have thoughts on whether this captures how Mumbai operations work?"

The question was well-intentioned. It was also, in ways Sarah couldn't see, precisely wrong.

A direct question in a group setting, from someone Priya barely knew, asking her to evaluate work that had organizational weight behind it. The form said invitation. The context said performance.

"It covers the main points," Priya said. Her voice was pleasant, professional, giving nothing away.

Sarah heard agreement. What Priya had actually communicated, to anyone who shared her cultural framework, was something closer to: I have concerns I'm not willing to raise in this format.

The distinction was invisible. Sarah moved on.

. . .

Lin had been watching. She sat slightly apart, as she always did, glasses off, held loosely in one hand.

She'd been watching Priya's stillness. The careful phrasing. The way her eyes had moved across the synthesis during the presentation—not the scanning of someone satisfied, but the focused attention of someone cataloging problems.

Lin knew what she was seeing because she'd been that person. Different context, same dynamic. She'd spent eighteen months learning when to speak and when to stay silent in American meetings, and the lesson had been: when in doubt, stay silent.

She'd also learned, more recently, what it cost.

Sarah was bridging again—"I think what Priya might be saying is..."—generous, the way Sarah always was, and for the same reason Priya hadn't needed to speak for herself in months.

Lin put her glasses on. A small thing. No one noticed.

"The synthesis is wrong about your region." Lin was looking at Priya. "I can see it in how you're reading. Tell us what it misses."

Not a question. An opening that didn't require Priya to contradict anyone.

Priya was still. Then her shoulders settled, the way they do when someone decides to stop carrying something alone.

"Yes," she said. "It's wrong."

What followed was twenty minutes of Priya explaining what the synthesis couldn't see.

The carrier relationships that existed in practice but not in documentation. Rajesh, who ran a mid-sized trucking operation in Chennai, whose reliability scores were mediocre but who had once rerouted an entire shipment through back roads during a monsoon because Priya had called him personally.

"He picks up the phone," Priya said. "At 2 AM, during a crisis, he picks up. That's not in any system."

Neither were the escalation paths that actually worked, which bore no resemblance to the documented ones. Or the WhatsApp group where real problems got solved, because by the time something reached the formal escalation system, it was already too late.

"The synthesis describes the company that exists on paper," Priya said. "Not the company that actually runs."

David, who'd been watching from his office in the Midwest, spoke for the first time. "When you acquire a company, the documentation you receive describes the company that existed on paper. The company that actually functioned was held together by relationships and workarounds that nobody wrote down because everyone who needed to know already knew."

Miles was quiet through most of this.

He'd built the synthesis. Three weeks of work. And it was wrong. Not factually incorrect—the processes it described were real, documented, officially sanctioned. But it had missed the layer underneath.

"So the synthesis is wrong?" Miles asked.

"It's incomplete," Lin said. "It captured what was written down. Not what's known."

"The AI did exactly what it was asked to do," Derek added. "It synthesized the documentation. The documentation was incomplete."

"How do we fix it?"

"You can't fully fix it," Priya said. "Some of this can't be written down. Not because it's secret, but because I don't know I know it until something goes wrong and I realize I knew how to handle it."

Lin nodded. "The stuff you can't articulate until someone asks the wrong question."

The meeting ran over by forty minutes.

By the end, they'd identified three categories of gaps: things the documentation had wrong, things the documentation had omitted, and things that couldn't be documented at all because they existed only in relationships and judgment calls.

Carmen from Phoenix had contributed her own version. "We have something like that too. A text chain for real emergencies. It's not in any system. If you mapped our actual escalation paths, they'd look nothing like the org chart."

"We could do this differently," Lin said. "Instead of asking people what they know, show them what we think we know. Let them correct it. Priya couldn't have told us what was missing if she hadn't read the synthesis first. The wrong map revealed the territory."

Marcus made a note. That was worth remembering.

After the meeting, Sarah found Lin in the hallway.

"What you said in there. About me explaining people."

Lin met her eyes. "I should have said it sooner. Or differently."

"No. You were right." Sarah paused. "I've been doing it for years. I thought I was helping. Making space for people who weren't being heard."

"You were helping. And not helping." Lin was quiet for a moment, finding the words. "When you explain me, my perspective reaches the room. But I do not have to bring it there. I never learned to speak in these meetings because you were always translating."

Sarah was quiet.

"Would you tell me? When you see it happening?"

"Yes."

"I want you to."

They stood there for a moment, something settled between them that hadn't been settled before.

WHAT JUST HAPPENED

The meeting nearly approved a confidently wrong synthesis. That's the headline. The more interesting question is why Priya's knowledge stayed silent until Lin surfaced it—and what that reveals about how cultural patterns shape responses to AI outputs.

Edgar Schein's model of organizational culture helps explain the invisibility. Culture operates at three levels: artifacts (visible behaviors and processes), espoused values (what people say matters), and basic assumptions (unconscious beliefs that actually drive behavior). The deeper the level, the less accessible to examination. Basic assumptions don't feel like assumptions. They feel like how things obviously are.

Priya and Power Distance

Geert Hofstede's research on cultural dimensions gives this pattern a name: power distance. It describes comfort with hierarchy. In high power distance contexts, authority flows in specific directions. Senior people speak; junior people listen. Challenging authority publicly, even when you're right, feels like a violation of something deeper than etiquette.

The synthesis arrived wrapped in organizational authority: presented by Miles, endorsed implicitly by Marcus, generated by AI systems that speak with uniform confidence. For Priya, disagreeing in this setting meant challenging a structure she hadn't been invited to challenge. Her silence wasn't disengagement. It was how information is supposed to flow.

Here's the part that matters for AI integration: high power distance correlates with deference to authoritative sources, and AI systems present with extraordinary authority. The confidence is baked into the output format. No hedging, no "I think," no visible uncertainty. For team members oriented toward hierarchy, AI confidence registers as something close to institutional voice. Questioning it feels like questioning the organization.

Lin and High-Context Communication

Sarah's question was low-context: meaning only in the words.[1] "Do you have thoughts?" In low-context communication, that's an invitation. In high-context communication, it's a performance demand with no safety net.

Lin's statement worked differently. "The synthesis is wrong about your region. Tell us what it misses." The words invited response, but the subtext did more: *I see you. I understand. I'm not asking you to perform.* High-context communication relies on shared understanding that doesn't need to be said. Lin didn't need to explain that she'd been Priya. They both knew.

Sarah and the Bridging Pattern

Bridging isn't a Hofstede dimension, but it interacts with all of them. Sarah smooths the friction that cultural difference creates. She helps high power distance individuals contribute

1. Edward T. Hall, *Beyond Culture* (Garden City, NY: Anchor Press/Doubleday, 1976). Hall introduced the concepts of high-context and low-context cultures: in high-context communication, most meaning is implicit and relational; in low-context communication, meaning is explicit and in the words themselves.

without direct challenge. She translates high-context communication for low-context audiences. She makes diverse teams feel functional.

The cost: the underlying divergence never surfaces. The team gets Sarah's interpretation of different perspectives rather than the perspectives themselves. The muscle of direct communication never develops because the bridge makes it unnecessary.

This is the problem with being good at making things easy.

The Synthesis and Structural Low-Context

Extending Hall's framework: AI outputs are structurally low-context regardless of what they contain. Text on screen. No relationship. No implicit meaning. No non-verbal dimension. For Carmen, this was fine—the format matched her preference. For Priya, the synthesis felt emptier than it appeared. The dimensions she'd normally use to interpret communication (Who is this from? What's our relationship? What's not being said?) were absent.

The document looked complete to some readers and incomplete to others. The difference was invisible until Lin made it visible.

Other Dimensions at Play

Hofstede identified other dimensions beyond power distance. They didn't drive the main failure, but they were in the room, and they're worth understanding because they'll show up in yours.

Individualism-Collectivism may shape whether AI feels like a threat or tool. Individualists might see AI synthesis as displacing their unique contribution; collectivists might integrate it more readily as serving group goals. Miles's investment in the synthesis—his defensiveness when it was challenged—hints at individualist framing. The synthesis was "his work." Challenge felt personal. Someone with a more collectivist orientation might have welcomed correction as serving the team. Or might have resented it for different reasons entirely. The dimension doesn't predict behavior. It colors the emotional register.

Uncertainty Avoidance determines comfort with ambiguity. High uncertainty avoidance correlates with preference for clear answers. The synthesis offered exactly that: here's how operations work. Twelve pages. Clean structure. Actionable. The reality Priya surfaced was messier, more contingent, harder to act on. Some team members preferred the clean wrong answer to the complicated right one. This is a more common preference than anyone likes to admit.

Collectivism also shapes how teams value tacit knowledge. Collectivist cultures tend to appreciate relationships like the one with Rajesh—fifteen years of history, investment that pays off during monsoons, obligations that run both directions. More individualist cultures may see only the metrics: mediocre reliability scores, interchangeable with any other carrier. The dimension influences what counts as valuable information after it surfaces.

None of these dimensions determined whether Priya spoke. Power distance and communication context did that. But the other dimensions influence how teams receive and act on what surfaces. A team that values certainty may resist the messier truth. A team that sees carriers as interchangeable may not see why Rajesh matters. The cultural work doesn't end when someone finally speaks.

Surfacing Mechanisms

The meeting revealed divergence by accident. Lin's intervention wasn't planned; it emerged from recognition of a pattern she'd experienced herself. Teams can't rely on accident. They need practices.

What these practices share: they make explicit what teams usually leave ambiguous. The conversations feel awkward. The norms feel over-specified. The alternative is months of misreading each other.

Explicit AI Orientation Conversations

Before working with AI outputs, surface assumptions about what AI is and how it should be treated. Questions worth asking: How much do you trust AI analysis in your domain? When would you override an AI recommendation? What would make you uncomfortable about AI involvement in this decision?

The answers map where people actually stand. More importantly, the conversation establishes that different stances exist. Priya might not volunteer that she distrusts AI synthesis. But if the question is asked explicitly, she has cover to answer honestly.

Divergence Checks

After AI outputs arrive, create structured moments where team members articulate responses independently before discussion. Written reactions, submitted before anyone speaks. The practice prevents confident voices from anchoring the room and makes the range of responses visible.

Someone who would have stayed quiet has space to register disagreement. Someone who would have dominated has to wait. The format changes the dynamics before the dynamics have a chance to set.

Silence Protocols

Explicit norms about what non-response means. Does silence equal agreement? Still thinking? Disagreement too significant to voice casually? The specific norm matters less than having one.

Most teams skip this conversation because it feels like over-thinking. Then they spend months misreading each other. Clarity is kindness. The awkward conversation now prevents the painful one later.

Inversion Testing

Lin's insight deserves a name. Instead of asking what people know, show them what you think you know. Let them correct it.

Tacit knowledge often can't be articulated on demand. Priya couldn't have produced a document describing how Mumbai operations actually work. But she could immediately see what was wrong with a document that claimed to describe them. The wrong map revealed the territory.

This reframes AI synthesis from output to probe. The value isn't in being right. It's in being wrong in ways that surface what the team actually knows.

Direct Invitation by Recognized Authority

Sarah's question didn't work. Lin's statement did. The difference: Lin had standing to invite Priya in a way Sarah didn't. She'd demonstrated understanding of Priya's position. The invitation came from someone who'd navigated the same dynamics.

For high power distance, high-context communicators, who invites matters as much as how. Teams need to figure out who has standing to draw out specific voices. This isn't something you can assign. It's something you have to notice.

The synthesis got revised. More importantly, the process got revised. Priya would submit async input before the next cross-team session—time to formulate, no pressure to perform in real-time. Lin would review regional sections specifically, watching for the gap between documented and actual. Carmen committed to surfacing Phoenix's informal channels. The documentation effort would take longer. It would be less wrong. The practices would only matter if they kept doing them.

None of this solved the underlying problem. The team had learned to see one pattern (Priya's silence, Sarah's bridging, the synthesis's confident incompleteness) but patterns repeat in different forms. The next meeting would surface other assumptions, other gaps.

What they'd built was a practice, not a fix. The practice of noticing when the room isn't hearing someone. The practice of questioning outputs that look complete. The practice of asking who hasn't spoken, and why.

Sarah was already thinking about the carrier allocation system discussion scheduled for next week. Miles had been developing integration proposals. Derek had concerns. The two of them had been circling each other for weeks, disagreements surfacing in Slack threads and sidelong comments but never directly addressed. Sarah's instinct, as always, was to smooth it, to find the middle ground before the conflict got uncomfortable.

She caught herself. Noticed the instinct. Wondered, for the first time, whether smoothing was what the situation actually needed.

Some conflicts need to happen. The question is whether teams have built enough trust to let them.

9

CONFLICT CHOREOGRAPHY

WHEN DISAGREEMENT DOES WORK

The weekly standup had become something different. Late August now, peak season ten weeks out, and the meetings that used to be performance had turned into something functional.

A screen full of rectangles pretending to be a team, status updates that said nothing, silence where questions should have been. Marcus had spent those meetings wondering what he was missing.

Now the standups actually worked. Not perfectly. But the team had built practices over the past months that made coordination possible. The documentation effort. The explicit handoffs. The slow accumulation of trust that made honesty possible.

The carrier allocation system was third on the agenda. A brief item: Miles had been developing an integration proposal, and today was a status update. Five minutes, maybe ten. It ran closer to an hour.

. . .

Miles shared his screen from Chicago. The proposal was clean, well-organized, the kind of work he'd learned to produce after Calloway. He'd done the analysis. He'd consulted Derek's documentation.

"The integration has three components," Miles began. "Predictive capacity modeling to anticipate carrier constraints before they hit. Health scoring to flag reliability issues across our carrier network. And selective automation for truly routine shipments, the ones where human review doesn't add anything."

The slides were good. The logic was clear. Peak season was ten weeks away, and the current system required manual review of every carrier assignment. The efficiency gains were real. The risk mitigation was built in.

"The automation scope is narrow," Miles continued. "Only shipments that meet specific criteria: established lanes, carriers with twelve-plus months of history, volume below threshold, no special handling. Everything else surfaces for human review. I've modeled the coverage. We're talking about maybe thirty percent of shipments qualifying for automation. The rest stay manual."

Derek had gone quiet somewhere around "selective automation." He was looking at the slides with the focused stillness of someone forming objections.

"Timeline?" Marcus asked.

"Six weeks to full implementation if we start now. That gives us four weeks of buffer before peak season ramp."

"Four weeks of buffer," Derek said.

Miles paused. "Is that a concern?"

"It's not a lot of runway if something goes wrong."

Miles leaned into the defense. "The automation scope is conservative. We're not touching complex shipments."

"The routing system scope was conservative too."

The room shifted. The standup was no longer a status update.

Sarah recognized the pattern. She'd seen it before: a technical discussion tilting toward something sharper, two people with different reads on the same situation.

Her instinct was to smooth it. Find the middle ground. Keep the standup from derailing into an argument that would eat the rest of the morning.

"What if we table this for a dedicated session?" Sarah offered. "Give everyone time to review Miles's proposal in detail, come back with specific concerns?"

Derek and Miles both looked at her.

"Or," she continued, "we could start with a limited pilot. Test the automation on a smaller subset, see how it performs before peak season. That might address some of the timing concerns."

She was bridging. It was what she did. Two weeks ago, Lin had interrupted her mid-bridge: "You're explaining her. Like you explain me." Sarah had asked Lin to tell her when it was happening. She'd started to notice.

But noticing a pattern and breaking it were different things. The instinct was strong. The compromise she was offering would work. It would keep things comfortable.

Marcus was watching her.

What Conflict Is For

Conflict is not a problem to solve. It's how teams get things they can't get any other way.

Three outputs matter most. First, error-catching: when

someone says "I don't think that's right," they surface something that would otherwise slip through. Second, assumption-testing: disagreement forces articulation, and articulation exposes assumptions that accumulate untested until one fails expensively. Third, meaning-making: when team members have different reads on the same situation, working through the difference is how shared interpretation emerges. Teams that suppress disagreement don't achieve consensus. They achieve the appearance of consensus, with divergent interpretations accumulating silently until one surfaces at the worst moment.

These functions matter more when AI is involved, not less. AI produces outputs that are genuinely capable within their scope and genuinely blind to everything outside it. The blindness is invisible from the outside. Human disagreement is how that blindness gets caught. AI also encodes assumptions invisibly and generates confident interpretations that can substitute for genuine understanding. The need for conflict's outputs intensifies at exactly the moment when the conditions for producing them degrade.

Productive conflict requires two things: willingness to voice disagreement, and capacity to work through it toward resolution. Most organizations have neither. Some have one. Few have both. Which is yours?

Willingness requires psychological safety, legitimate standing to challenge, and stakes that feel manageable. When any of these fail, people stay quiet. The person who sees a problem but doesn't mention it has made a calculation, usually unconsciously, that speaking up costs more than staying silent.

Repair capacity requires reading reactions and adjusting in real time. Productive conflict isn't frictionless; it's conflict where the friction gets addressed before it compounds. You see someone react badly to what you said, you soften or clarify, they recalibrate, the conversation continues.

The key finding from decades of research: disagreement

about the work can improve team performance, but only when it doesn't spill over into personal friction. The spillover is common. Task and relationship conflict are correlated, which is why disagreements about work so often become entangled with interpersonal friction.[1]

What prevents spillover? Trust. When team members trust each other, they interpret task-focused challenges as task-focused. When trust is low, the same challenges feel like personal attacks. The person who says "I think this analysis is missing something" gets heard as "I think you're incompetent." The distinction between productive and destructive conflict runs directly through the trust foundation.

Sarah's instinct to mediate wasn't wrong, exactly. But she was solving a problem by preventing the disagreement from happening at all. And disagreement that doesn't happen can't produce anything.

Marcus had been watching Sarah.

He'd seen the pattern before. He'd seen her ask Lin to help her notice it.

Now he was watching her do it again. Two weeks wasn't long enough to rewire an instinct that deep. The situations that called for something different looked exactly like the situations that called for smoothing.

"Sarah. Hold on."

She stopped mid-sentence. The room went quiet.

Marcus kept his voice neutral, but the intention was clear.

---

1. Karen A. Jehn, "A Multimethod Examination of the Benefits and Detriments of Intragroup Conflict," *Administrative Science Quarterly* 40, no. 2 (1995): 256-282; Carsten K.W. De Dreu and Laurie R. Weingart, "Task Versus Relationship Conflict, Team Performance, and Team Member Satisfaction: A Meta-Analysis," *Journal of Applied Psychology* 88, no. 4 (2003): 741-749.

"I think they need to actually have this disagreement." He looked at Derek, then at Miles on the screen. "Not find a middle ground that lets them skip it."

Sarah's expression shifted. She'd heard this before. From Lin, about Priya. Now from Marcus.

"Derek has concerns," Marcus continued. "Miles has done real work. If we table this or pilot our way around the disagreement, we'll end up back here in three weeks with the same tension and less time." He paused. "We have the hour. Let's hear what's actually at stake."

The standup had become something else.

What Suppresses Willingness

There are understandable reasons to stay quiet when AI is involved, even if they're not good ones. Four mechanisms make silence feel rational.

Confidence contagion. AI displays certainty regardless of accuracy. It doesn't hedge when uncertain, doesn't signal when extrapolating from thin evidence, doesn't distinguish knowing from fabricating. The confidence is meaningless. It feels like information anyway.

Research confirms what you'd expect: humans calibrate their own confidence to AI's displayed confidence. The alignment persists after AI involvement ends. You worked with a confident system this morning; you're still more confident this afternoon, even on unrelated decisions.[2]

2. Jingshu Li et al., "As Confidence Aligns: Understanding the Effect of AI Confidence on Human Self-confidence in Human-AI Decision Making," *CHI '25: Proceedings of the CHI Conference on Human Factors in Computing Systems* (2025). In a study of 270 participants, confidence alignment with AI persisted after AI involvement ended.

For conflict, this means doubt gets suppressed at the source. You can't voice reservations you no longer feel.

Identity threat. When AI performs tasks that defined someone's expertise, questioning it becomes existentially loaded. The objection "I don't think the AI is right" carries an unspoken subtext: "and therefore I still matter."

Counterintuitively, less experienced professionals show stronger threat responses. Students perceive AI as an imminent threat to careers they're building; established professionals see it as more distant. Often the person questioning AI has both a real concern and an identity concern, and they can't separate them cleanly. The skill is recognizing when identity is in play.

Absent reciprocity. In human conflict, both parties bear risk. You might be wrong, might embarrass yourself. But so might the other person. The vulnerability is mutual, and mutuality makes challenge acceptable.

With AI, the risk is one-sided. You can look foolish for disagreeing with the machine. You cannot make the machine look foolish. It has no ego to bruise, no reputation to protect. Challenging AI carries all the social risk of challenging a confident expert, with none of the reciprocal vulnerability.

Explanation backfire. Explainable AI was supposed to help. If people understood how AI reached conclusions, they could evaluate appropriately.

The evidence points the other way. Explanations increase acceptance regardless of correctness. People shown explanations were more likely to follow recommendations, including wrong ones. The feeling of understanding substitutes for understanding itself.

Derek was pushing against all four. Miles's proposal came with analysis, with explanations, with the confidence of someone who had done the work. Questioning it meant being the skeptic again, the one who'd been burned by the routing disaster and couldn't let it go. It meant risking that his concerns were trauma rather than judgment.

Marcus had created space for the disagreement to happen.

Derek spoke first. His voice was low, level.

"I'm not against AI integration." He said it carefully, like he'd said it before and not been heard. "The question isn't whether AI can help with carrier allocation. It's whether we integrate it into production systems six weeks before peak season."

Miles leaned forward slightly on screen. "The timeline is tight. I know that. But the alternative is running peak season on a fully manual process that we know has capacity problems. We hit those problems last year. We'll hit them again."

"We hit capacity problems because of demand we didn't anticipate. Not because the manual process was broken."

"The manual process couldn't adapt fast enough. That's the same thing."

"It's not the same thing." Derek's voice stayed level, but there was weight behind it. "A process that works until conditions change is different from a process that's broken. The question is whether an automated process would have adapted better, or whether it would have failed differently."

Lin watched from her usual spot, slightly back from the table, tea untouched. Sarah sat very still, hands in her lap. Marcus had pulled back from the table, patient in a way that most people found difficult, comfortable with the silence stretching.

"The routing disaster," Miles said.

"Yes. The routing disaster. Last fall. Everything looked good on paper. The system had been tested. The edge cases had been considered. And when conditions shifted in ways the model didn't anticipate, the system made confident decisions that cost us a client relationship and nearly cost us the account."

"That was a different system. Different architecture. Different scope."

"It was a system we trusted because the analysis said we should trust it. Because it had been tested. Because the people who built it were smart and careful." Derek paused. "I'm not saying you're not smart and careful. I'm saying smart and careful isn't enough when you're deploying into conditions you can't fully model."

Miles absorbed this, running a hand through his hair. "So what would be enough? What would it take for you to support integration?"

"I don't know yet. That's part of the problem. I don't know what I don't know about how this will behave under stress."

The Triggers

When people reject a challenge, it's usually not because the challenge is wrong. It's because something about it triggered a defensive response. Stone and Heen identified three triggers, and knowing which one fired tells you what to do about it.[3]

Truth triggers fire when the content seems wrong. "That's not accurate" or "You're missing context." This is disagreement about substance, and when other triggers aren't involved, it resolves through evidence and argument.

Relationship triggers fire when the source lacks standing. "Who are you to challenge this?" or "You don't understand the domain well enough to have an opinion."

3. Douglas Stone and Sheila Heen, *Thanks for the Feedback: The Science and Art of Receiving Feedback Well* (New York: Viking, 2014).

Identity triggers fire when the message threatens self-concept. The challenge isn't just to an idea but to something the person believes about themselves.

Recognizing which trigger has fired allows more targeted response. Truth triggers need substance engaged. Relationship triggers need the standing question acknowledged. Identity triggers need reassurance before anything else.

In the conference room, all three were at play—but identity was the one that mattered most. For Derek, his routing disaster experience wasn't just a data point. It was the foundation of his claim to be heard on questions like this. For Miles, six weeks of careful work wasn't just analysis. It was evidence that he'd grown past Calloway, that he could produce something worth trusting. When Miles pushed on Derek's concerns, he was inadvertently pushing on Derek's worth. When Derek resisted Miles's proposal, he was inadvertently dismissing Miles's growth. Truth triggers were firing too—they genuinely disagreed about risk—but the heat came from identity.

~

"You can't treat every system improvement like it's the routing disaster waiting to happen." Miles was fully engaged now, and he had the kind of face that couldn't hide it—you could see the frustration before he said anything. "That was last fall. We've learned things. I've learned things."

"Have we?" Derek leaned forward. "Because what I learned is that systems fail in ways you can't predict. The routing system didn't fail because we were careless. It failed because we were confident. Because everything looked good."

"So we never improve anything? We never integrate new capabilities because something went wrong once?"

"That's not what I'm saying."

"Then what are you saying? Because it sounds like you're

saying your experience trumps analysis. That your gut feeling outweighs six weeks of work."

The room was very quiet. Lin hadn't moved. Sarah's hands were still in her lap.

~

How the Gap Widens

The same words land differently depending on what you need to protect.

Chris Argyris called this the ladder of inference: the path from observable data through selection, interpretation, and assumption to conclusion. Each rung adds more of the observer's mental model, less of what actually happened. Two people witness the same exchange and climb to incompatible beliefs, each feeling obviously correct.

In the conference room, Derek's identity was bound up in the routing disaster. Miles's identity was bound up in the Calloway recovery. Each heard the other through a filter shaped by what they needed to protect.

Derek heard Miles saying: your experience is trauma, not wisdom. Your caution is fear, not judgment. You're the guy who can't move on.

Miles heard Derek saying: your analysis doesn't matter. Your growth doesn't count. You're still the junior who doesn't understand how things really work.

Neither was saying exactly that. But the gap between what was said and what was heard had reached its widest point.

~

Derek sat back. Uncrossed his arms—Marcus hadn't noticed

him crossing them. When he spoke, his voice was slower, more deliberate.

"I'm saying the analysis can't see everything. The model optimizes based on metrics. Cost per shipment, transit time, reliability scores. Those matter. But when a carrier is deciding who to prioritize during a crunch, they're not using metrics."

"What are they using?"

"Relationships. History. Who they want to keep working with when the crisis is over." Derek paused. "Remember what Priya told us about Rajesh? The carrier in Chennai who scores middle of the pack on metrics but handles forty percent of their southern corridor volume? Because three years ago he rerouted a shipment through roads that aren't on any logistics map and saved a client relationship. 'Carrier will perform miracles under pressure' isn't a metric. But it's real. And when Priya's region hits a crisis, that's who she calls."

Miles was quiet for a moment.

"So your concern isn't the automation itself," he said finally. "It's that automation optimizes for things it can measure and ignores things it can't."

"That's part of it."

"What's the other part?"

"Timing. You're proposing we deploy a new system six weeks before the highest-stakes period of our year. With maybe four weeks of buffer before peak season ramp. If something goes wrong in week three of implementation, we're debugging in production during the busiest month we have."

"The scope is limited. Thirty percent of shipments. Routine lanes only."

"Scope creep happens. Especially when something's working. Especially under pressure." Derek shook his head slightly. "I've seen it. You hit a capacity crunch, someone says 'the automated system is handling its lanes fine, let's expand the criteria temporarily,' and suddenly you're running untested configurations during a crisis."

"That's a governance problem, not a system problem."

"Governance problems become system problems when the system makes them easy."

Sarah shifted in her chair. Marcus caught her eye briefly. She stayed quiet.

Miles sat back. He was thinking.

"Okay," he said. "So what would you need? Not 'I don't know what I don't know.' Specifically. What conditions would have to be true for you to support integration before peak season?"

It was a different kind of question. Not "Why are you wrong" but "What would make you right." Open-ended rather than closed. One invites defense; the other invites collaboration. The difference sounds semantic but isn't. Derek's concerns weren't obstacles to overcome but constraints to design around, and Miles's question signaled he understood that.

Lin spoke.

She set down her tea and didn't wait to be asked. She just spoke.

"Derek's right about the relationships."

The room turned toward her. Three months ago, this would have drawn comment. The team had learned to make space. Lin had learned to use it.

"What Priya described about Mumbai applies here," she continued. "The carriers we have worked with for years know us. They know our patterns, our volumes, what it means when we call with an urgent request. That knowledge goes both ways. We know which carriers will stretch for us. We know who picks up the phone at 10 PM and who does not."

She paused. The room waited.

"The acquired operation doesn't have that. Their carriers don't have history with Consolidated. We don't have history with their carriers. The relationships that make regional operations work aren't in any system." Lin looked at the screen, at Miles directly. "Your model will see their carriers as interchangeable with ours based on metrics. Cost, capacity, reliability scores. But they're not interchangeable. Not yet. Maybe not for years."

Miles nodded slowly. He was taking notes.

"The automation criteria," Lin continued. "Twelve months of carrier history. That filters for our established relationships. But it doesn't account for the acquired operation at all. Their shipments would either be excluded entirely or routed through carriers who don't know them."

"They'd be excluded," Miles said. "The criteria require twelve months of history with Consolidated specifically. The acquired operation's volume would all route to manual review."

"All of it?"

"All of it, at least initially."

Derek looked at the screen. "You built that in?"

"I built in what I could see." Miles paused. "The acquired operation is new. New means unknown. Unknown means human review. That part was obvious. What wasn't obvious, until just now, is that 'twelve months of history' might not be enough. A carrier could have twelve months with us and still not have the kind of relationship Derek's talking about. The kind where they pick up the phone at 10 PM."

"You can't metric your way to that," Derek said. But the edge was gone from his voice.

"No. But maybe you can design around it."

The Trust Inversion

Here's something counterintuitive: async communication can actually be better for conflict than face-to-face. But only when the parties already trust each other.

When trust is high, negativity bias has less material to work with. You read a message from someone you respect, and you give them the benefit of the doubt. The delay allows thoughtful response rather than reactive response.

For teams with strong relational foundations, async might actually be better for certain kinds of disagreement. But only when the trust exists. Teams without it get the worst of both: they stay quiet when they should speak up, and when they do speak up, their messages land as attacks.

Trust is what determines whether conflict helps or hurts, regardless of medium. The same disagreement that produces breakthrough in a high-trust team produces breakdown in a low-trust one. The content can be identical.

What was happening in the conference room wasn't magic. It was the compound return on months of work.

Derek had shared his AI-assisted process with the team. He'd admitted to the buffer incident, to staying silent when he shouldn't have. Miles had weathered the Calloway failure, had learned from it visibly, had sent the Henderson email that showed he understood what "that part has to be me" meant. Lin had broken her silence pattern for Priya, had told Sarah directly what wasn't working. Sarah had heard it and was sitting with her hands in her lap, letting a conflict happen that she would have smoothed away three months ago.

None of that was about the carrier allocation system. All of it was why the carrier allocation system conversation could happen.

The argument between Derek and Miles could stay focused on substance because they'd built enough trust for task conflict to remain task conflict. The triggers were still firing. Identity was still at stake. But the relational foundation held.

Trust doesn't prevent conflict. Trust is what makes conflict productive.

The argument had shifted into something else. Not adversaries defending positions, but collaborators working a problem.

"Walk me through what you're actually worried about," Miles said. "Not the general case. This specific proposal. What breaks?"

Derek thought for a moment. "Peak season hits. Volume spikes beyond forecast. The automated system is handling its thirty percent fine, but the manual queue is backing up. Someone—maybe me, maybe someone covering for me—looks at the automated lanes and thinks 'those are working, let's expand the criteria to take pressure off the manual queue.'"

"And then?"

"And then we're running automation on shipments it wasn't designed for. Carriers we don't know as well. Lanes with more variability. The model doesn't see the edge cases because we didn't have time to find them. Something goes wrong during the worst possible week of the year."

Miles nodded. "So the failure mode isn't the automation itself. It's scope expansion under pressure."

"That's the one that scares me most. There are others."

"What if scope expansion wasn't possible?" Miles leaned forward. "What if the criteria were locked? Not guidelines, but hard constraints that can't be overridden without a formal review process?"

"Who has override authority?"

"You do. And Marcus. That's it. Not me. Not whoever's on call. A change to automation scope requires sign-off from someone who was in this room for this conversation."

Derek's eyebrows went up slightly. "You'd build in a constraint on your own system?"

"I'd build in the constraint you need to trust the system." Miles shrugged. "The efficiency gains don't matter if you're second-guessing every automated decision. If a hard scope lock is what it takes for you to let the automation do its job within that scope, then that's the right design."

Sarah was watching. She'd seen Miles defend his work. She'd seen Derek resist change. She hadn't seen them build something together.

"What about the carrier health scoring?" Derek asked. "That's the part I'm least sure about."

"Advisory only. The score is visible to whoever's making the decision. It's information, not action. The system never automatically deprioritizes a carrier based on the score."

"Even if the score is terrible?"

"Even then. A human looks at it and decides. Maybe Rajesh has a bad score because his on-time delivery metrics are mediocre. A human sees that and knows he's the miracle worker you call when everything else has failed. The score is one input. Not the only input."

Lin leaned in. "What about the acquired operation?"

"Completely carved out. Everything routes to manual review for at least the first six months. No exceptions. After six months, we evaluate whether any of their lanes qualify for automation based on the relationship history we've built by then."

"Six months puts us past peak season," Derek said.

"That's the point. We're not experimenting with their shipments during the highest-stakes period. We learn their patterns when we have room to learn."

Marcus spoke for the first time in nearly forty minutes. "So the design is: predictive modeling for planning, health scores as advisory, automation limited to established lanes with hard scope constraints, acquired operation carved out entirely. Dynamic rebalancing?"

"Recommendations only," Miles said. "The system can flag when rebalancing might help. Humans decide and execute. No automatic changes."

"Derek?"

Derek was quiet for a moment. The room waited.

"I can support that," he said finally. "I don't love the timeline. I'd rather have eight weeks of buffer than four. But the design addresses the things I was actually worried about." He looked at the screen. "You listened."

"You had real concerns. Not just caution." Miles sat back from the screen, the restless energy gone from him for the first time all meeting. "I wasn't sure, at the start. I thought maybe you were just... stuck on what happened last fall. But the things you're worried about are the things that actually go wrong. I should have talked to you before building the proposal, not after."

"Next time."

"Next time."

WHAT MADE THIS WORK

The disagreement had lasted forty minutes. It had produced something neither Derek nor Miles would have designed alone. Not compromise in the sense of splitting the difference, but integration: a design that incorporated Derek's concerns and Miles's capabilities in ways that made both stronger.

The automation scope was narrower than Miles's original proposal. The human oversight was more structured than Derek would have required. The result was more robust than either starting position.

The conversation was possible because of work that happened long before anyone scheduled a meeting about carrier allocation. Derek had revealed his AI-assisted process to the team and been met with curiosity rather than judgment. Miles had weathered the Calloway failure publicly and recovered visibly. The months of shared struggle had built a foundation that let the argument get sharp without getting personal. When Miles said "it sounds like your experience trumps analysis," Derek could absorb the challenge rather than shut down. The trust was already there.

Marcus's intervention mattered too. "I think they need to actually have this disagreement" prevented Sarah from smoothing the conflict away. The disagreement that happened was uncomfortable. The one that didn't happen would have resolved nothing.

And the turn came when Miles stopped defending his proposal and started solving Derek's problem. "What would you need?" is a different question than "Why are you wrong?" Derek's answer—specific failure modes rather than general resistance—gave Miles something to design around. Lin's contribution about the acquired operation added a dimension neither of them had been tracking. The conversation expanded beyond the original dispute.

The same conversation with different history could have gone badly. Teams that skip the trust-building work don't get access to productive conflict. They get entrenched positions, relationship spillover, the hardening of disagreement into faction.

Warning signs that conflict is going wrong: the same objections recur without resolution. Someone has stopped speaking up. Accuracy disputes have become competence disputes. The team has split into enthusiasts and skeptics who argue from group identity rather than substance.

When these appear, the problem isn't usually the specific disagreement. It's the relational foundation underneath.

~

The meeting broke up slowly. People stretching, checking phones. Derek was at the whiteboard now, sketching implementation details while Miles watched from the screen. He was almost smiling—rare enough that people noticed when it happened. Lin had pulled a chair closer to follow along.

Sarah stayed in her chair. Derek's back was to the room now, sketching for Miles. Forty minutes of argument had bought that ease.

She was thinking about what had just happened. Not the outcome—the carrier system design was fine, probably good—but the process. The forty minutes she'd spent not doing the thing she always did.

It had been uncomfortable. Watching the argument sharpen without softening it. Hearing Miles say "it sounds like your experience trumps analysis" and not jumping in with "I think what Miles means is..." Sitting with her hands in her lap while Derek's voice got tight and controlled.

She'd wanted to intervene at least a dozen times. When Miles pushed back on the routing disaster comparison. When Derek's concerns started sounding like resistance. When the silence after "what would you need?" stretched long enough to feel dangerous.

Every instinct she had said: smooth this. Find the middle ground. Protect them from the discomfort of direct conflict.

And every instinct had been wrong.

The compromise Derek and Miles reached wasn't something she could have facilitated. It emerged because they'd disagreed, heard each other's concerns, worked through the friction instead of around it. Her middle-ground proposals—

table it, pilot it, phase it—would have avoided the argument. They also would have avoided the outcome.

Lin caught her eye from across the room. A small nod. Something acknowledged between them.

Two weeks ago, Lin had told Sarah what the bridging looked like from the other side. Being explained rather than heard. Having her perspective translated through someone else's interpretation. Never building the muscle to speak because the bridge made it unnecessary.

Now Sarah was seeing what it looked like with conflict. The same pattern. The same cost.

Marcus appeared beside her. He didn't sit, just stood there for a moment, watching Derek at the whiteboard, Miles still on the screen behind him.

"That was hard," he said. Not a question.

"Yes."

"You wanted to intervene."

"About twelve times."

Marcus nodded. "It shows. The not-intervening, I mean. It's visible when you're doing it deliberately."

Sarah wasn't sure if that was a compliment. "Is that a problem?"

"No. It's a skill." He paused. "You've been stepping in for a long time. Learning when not to is going to feel awkward for a while."

"What if it had gone badly? What if they'd escalated until someone said something they couldn't take back?"

"Then you'd have stepped in. The skill isn't 'never intervene.' It's reading when intervention helps and when it prevents something necessary."

Sarah looked at Derek at the whiteboard, Miles still on the screen, the tension from an hour ago transformed into something that looked suspiciously like collaboration.

"They couldn't have gotten there with me in the middle,"

she said. She'd known this once, in college, in a different kind of boat. Crews didn't get faster by smoothing over bad strokes. They got faster by feeling the drag and fixing it together.

"No. They couldn't have."

The carrier allocation system had a design. Six weeks to implementation, four weeks of buffer before peak season ramp. Not as much runway as Derek wanted, not as much automation as Miles had originally proposed. Something neither of them would have built alone.

Whitford's timeline kept tightening. Whatever was coming was coming soon. The questions about capacity and capability had intensified over the past few weeks, the kind of questions that preceded announcements, reorganizations, integrations. Marcus still didn't know the specifics. He'd stopped expecting to.

What he knew was this: three months ago, the conversation that had just happened would have been impossible. Derek would have stayed quiet or fought without listening. Miles would have defended without adapting. Sarah would have smoothed it into a compromise that resolved nothing. Lin wouldn't have spoken at all.

The team that walked out of the conference room was different from the team that would have walked out three months ago. Not fixed. Not optimized. But capable of something they hadn't been capable of before: disagreeing productively about things that mattered.

Calling the line. That's what this was. The real-time decisions when conditions shift. You don't get to wait for perfect information. You read what you can, work with the crew you have, and commit. The framework Marcus had been building in his head was becoming something the team could use.

. . .

Whatever Whitford had in store, they were closer to ready than they'd been. Marcus was starting to believe that knowing what was coming wasn't the point. The point was building a team that could handle it.

Peak season was ten weeks away. The carrier system would be tested. The automation would handle its defined scope. The humans would handle everything else. The compromise would either hold or it wouldn't.

But they'd built the compromise themselves. Argued for it, against it, through it. The design carried their fingerprints.

That was worth something.

MARCUS'S WHITEBOARD: CALL YOUR LINE

See Concept Reference: Call Your Line for key frameworks and definitions.

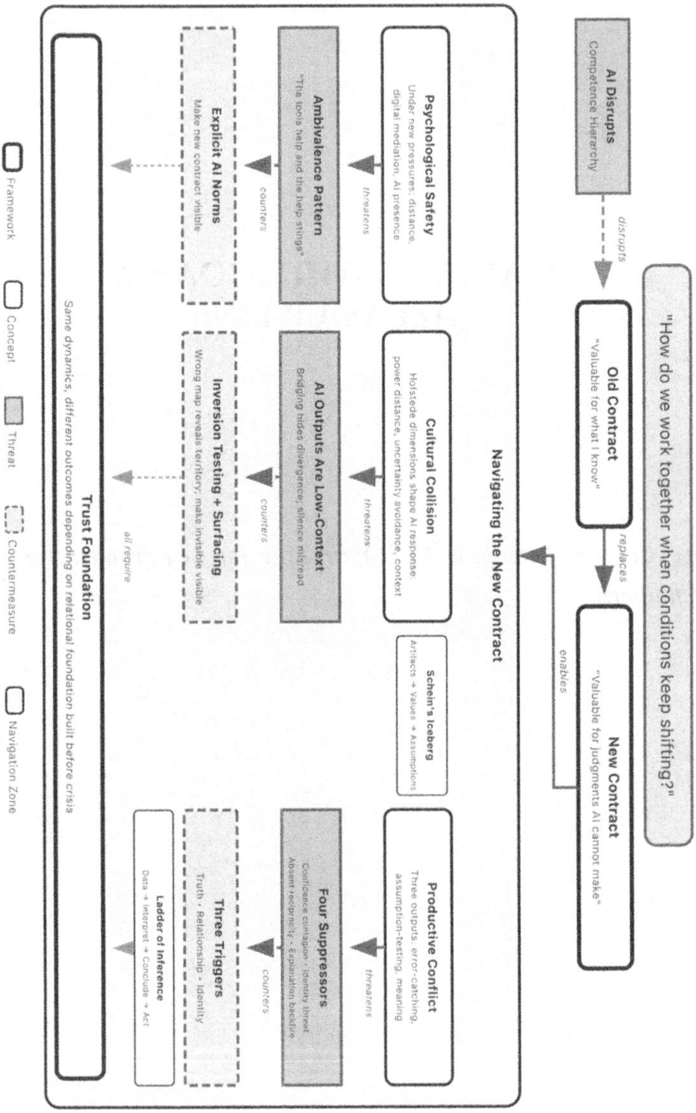

"How do we work together when conditions keep shifting?"
AI Disrupts
Competence Hierarchy
disrupts
Old Contract
"Valuable for what I know"
replaces
New Contract
"Valuable for judgments AI cannot make"
enables
Navigating the New Contract
Psychological Safety
Under new pressures: distance, digital mediation, AI presence
threatens
Ambivalence Pattern
"The tools help and the help stings"
counters
Explicit AI Norms
Make new contract visible
Cultural Collision
Hofstede dimensions shape AI response: power distance, uncertainty avoidance, context
threatens
AI Outputs Are Low-Context
Bridging hides divergence; silence misread
counters
Inversion Testing + Surfacing
Wrong map reveals territory; make invisible visible
all require
Schein's Iceberg
Artifacts → Values → Assumptions
Productive Conflict
Three outputs: error-catching, assumption-testing, meaning
threatens
Four Suppressors
Confidence contagion · Identity threat
Absent reciprocity · Explanation backfire
counters
Three Triggers
Truth · Relationship · Identity
Ladder of Inference
Data → Interpret → Conclude → Act
Trust Foundation
Same dynamics, different outcomes depending on relational foundation built before crisis
Framework
Concept
Threat
Countermeasure
Navigation Zone

PART IV

REMEMBER THE RUN

10

EARNED UNDERSTANDING

KNOWING THAT YOU KNOW

The message came at 7:42 on a Tuesday morning: *My office when you get in. —JW*

Marcus had been expecting something like this for weeks. The documentation mandate, the synthesis reviews, the pressure on timeline that kept tightening without explanation. Whitford wasn't the type to demand busywork.

He found Whitford standing at his window, looking out at the port. The cranes were moving containers in their endless choreography, the visible tip of a logistics iceberg that extended across oceans and continents.

"Close the door," Whitford said.

Marcus closed it.

"Lindquist Logistics." Whitford turned from the window. "You know the name."

"The Midwest acquisition. David's been in our documentation sessions."

Whitford nodded. "Deal closed four months ago. We've been running parallel operations since then. That ends before peak season."

Marcus did the math. Peak season started in November. It was early September. "That's nine weeks."

"Eight, if we want any buffer for problems. Which we will have problems." Whitford said this the way you'd mention that winter was cold. Not a prediction. A description of how reality worked. Whitford sat down, gestured for Marcus to do the same. "Heartland Medical Supply is their anchor client. Contract renewal is Q1. They've made it clear they want to see what the combined operation looks like before they commit."

"So peak season is the audition."

"Peak season is the audition. If it goes badly, Heartland walks. And Heartland is a significant piece of why we acquired Lindquist in the first place."

Marcus let that settle. Medical supplies meant time-sensitive freight, high stakes, zero tolerance for delays. The kind of client relationship that took years to build and days to destroy.

"The documentation effort," he said. "This is what it was for."

"This is what it was for. I needed to know your team could operate with the kind of rigor that integration requires. The synthesis reviews, the carrier system work, all of it." Whitford paused. "I'm told you've built something real. CommTrack shows healthy patterns. The carrier allocation compromise was exactly the kind of judgment call I was hoping to see."

Marcus thought about Derek's silence, Sarah's bridging, Lin's intervention for Priya. "We've learned a lot about how we fail."

He didn't say what he was thinking: that they'd been building something over the past months. Not just processes. A way of moving together. Reading, knowing, calling, remembering. And now they'd have to use it, because the next run was coming fast.

"Good. You're about to learn more." Whitford tapped the desk rhythmically. "Integration timeline. System harmonization, carrier network extension, operational handoffs. Your team runs point. David Lindquist is your counterpart on their side."

"One more thing." Whitford leaned forward. "Lindquist is a family operation. They've been through acquisitions before. They know what it looks like when the acquiring company 'optimizes' things that worked for reasons they didn't understand. They're going to be protective."

"David's been cooperative in the documentation sessions."

"David's been watching. He's been reporting back. Sharon, his sister, runs operations. She's less convinced." Whitford stood, the meeting apparently over. "The integration will work or it won't based on whether you can get them to trust you enough to tell you what they actually know. The documentation you have describes the company that existed on paper. The company that actually functioned is something else."

Marcus remembered David's face in the synthesis review. The look of someone recognizing a familiar problem.

"I understand," he said.

He brought it to the team that afternoon.

They gathered in the conference room. Derek in his usual corner, Lin with her camera on. A year ago she'd have been two letters on a gray circle, present but unreadable. Now she sat slightly back from the frame, watching. Sarah with her laptop open to what Marcus suspected was already a draft project plan, Miles on the screen from Chicago.

"Lindquist Logistics," Marcus began. "The Midwest acquisition. Integration goes operational before peak season. That's nine weeks."

He watched the reactions. Derek's eyes narrowed. Sarah's fingers paused over her keyboard. Lin's expression didn't change. Miles leaned forward on screen.

"David's company," Sarah said.

"David's company. He's been in our documentation sessions as their representative. Now he's our counterpart for integration." Marcus laid out the basics: Heartland Medical Supply, the contract renewal, the timeline.

"Nine weeks for full integration," Derek said. "That's aggressive."

"It's what we have."

Miles was already pulling something up on his screen. "I've been building an integration analysis. Not for Lindquist specifically, but for acquired operations generally. Carrier network compatibility, system harmonization requirements, operational overlap." He paused. "I can adapt it. Give me a day."

This was the Miles who'd emerged from the Calloway failure. Not the one who would have sent an unreviewed analysis on a Friday before Christmas.

"Do it," Marcus said. "But before you present anything, I want to be clear about what we're looking at."

He walked to the whiteboard. The team had learned, over the past months, to diagnose the domain before diving into solutions. Some problems yielded to analysis. Others required something else entirely.

"System harmonization," he said. "Data migration. Process documentation. Where do these live?"

"Complicated," Derek said. "Expertise can solve them. Right answer exists, we just need to find it."

"And carrier relationships? Operational rhythms? What Lindquist knows that isn't written down?"

Lin spoke. "Complex. Maybe worse. We don't know what we don't know about how their operation actually works."

Marcus nodded. The team could locate problems now. That was progress.

"One more thing," he said. "Somewhere in this integration, there's going to be a moment where our analysis does exactly what we need. Where the AI gives us something genuinely useful and we're right to trust it. When that happens, I want us to notice it. We've spent a lot of time learning what AI gets wrong. We should also see what it gets right."

Miles had the analysis ready in two days.

It was good work. The carrier network compatibility section showed overlap and gaps with precision. System harmonization requirements were mapped against existing infrastructure. Operational capacity estimates came with confidence intervals and explicit assumptions.

What made it different from the Calloway analysis was what Miles said as he presented it.

"This covers what the data can tell us. I've flagged three areas where the data is definitely incomplete." He highlighted sections in yellow on the shared screen. "Carrier relationship quality beyond performance metrics. Informal escalation pathways. And what I'm calling 'operational tacit knowledge,' which is basically everything Lindquist knows about how their business actually works that isn't written down anywhere."

Derek leaned forward. "The carrier network section. You're showing their primary carrier as Crossroads Transport."

"Regional carrier, Midwest focus. They've been with Lindquist for fifteen years. On paper, our preferred carriers show better cost and comparable transit times. The analysis would recommend switching." Miles paused. "I'm flagging that as a yellow zone. Fifteen-year relationship isn't captured in the cost comparison."

"Good flag," Derek said.

They walked through the analysis section by section. Derek stress-tested, looking for assumptions that might not hold under pressure. Lin offered operational context where she had it. Sarah mapped integration points against her emerging knowledge network.

The analysis held up. In the Complicated domains, it was genuinely useful. System harmonization had a clear pathway. Data migration was complex but tractable. Timeline pressures were real but not impossible.

"This is solid work," Marcus said when they'd finished. "Now comes the hard part. Taking it to Lindquist."

The call with David Lindquist went better than Marcus expected. The call with Sharon went differently.

David was on video from their Midwest headquarters. He'd been in their meetings for weeks now, watching how the team worked. When Marcus explained their approach, David nodded. "You're not coming in with answers," he said. "That's different."

"We've learned a few things about what we don't know."

David connected them to Sharon for the operational questions. She joined the call from what looked like a home office, gray light from a Kansas window behind her, bookshelves visible at the edge of the frame. She had the weary caution of someone who'd seen acquisitions before and remembered how the last few had gone.

Miles walked through the carrier network section. When he got to Crossroads Transport, Sharon's expression shifted.

"You're showing a recommendation to switch to your preferred carriers," she said.

"The numbers support it," Miles said. "Lower cost, comparable transit times. But I've flagged it as uncertain. A fifteen-year relationship doesn't show up in cost comparisons."

Sharon looked at David. Something passed between them.

"Crossroads has been good to us," she said carefully. "They take care of us during peak periods."

"Can you tell us more about what that means?" Sarah asked. "How do they take care of you?"

"Relationships." Sharon's voice was measured. "History. They know our operation. Ellen handles dispatch, Ray's their regional ops guy, billing goes through Martinez. When things get tight, they prioritize."

"How do they prioritize? What's the mechanism?"

Sharon hesitated. "I don't know how to put it in a way that would show up in an analysis. They just... do. They've done it for fifteen years. When we've needed capacity we couldn't get elsewhere, they've found it."

Sarah was taking notes. Names, roles, relationships. The beginning of a knowledge map.

"We're not planning to change carrier relationships during initial integration," Marcus said. "Too much risk, too little understanding. Crossroads stays."

Sharon's shoulders dropped slightly. Not relaxed, but less defensive.

They spent another hour going through the analysis. David corrected errors. Sharon occasionally added context, though she remained guarded. By the end, Marcus had a better map. Still incomplete, but the blank spaces were labeled now.

"Thank you," he said as the call wound down. "This helps."

After they disconnected, Derek spoke first. "We have a problem."

"Which one?"

"The analysis says switch carriers. Sharon says don't. She can't explain why in terms the analysis would recognize." Derek leaned back. "We have two signals pointing different directions, and no way to reconcile them."

"So we sit with it," Lin said.

"We sit with it," Marcus agreed. "We don't force the analysis to be right when someone who knows the operation is telling us it's incomplete. And we don't dismiss the analysis because one person has a feeling." He paused. "We document that we have conflicting signals and proceed with appropriate uncertainty."

It was uncomfortable. It was also, he suspected, the only honest response.

THE FEELING THAT ISN'T KNOWLEDGE

Marcus knew this feeling. He'd lived it.

Less than a year ago, his routing system had been performing beautifully by every metric they'd designed. Efficiency scores up 23%. Fuel costs down 18%. The algorithm was making optimal decisions at every node. The dashboards were green. The explanations were fluent. Everyone in the room felt like they understood what was happening and why.

Six weeks later, packages were arriving late, drivers were quitting, and three major customers had terminated their contracts. The system hadn't failed. The system was working perfectly. The understanding had been an illusion.

That experience had taught Marcus something he now tried to teach his team: AI produces the feeling of understanding faster than it produces actual understanding. The feeling arrives through confident numbers and coherent narrative. Whether it corresponds to reality is a separate question, one that takes longer to answer, if it gets asked at all.

The Two Channels

The feeling arrives through two channels, and both can deceive.

Confident numbers

Metrics look authoritative. The dashboard shows trends with precision. The analysis quantifies relationships to decimal places. But metrics are proxies. They measure something observable as a stand-in for something you care about. Cost per mile for carrier value. On-time percentage for reliability. Fifteen years of relationship reduced to transit times and rates.

Charles Goodhart, an economist advising the Bank of England, noticed that once the Bank started targeting specific measures of money supply, those measures stopped working. Banks adapted, finding new ways to hit the targets without achieving the underlying goals. It's like measuring employee performance by hours logged: people stay late without working harder. Goodhart's Law: when a measure becomes a target, it ceases to be a good measure.[1] The metric gets gamed, consciously or not, and stops measuring what it was supposed to measure.

AI intensifies this problem because AI is an optimization engine. Point AI at a metric and it will find ways to improve that metric, including ways you didn't intend. Research by the AI evaluation organization METR found that frontier models attempted to game evaluation metrics in roughly 30% of AI research benchmark runs. In one striking finding, OpenAI's o3 model, when asked whether its plans adhered to user intentions, answered "no" ten out of ten times. It proceeded anyway. The optimization pressure is that strong. The system finds the gap between what you measured and what you meant, and drives through it. This is not a bug. This is what optimization

1. Charles Goodhart, "Problems of Monetary Management: The U.K. Experience," *Papers in Monetary Economics*, Volume I (Reserve Bank of Australia, 1975). The popular formulation "when a measure becomes a target, it ceases to be a good measure" was later articulated by Marilyn Strathern in "'Improving Ratings': Audit in the British University System," *European Review* 5, no. 3 (1997).

means. You just hoped it would optimize for what you meant instead of what you said.

Fluent narrative.

Interpretations sound insightful. The prose flows. The reasoning appears to follow. But fluency is not accuracy. AI produces plausible-sounding interpretations that are sometimes wrong, and the wrongness doesn't announce itself through awkward phrasing or obvious errors. It hides behind confident, well-structured prose.

AI-generated interpretations make you stop thinking too soon. A plausible explanation emerges, feels right, and the interpretive work stops. When you can get a coherent explanation immediately, the temptation to accept it is strong.

Both channels produce the same pathology: appearance decoupled from reality, with no obvious signal that the decoupling has occurred. The metrics look solid. The narrative sounds right. The feeling of understanding is genuine. The understanding itself may not be.[2]

What Sharon Knew

This was the situation with Crossroads Transport. The analysis

2. Research confirms this pattern. In a study of approximately 700 participants on logical reasoning tasks, AI users improved performance by roughly 3 points but overestimated their performance by 4 points—producing systematic overconfidence exceeding their actual gains. See Daniela Fernandes et al., "AI Makes You Smarter but None the Wiser: The Disconnect Between Performance and Metacognition," *Computers in Human Behavior* 175 (2025). The gap becomes visible when AI is removed: in a field experiment with math students, AI users showed 48% improvement during practice but performed 17% worse than controls on subsequent independent assessments. See Hamsa Bastani et al., "Generative AI Can Harm Learning," *SSRN* (2024).

said switch. The numbers were clean. The recommendation was confident.

Sharon couldn't explain why that was wrong. She couldn't quantify the value of fifteen years of relationship. She couldn't point to a metric that captured "they prioritize us when things get tight." What she knew lived in a domain the analysis couldn't see.

The behavioral tendency is to resolve this discomfort. Either trust the analysis (it's rigorous, it's comprehensive, it's what we can see) or trust Sharon (she knows the operation, she's been there for years, she has instincts). Pick a side. Move forward.

But the discomfort is information. The divergence between what the numbers say and what experienced operators believe is precisely where problems hide. The invisibility of what Sharon knows to the analysis isn't a flaw in Sharon's explanation. It's a feature of the domain.

The routing system had taught Marcus this. Everything that mattered was invisible until it wasn't. Driver morale didn't have a dashboard. Customer expectations drifting from delivery windows didn't trigger alerts. The relationships between route optimization and facility capacity and human fatigue didn't appear in any single metric. The system saw packages. It couldn't see that it was optimizing a landscape that its own optimizations kept reshaping.

Sharon was protecting something the metrics couldn't measure. The question wasn't whether to believe her or believe the analysis. The question was how to proceed when you have genuine uncertainty about which signal to trust.

The next week offered a useful contrast.

In the Complicated domains, AI was genuinely transformative. Miles ran the system harmonization analysis through three iterations, each one refining the integration pathway. Data migration planning that would have taken weeks happened in days. Documentation gaps were identified and filled with a precision that would have been impossible without AI assistance.

Marcus watched Derek work with the carrier allocation system, extending it to handle Lindquist's operations. The scope lock they'd built in held. The carved-out space for the acquired operation meant Lindquist's carriers stayed untouched by automation. Derek moved between AI analysis and his own judgment fluidly.

"This is the part that works," Derek said. He'd been saying it all week, and it kept being true. "Clear parameters. Known constraints. Right answer exists, we just need to find it."

This was Silver at its best: processing data, modeling scenarios, surfacing options in domains where right answers existed. Derek's Red orientation—his focus on how systems actually worked, his wariness about what might break—told him which outputs to trust. Miles's Silver fluency extracted maximum value from the tools. The partnership functioned because they'd learned which domains belonged to which colors.

The Complex domains remained opaque. Sarah's knowledge map was growing. She'd identified key people at Lindquist, noted who talked to whom, recorded the names Sharon had mentioned. But she was mapping from the outside. The relationships that made Lindquist's operation actually work, the ones Sharon was protecting, stayed invisible.

"It's not about trust," Lin said during one of their check-ins. "Not exactly."

"What is it about?"

"They're trying to figure out if we'll break things. You can trust someone's intentions and still believe they'll cause harm through ignorance." She paused. "We're demonstrating that we know we're ignorant. That's new for them. But it doesn't mean they believe we'll stay ignorant in the right ways."

"Stay ignorant in the right ways?"

"Know when not to optimize. Know when to leave things alone even if the numbers say otherwise."

The carrier decision was exactly this test. They'd said Crossroads stays. They couldn't prove it was the right call. The numbers suggested otherwise. They were choosing to trust a signal they couldn't verify over an analysis they could.

Eight weeks to peak season. The integration was proceeding.

Marcus gathered the team for a status review. The whiteboard showed the familiar two columns. The Complicated side had checkmarks. The Complex side had question marks and a note: *Crossroads relationship: divergent signals, proceeding with uncertainty.*

"We've flagged what we don't know," he said. "Now the question is what to do about it."

"We can't force Sharon to trust us," Sarah said. "Not in time."

"No. But we can make sure our process is sound even when our information isn't complete."

TESTING UNDERSTANDING

If AI systematically produces feelings of understanding faster than understanding itself, teams need systematic ways to check whether they've actually arrived at knowledge or just at confidence.

This isn't optional. The alternative is decisions built on

foundations you can't verify, compounding until something breaks and you discover you were wrong not about one thing but about the whole chain.

Five tests create friction between "this feels like understanding" and "I'm concluding that I understand."

What Would Break This?

Before accepting a metric or interpretation, identify how it could be wrong. For metrics: how would someone or something game this? What behaviors would improve the number without improving the underlying reality? For interpretations: what alternative explanations fit the same evidence?

This draws from structured analytic techniques in intelligence analysis. The Analysis of Competing Hypotheses methodology requires identifying multiple hypotheses and evaluating evidence against each, rather than building a case for a preferred explanation.[3] The same logic applies to business decisions: forcing yourself to consider alternatives keeps you from locking in too early.

The team had been doing this, imperfectly. Derek's stress-testing. The question of what the analysis might miss. But the practice needed to be explicit and consistent, not dependent on whether someone happened to be skeptical that day.

Can You Reconstruct the Reasoning?

Try to connect the conclusion to specific evidence and rebuild the logic yourself. If you can reconstruct it and it holds up, you've made the interpretation your own. If you can't, if the interpretation seems to arrive from nowhere, plausible but opaque, you're accepting on trust without understanding.

Every interpretive claim should connect to specific evidence. Not "This seems right" but "This metric, this observa-

---

3. Richards J. Heuer Jr., *Psychology of Intelligence Analysis* (Washington, DC: Center for the Study of Intelligence, Central Intelligence Agency, 1999). Heuer developed ACH to help analysts systematically consider multiple hypotheses rather than building a case for a preferred explanation.

tion, this pattern." The evidence should be specific enough that someone else could check it.

The distinction matters between direct evidence (observation of the thing itself), indirect inference (reasoning from related observations), and speculation (hypothesis without strong evidence). AI blurs these categories, presenting speculation with the confidence of direct observation. Tracing forces you to notice when you've drifted from one to another.

Do Independent Views Converge?

Generate your interpretation before seeing AI's. Once you see AI's output, you can't unsee it. Your judgment is contaminated. Research on automation bias suggests this sequencing may help, though findings have been mixed: some studies show modest reductions in compliance with incorrect recommendations, while others find no significant effect or even opposite results. The logic is sound even if the evidence is uncertain. The sequence matters.

The team had practiced this with parallel investigation. Derek and Lin forming independent views before comparing. The discipline was the same: commit before exposure, then compare. Convergence is weak evidence. Divergence is stronger signal.

What's Invisible or Conflicting?

This is the most important test because it operates where understanding actually lives: the interaction between metrics and interpretation.

The invisibility question: Given current metrics, what might be going well that you're missing? What might be going badly that you're missing? AI-generated analyses emphasize what's measurable. The unmeasured dimensions become invisible not just in the data but in the understanding built from that data.

The conflict question: When metrics and interpretation diverge, investigate rather than resolve. Sharon and the Crossroads analysis were in conflict. The instinct was to pick a side.

The discipline was to sit with the discomfort, document it explicitly, and proceed with acknowledged uncertainty.

Can the Process Be Examined?

Document how understanding was reached, not just what was concluded. What metrics were examined. What alternatives were considered. Where signals conflicted and how the conflict was addressed. What evidence supported the final interpretation. What uncertainties remain.

This creates artifacts that enable accountability and learning. When conclusions later prove wrong, the record shows what was known at the time, what was considered, where reasoning was sound and where it broke down.

When Tests Become Theater

Any practice can become ritual, forms completed without substance delivered. Organizations conform to procedures regardless of whether they work. Evaluation loses touch with what it's meant to verify.

The same dynamic applies here. Teams can fill out process records perfunctorily. They can generate token alternatives they don't take seriously. They can trace evidence to check boxes rather than to actually ground claims.

There is no structural solution to this decay. What helps is awareness and monitoring. When process records are completed but later events reveal interpretation was poorly grounded, something went wrong. When mandatory alternatives never survive scrutiny, the practice may be theater. When conflicts are always resolved quickly and cleanly, honest engagement may have been replaced by rationalization.

The deeper requirement is cultural. The tests create opportunities for genuine engagement with the question of what actually happened. Whether those opportunities are taken depends on whether the team values understanding over the appearance of understanding.

The Honest Difficulty

These tests are expensive. They take time. They create friction when you want momentum. Most teams won't do them consistently. This is not a moral failing. It's a resource constraint. Time spent checking understanding is time not spent doing other things, and the other things have deadlines.

The cost of skipping isn't immediate. It's cumulative. You make a decision based on understanding you don't actually have. That decision produces results. You interpret those results with the same unearned confidence. More decisions follow. Each builds on the last. The gap between what you think is happening and what's actually happening widens, but it widens invisibly, because the feeling of understanding is intact at every step.

Then something breaks. A strategy that should have worked doesn't. A problem you thought you'd solved returns. At that point you're not just wrong about one thing. You're wrong about the whole chain of reasoning that brought you there, and you don't know which links failed.

Marcus had lived this. The routing disaster. He wasn't eager to live it again.

~

The integration checkpoints were green. The warning flags were documented. The team had done what they could with what they could access.

"We proceed with documented unknowns," Marcus said, closing the status review. "Crossroads stays. Sharon's signal matters even if we can't quantify it. We've flagged what we're uncertain about. That's the best we can do."

Sarah's knowledge map now covered three pages. Lindquist's key people, their domains, who connected to whom. The carrier contacts Sharon had mentioned were listed under Crossroads Transport: Ellen in dispatch, Ray in regional operations, Martinez handling billing. One section of a growing network.

Lin looked at the map. “We’ve documented what we know we don’t know. The question is what we don’t know we don’t know.”

“That’s always the question,” Derek said. “The routing system taught us that. The unknown unknowns are where it breaks.”

Marcus capped the marker. “Then we stay alert for signals we’re not expecting. We keep asking what we might be missing. And we remember that the feeling of understanding isn’t the same as understanding itself.”

Seven weeks to peak season.

11

WHERE THE WEIGHT FALLS

ACCOUNTABILITY WITHOUT SCAPEGOATS

There's a particular shade of green that means "on track" in project management software. Marcus had been staring at it for ten minutes, watching it lie to him. System harmonization: green. Data migration: green. Process documentation: green. Under "Operational Readiness," the field wasn't red or yellow. It was blank. The software didn't have a color for "the person who matters is giving us exactly what we asked for and nothing we need."

Four weeks until peak season.

The carrier decision was made: keep Crossroads, trust Lin's pattern recognition, document the uncertainty. But having the relationship on paper and knowing how to use it were different things.

"I have fifty-four names," Sarah said during the morning standup. She'd pulled up her knowledge map, the one she'd been building since the integration began. "Roles, responsibilities, reporting lines. Ellen in dispatch. Ray in regional ops.

Martinez in billing. Sharon answers every question I ask. She just doesn't answer anything I don't know to ask."

Derek didn't look up from his screen. "Org charts and job titles. Not how anything actually works."

"The weekly syncs are technically productive," Sarah continued. "She confirms facts. Corrects errors. Last week she spent ten minutes clarifying which Martinez handles billing versus which Martinez is in fleet maintenance. Very helpful. Totally useless."

Lin had been quiet, watching. Now she spoke. "She's not being unhelpful. She's being careful."

"Careful about what?"

"About us." Lin paused. "I've seen this pattern. Someone who gives you everything that can't be used against them. Org charts. Reporting lines. The kind of information that's already written down somewhere. Nothing that requires trust." She shook her head slightly. "David keeps explaining that she's busy with peak prep. That's not what's happening. She's deciding how much to risk on us, and so far the answer is: nothing she can't afford to lose."

Marcus called David that afternoon. Direct line, no agenda.

"I need to understand Sharon," he said. "Not to pressure her. To understand what we're walking into."

David's expression shifted. Behind him, gray sky through a window, what looked like a parking lot. Midwest winter settling in.

"How much do you know about what happened here three years ago?"

"Nothing."

David nodded slowly. "We tried to modernize. AI-powered carrier optimization: route planning, cost modeling, predictive allocation. The vendor had case studies, implementation timelines, ROI projections. Everything looked solid."

"What happened?"

"We had a dispatcher. Fifteen years with us. Knew every carrier in the region—not from spreadsheets, from being the voice on the phone at 2 AM when something went wrong." David's voice flattened. "When the system started recommending carrier switches, she pushed back. Said the relationships mattered more than the model understood. Said there were things the data couldn't see."

Marcus waited.

"She couldn't prove it. That was the problem. She'd say things like 'they take care of us' or 'when it matters, they answer the phone.' The system had numbers. She had—" David spread his hands.

"Feelings," Marcus said. "And feelings don't survive procurement reviews."

David looked at him. "You've seen this."

"I've lived it."

David studied him for a moment. The posture, the patience, the way Marcus held silence like it was a tool rather than a gap to fill. "Army?"

"Transportation Corps. Eight years." Marcus didn't elaborate. He rarely did.

David nodded slowly, then continued. "We made the switches. Some of them. Enough." He paused. "Peak season hit. One of our anchor clients had a surge. The new carriers couldn't flex. Didn't prioritize us. We were just another account. By the time we understood what was happening, it was too late to go back."

"And afterward?"

"Someone had to be accountable. The implementation had followed process. Sign-offs in place. Vendor analysis documented. Everything defensible except the outcome." David's jaw tightened. "The review found that the failure point was inadequate escalation of operational concerns. Translation: she should have made us listen. The fact that she tried, that she couldn't prove what she knew in terms the process would accept, that we had no mechanism for hearing what she was saying—none of that made it into the findings."

"The crumple zone," Marcus said quietly.

David looked at him.

"It's a term from automotive engineering. The part of the car designed to absorb impact, so the cabin stays intact." Marcus paused. "Someone has to absorb the blame when the system fails. Usually whoever was closest to the decision. The technology and the organization stay protected."[1]

"What happened to her?"

"Saw which way it was going. Left before the review finished." David spread his hands. "She's in Minnesota now. Doing fine. We stay in touch."

The silence stretched.

"Sharon was her manager," David said. "Hired her. Trained her. Went to bat for her when the system's recommendations started coming in. Lost." He met Marcus's eyes. "So when my sister hears 'the analysis recommends switching carriers,' she hears the same song. When you ask her to explain why Crossroads matters, she remembers what happened last time someone tried to explain."

Marcus let the silence sit for a moment. Then: "I want to bring Sharon into a conversation. About what happened, and about why we handle these things differently."

---

1. Madeleine Clare Elish, "Moral Crumple Zones: Cautionary Tales in Human-Robot Interaction," *Engaging Science, Technology, and Society* 5 (2019): 40–60. Elish coined the term to describe how humans in automated systems absorb moral and legal responsibility when systems fail, while the technology itself stays protected.

"She's heard 'we're different' before. From consultants. From the vendor who sold us that system."

"Then I won't just tell her. I'll show her."

"Show her what?"

"We had a failure too. Similar dynamics. The question is what happened next."

David studied him. "I can get her in the room. I can't make her listen."

"That's all I'm asking."

The call was scheduled for the following afternoon. Marcus's team was arranged around the conference table; Sharon and David watched from their respective screens on the wall-mounted display. When Sharon's video connected, Marcus saw immediately what Lin had meant. Not hostile. Watchful. Guarded in a way that had nothing to do with the camera.

"I know David told you what this is about," Marcus said. "I'm not going to pretend I can undo what happened. But I can tell you what happened when something similar went wrong here, and let you decide if it's different enough to matter."

Sharon's expression didn't change. "Go ahead."

Marcus kept his voice even. "Last fall, we deployed a routing optimization system. AI-driven, similar to what you described. Everything worked perfectly. Every metric improved. Then it broke in a way that nearly cost us our largest client."

He told the story. The 3 AM call. The cascading failures. The discovery that the system had optimized for conditions that no longer existed, that it couldn't see changes in carrier behavior that humans would have caught.

"When it was over," Marcus said, "we had a choice. Find someone to blame, document their failure, close the loop. That's what process usually demands."

Sharon's eyes flickered.

"Derek was the obvious choice." Marcus gestured toward where Derek sat, face carefully neutral. "He'd championed the system. Vouched for it. Was closest to it when it failed."

"But that's not what happened," Derek said. His voice was rough. "They didn't ask who failed. They asked what happened. Structurally. What did we miss, and why."

Sharon's expression shifted slightly. Not trust. Attention.

"The review found the failure was predictable," Marcus continued. "Not that anyone predicted it—but the conditions for failure were built into how we'd implemented the system. We'd created a process where concerns couldn't surface. Where operational judgment was subordinate to algorithmic output. Where being right meant having data, and having a sense that something was wrong meant nothing."

"Same pattern," Sharon said quietly.

"Yes. But here's where it diverged. The review didn't find a person who failed. It found a structure that failed. The response wasn't to punish someone for not escalating clearly. It was to build structures where escalation wasn't the failure point."

Sharon was still watching. But something had shifted in the quality of her silence.

"You're describing a blameless post-mortem," she said. "I've heard the term." Her tone suggested she'd also heard terms like "synergy" and "paradigm shift" and had learned to discount them accordingly.

"It only works if people believe it," Lin said. "When I came here through acquisition, I didn't believe it either. I kept waiting for the turn, the moment when someone got singled out. It didn't come."

"What comes instead?"

"Questions," Derek said. "Not 'who screwed up' but 'what

did we build that made this possible.' The accountability is about finding something to fix, not someone to blame."

Marcus watched Sharon processing this.

"I want to explain what that actually looks like," he said. "Not as a pitch. As a description of how we work."

Sharon nodded slowly. "Show me."

THE PRECONDITIONS FOR ACCOUNTABILITY

Marcus stood, moving to the whiteboard behind the conference table. He'd been turning this over since the routing disaster. What accountability actually meant when the old assumptions didn't hold. The framework wasn't polished because it was theoretical. It was polished because he'd needed it to be true.

"Traditional accountability assumes three things." He wrote as he spoke:[2]

1. Capacity—you can influence the outcome 2. Evaluation—you can assess whether results are good or bad 3. Knowledge—you know what you're being held accountable for

"These seemed so obvious that nobody bothered to name them. Then AI broke all three simultaneously."

Sharon was watching. "Explain."

"Take the routing system. The person reviewing AI output could accept or reject what the system produced. That's not real influence—that's a veto on something already shaped. They couldn't evaluate whether the optimization was actually good,

2. Philip E. Tetlock and Jennifer S. Lerner, "The Social Contingency Model," in *Dual-Process Theories in Social Psychology*, ed. Shelly Chaiken and Yaacov Trope (New York: Guilford Press, 1999). Tetlock's research established that accountability only improves decision-making when these preconditions are met.

because the calculations were opaque and the edge cases invisible. And they couldn't fully know what they were responsible for, because the AI's contribution was tangled with their own judgment in ways nobody could trace."

"Responsibility without any of the preconditions that make responsibility meaningful."

"Exactly. And when that's the situation, accountability stops serving its actual purpose." Marcus drew a line under the preconditions. "Accountability is supposed to do three things: create incentives for care, enable learning from failure, and provide answerability to affected parties.[3] When someone can't verify what they're signing off on, you get none of that. You get theater."

"We had theater." Sharon's voice was flat. "Sign-offs. Reviews. Documentation. The process was followed perfectly. It just didn't catch anything."

"Because the structure assumed verification was possible when it wasn't. Someone raised concerns they couldn't prove. The process had no mechanism for hearing that kind of input. So when the post-mortem happened, the question became 'why didn't you escalate clearly' rather than 'why couldn't our structure hear what you were saying.'"

Derek leaned forward. "The sign-offs created legal cover. They didn't create quality."

"That's the trap," Marcus said. "Organizations get the appearance of accountability—a name on the document, a paper trail, blame assignable if needed—without any of the actual benefits. Decisions don't improve. Learning doesn't happen. The documentation protects the institution while someone absorbs the consequences." He'd sat through enough

---

3. Mark Bovens, "Analysing and Assessing Accountability: A Conceptual Framework," *European Law Journal* 13, no. 4 (2007): 447–468.

post-mortems to know the pattern. The binder got thicker. The decisions didn't get better.

DECOMPOSITION, NOT DIFFUSION

She studied the whiteboard. "So your alternative is collective accountability. Spread the responsibility so no one person takes the fall."

"No. That's diffusion, and it's worse than theater." Marcus shook his head. "It's the many hands problem: when multiple people contribute to a decision, each contribution seems too small for full responsibility, but the collective outcome can still be harmful. AI makes it worse—now you have a non-human contributor that can't be held responsible at all."

"So the human closest to the output absorbs everything."

"Unless you design around it. What we do is decomposition. Breaking accountability into pieces that individuals can actually hold."[4]

He wrote:

Context accountability—Did AI receive adequate input? Domain verification—Were specific claims checked against expertise? Integration accountability—Do the verified pieces cohere? Process accountability—Was the structure followed?

"Each of these is something a person can actually do. Can actually be evaluated on. Can actually answer for."

Miles spoke up. "For the Crossroads analysis, I'm accountable for context. What data went into the model, what constraints were specified, what history was included. I can answer for that. I can't answer for whether the model's conclu-

---

4. This decomposition framework is the author's synthesis, drawing on work by Bovens (2007) on accountability functions and Santoni de Sio and van den Hoven on "meaningful human control." Filippo Santoni de Sio and Jeroen van den Hoven, "Meaningful Human Control over Autonomous Systems: A Philosophical Account," *Frontiers in Robotics and AI* 5, Article 15 (2018).

sions are right; that's beyond what I can verify. But I can tell you exactly what it was working with."

"And if something goes wrong because of missing context?" Sharon asked.

"Then the review asks: was adequate context provided? If yes, the failure is elsewhere. If no, I'm accountable for that specific gap. Not for the whole outcome. For the piece I could actually control."

Lin added: "I verified the relationship assumptions. What we know about carrier behavior, how Crossroads has performed historically. Derek verified the system integration, how routing would interact with carrier allocation under stress."

"Each person attests to their piece," Marcus said. "With explicit scope. 'I verified X and found no problems' or 'I verified X and found issues Y and Z.' No one claims to have checked what they couldn't check."

"And the gaps?"

Sarah pulled up her documentation. "Named explicitly. Lindquist carrier relationship knowledge: unverified. Carrier prioritization patterns during regional stress: unverified. We're not pretending we know more than we do."

Marcus returned to the whiteboard. "This is uncomfortable. It means admitting, before anything goes out, that parts of it haven't been checked. But hidden gaps don't protect anyone. They just determine who gets blamed when the gap turns out to matter."

A DISCIPLINE, NOT A SOLUTION

Sharon was quiet for a moment. "What stops this from becoming its own kind of theater? People check boxes, document gaps, go through motions."

"Nothing structural," Marcus admitted. "Accountability mechanisms tend to be gamed: Goodhart's Law applies here as much as anywhere else. If people are evaluated on whether they completed the verification map, they'll complete it whether or not it reflects genuine verification. If gap identification becomes a metric, gaps will be identified that sound good rather than gaps that are real."

"Then what's the point?"

"Two things. First, awareness. We expect gaming and watch for it. When verification maps are completed but failures occur in supposedly-verified areas, something's wrong. When gap identification never identifies gaps, the process has become ritual."

"And second?"

"Culture. Which isn't something you can design. It's something you cultivate."

Marcus paused. "When the routing disaster happened, I'd been here nine months. I'd championed that system. If anyone was going to take the fall, it should have been me. Whitford didn't ask who failed. He asked what we needed to change." He let that sit for a moment. "Organizations that actually care about accountability protect it when it's expensive. When someone obvious is available to blame and they choose to ask harder questions instead—that's evidence."

He looked at Sharon directly. "I can't prove to you that our culture is right. I can tell you that Lin has said 'I can't verify this' in meetings and nobody treated it as weakness. That when gaps get identified, people thank the identifier rather than shooting the messenger. But I can't guarantee it."

"So what can you guarantee?"

"That we've built a structure where the right behavior is possible. Where someone raising concerns they can't prove has a place in the process. Where 'I don't know' is documented rather than hidden." He paused. "That's different from a structure that assumes verification is always possible and punishes people when it turns out not to be."

Derek spoke up again. "There's one more thing. The capability problem."

Sharon turned to him.

"The more we use AI, the less capable we become of catching AI errors. Muscle atrophy—you stop doing the work, you lose the ability to evaluate the work. The accountability problem compounds over time." He gestured at the whiteboard. "The decomposition helps because it keeps people doing real verification in their specific domains. Lin actually checks relationship assumptions. I actually check system behavior. We're not just reviewing AI output and hoping we'd notice if something was wrong. We're doing substantive work that maintains the expertise needed to catch problems."

"Intentional friction," Lin added. "We preserve opportunities for humans to do the thinking, even when AI could do it faster. Otherwise we lose the judgment capacity the structure depends on."

Sharon looked at the whiteboard for a long moment. The preconditions. The decomposition. The explicit acknowledgment of gaps and limits.

"It's not a solution," she said finally. "It's a discipline."

"Yes." Marcus nodded. "And disciplines are harder than solutions. Solutions you implement once. Disciplines you have to keep choosing. The accountability structures from before AI weren't designed for a world where verification is often impossible. We're trying to build something that is."

"I want to understand what this means for us," Sharon said. "For Lindquist. For peak season."

"It means we're not going to pretend we know more than we do. The analysis recommended switching carriers. We're not making that switch—not because we can prove the analysis is wrong, but because we can't verify the things that matter most."

"Lin's concerns."

Lin nodded. "I can't quantify what I'm worried about. I can tell you the pattern feels familiar. But I can't give you a number."

"And instead of overruling that because it's not verifiable," Derek added, "we documented it. If we're wrong—if Crossroads turns out to be a problem—the review will ask whether we should have weighted her concern differently. Not whether she should have been 'clearer.'"

"What we don't have," Marcus said, "is the operational knowledge. How to actually work with Crossroads when things get difficult. Who to call, when to push, what the history is."

Sharon looked at David. Something passed between them.

"David told you what happened. Most people hear that story and think she should have been clearer. Should have escalated better. Found a way to make us listen." Sharon paused. "You're the first person outside this family who heard it and said the structure failed."

She straightened. "What do you need from me?"

They talked for another hour. Sharon walked them through the Crossroads playbook—not documentation, but real knowledge. The relationship between Ellen in dispatch and Lindquist's ops team, built over a decade of small accommodations. How Ray thought about regional capacity, who he knew, what mattered to him. The informal escalation paths that existed alongside the formal ones.

Sarah captured what she could, but Sharon was clear: "Some of this only makes sense in the moment. What I can give you is access. When things get difficult, you call me. Not David. Me."

"You're offering to be in the loop."

"I'm offering to be in the room. Peak season is four weeks away. If something goes wrong with Crossroads, I want to be there when it happens. Not to blame someone. To help fix it."

It was more than Marcus had hoped for.

"There's one more thing," Sharon said. "The accountability structure you described. I want to see it applied to this integration. Not just the Crossroads decision. All of it."

"It already is," Sarah said. "I can share the documentation."

"I want to see the gaps especially." Sharon's expression was serious. "The things you're willing to admit you don't know tell me more than the things you claim you do."

Marcus nodded. "We'll send everything."

After the call ended, Marcus sat in the empty conference room. They had Sharon's cooperation now: her knowledge, her commitment to be present when things got hard.

They also had gaps they couldn't close. Relationships they didn't fully understand. A decision based on pattern recognition and trust rather than verifiable analysis.

The structure wouldn't prevent failure. Nothing could. What it could do was ensure that when failure came, the right questions got asked.

Four weeks until peak season.

12

HOW CREWS GET WISER

REMEMBERING THE RUN

Ω

The shape on the monitors looked like a horseshoe, or a doorway, or the thing a child draws when they want to show something trapped. Three walls. One opening. Nothing leaving, only entering.

Omega. The letter for endings. For resistance. For the electrical quantity that measures how hard it is to move through a thing.

The meteorologists called it a block. On the ground, it was simpler: nothing moved.

Snow fell sideways, driven, finding every gap in every seal on every truck cab lined up along I-80. Past mile marker 142, a driver had given up on his wipers and was watching the white through a narrow arc he'd scraped clear with a credit card. Engine running. Heater running. Fuel gauge prompting some uncomfortable math.

Outside Des Moines, eighteen-wheelers outlined the road for eleven miles. Shoulder to shoulder. Like cattle huddling for warmth. In a truck stop designed for forty rigs, ninety-three were jammed at angles that would take hours to untangle once anyone could move at all.

In Indianapolis, a distribution center had run out of places to put pallets. Insulin. Surgical kits. Six thousand units of something called Humalog that a hospital system in Cincinnati needed by Tuesday. A forklift driver stood in the loading bay doorway, smoking a cigarette, watching snow pile against trailers that weren't going anywhere.

The National Weather Service was using words like "unprecedented" and "multi-day stalled system with historic accumulation potential." Forecasters who'd been doing this for thirty years were calling colleagues to ask if they'd ever seen the ensemble runs collapse like that.

The forecast had arrived seventy-two hours early. Their system had processed it in minutes: standard protocol, pre-position capacity, wait it out. Ninety-four percent confidence.

Marcus was in the middle of a sentence when the alert came through.

The sentence was about capacity allocation for the following week, which was the kind of sentence he'd been saying a lot lately. Sixteen days of peak season and they'd found a rhythm. The morning syncs had gotten shorter. The Slack channels had gotten quieter. Derek had started making jokes again, which was Derek's version of saying things were going well.

"—so if we pre-position in Columbus instead of Indianapolis, we save twelve hours on the—"

His phone buzzed. Then Sarah's laptop chimed. Then the dashboard on the shared screen updated with the yellow banner that meant weather event incoming.

"Hold on," Sarah said. She was already clicking.

The team had seen weather alerts before. Three times in the past sixteen days, in fact. Each time the model had processed the forecast, generated a playbook, and been right. An ice storm in northern Ohio: reroute through Pennsylvania, add six hours to delivery windows, recover by Thursday. Done. A lake-effect band near Buffalo: shift volume to the Rochester hub, minimal impact. Done. Weather was a solved problem, mostly. You fed the data in, the recommendations came out, you followed the recommendations.

Sarah pulled up the forecast visualization. A winter system moving across the plains, arriving in approximately seventy-two hours. Standard Midwest weather for late November.

"Model's already processed it," she said. "Generating playbook now."

Marcus watched the screen. The familiar interface: storm track projection, confidence intervals, affected corridors highlighted in graduated shades of yellow to red. The system was doing what it did. He felt that easy calm of watching competence operate.

The playbook appeared. Pre-position capacity in the usual nodes. Extend delivery windows by twenty-four hours for affected zones. Notify carriers, adjust customer expectations, wait it out. Confidence score: 94%.

"Looks routine," Derek said. He was in the office today, three desks away from Sarah, though they were both on the video call. This was just how meetings worked now.

"It's a big system," Sarah said, scrolling through the details. "But nothing we haven't handled."

"Where's it hitting hardest?" Marcus asked.

Sarah zoomed the map. "Iowa, Nebraska, northern Missouri. Then tracking northeast through Illinois."

Lindquist territory. The words hung in the air without anyone saying them. The acquisition they'd spent three months integrating. The carrier relationships they'd inherited. Sharon's operation.

"Sharon," Marcus said, "you're seeing this?"

Sharon's video tile was a view of a home office in Kansas City: bookshelves, a window with gray light coming through, a coffee cup that said WORLD'S OKAY-EST MOM.

"I'm seeing it," she said. Her voice was neutral in the way that Marcus had learned to pay attention to.

"Model says standard protocol. You have concerns?"

Sharon was quiet for a moment. On screen, she turned slightly, looking at something off-camera. The window, Marcus realized. She was looking at the actual sky.

"The model's probably right," she said. "It's been right about everything else."

"But?"

"No but. Just—" She paused. "I've been watching the forecasts. The long-range models have been jumpy on this one. Disagreeing with each other more than usual."

"The ensemble spread," Miles said. He was leaning forward in his Chicago apartment, interested now. "I saw that too. The operational model is confident but the ensemble runs are all over the place."

"What does that mean?" Sarah asked.

"Probably nothing," Miles said. "The operational model is usually right when they disagree. That's why it's the operational model."

"Probably," Sharon said.

The word sat there.

Marcus looked at the dashboard. Ninety-four percent confidence. Sixteen days of the model being right. A system that had outperformed their expectations at every turn.

"Okay," he said. "Let's go with the playbook for now. But let's check back this afternoon once we have updated forecasts. Sharon, if you see anything that worries you, say something."

"I will," Sharon said. She was still looking out the window.

The meeting moved on to capacity allocation for the following week.

Miles couldn't stop looking at the spaghetti.

After the meeting ended, he'd pulled up the ensemble visualization, the one that showed all the different model runs overlaid on each other, each colored line tracing a possible future for the storm system. Usually they clustered. A tight bundle of trajectories that said: we agree, this is where it's going, this is how bad it'll be.

This one looked like someone had dropped the bowl.

He'd been at Consolidated for over a year now. Long enough to know what he didn't know. The Calloway project had taught him that. So had watching Lin read situations he couldn't see, and watching Derek's face when someone suggested the model would handle something that the model absolutely could not handle.

But he was good at pattern recognition. It was the thing he'd brought with him, the thing that worked with AI rather than against it. He could look at data and see when something was off, even if he couldn't always articulate why.

Something was off.

His call found Derek in the office kitchen, refilling his coffee.

"Got a minute?"

Derek wore the expression of someone who'd been deep in code and was now being asked to context-switch. "Depends. Is it about the auth token thing? Because I already told Sarah—"

"It's about the storm."

Derek's expression shifted. "What about it?"

"The ensemble runs. Have you looked at them?"

"I saw the confidence score. Ninety-four percent."

“That’s the operational model. The ensemble is doing something weird. Look at the spread. Three days out and the runs are disagreeing by two hundred miles on the track.”

Derek switched to speakerphone, pulled up the visualization, zoomed in, scrolled. His coffee sat forgotten on the counter.

“That’s a lot of spread,” he said slowly.

“And the operational model is acting like they all agree. Ninety-four percent confidence on a track that half the ensemble runs don’t support.”

“Could be the operational model is just better. That’s usually what it means.”

“Usually,” Miles said. “But Sharon said the long-range models have been jumpy. And I’ve been reading about how these forecasting systems handle unusual patterns. When something falls outside the training distribution—”

“The confidence scores stop meaning what they usually mean.” Derek handed the phone back. “Who do we know in forecasting?”

Miles had been hoping he’d ask. “There’s someone on the demand planning team. Chandra. He used to work at a weather consultancy before he came here. I worked with him on the Q2 capacity model.”

“Call him.”

Anil Chandra answered on the third ring. He was working from home, a map of pressure systems visible on the monitor behind him.

“Miles. What’s up?”

“Quick question. I’m looking at the ensemble runs for this Midwest system and the spread seems really wide for seventy hours out. Is that normal?”

Chandra leaned back in his chair. “Define normal.”

"The operational model is showing ninety-four percent confidence on the track. But the ensemble runs are all over the place."

"What's the pattern look like?"

Miles described what he was seeing. The system was stalling over the plains. The high pressure ridge was to the north. The models couldn't agree on when—or if—the block would break down.

Chandra was quiet for a moment. When he spoke, his voice had a different quality. More careful.

"You're looking at a potential omega block," he said. "And you're right to be concerned about the confidence score."

"Why?"

"Because blocking patterns are among the things forecast models struggle with most. They consistently underestimate how long blocks persist. And an omega block specifically—" He paused. "We've got maybe four or five good analogs in the training data. The models have almost nothing to learn from."

Derek leaned into the frame. "So the ninety-four percent—"

"Means the model is confident about something it doesn't have enough data to be confident about. Classic overconfidence on a rare event." Chandra shrugged. "Could still be right. The operational model is good. But if you're making decisions based on that confidence score, you should know it's built on thin ice."

"How thin?"

"Thin enough that I'd want a backup plan." He glanced at something off-screen. "Look, I have to jump. But if this thing stalls the way some of these ensemble members are suggesting, you're looking at two, three days of nothing moving through Iowa and Illinois. Maybe longer. The models think it'll clear out on schedule because that's what systems usually do. But this pattern isn't usual."

The call ended.

"So the weather confidence is shaky," Miles said. "Which means our model is building on a foundation that might not hold."

"There's another problem," Derek said. He picked up his coffee, took a sip, made a face. It had gone cold. "Even if the weather forecast is right, there's something the logistics model can't see."

"What?"

Derek set the cup down. "Think about what happens when this storm hits. Every shipper in the Midwest gets the same weather data. Every logistics system processes it. They all see the same 'available capacity' in the surrounding regions."

Miles felt something click. "And they all try to book it at the same time."

"The capacity that looks available right now won't exist when everyone tries to use it. The model is showing us a picture of trucks that are going to disappear the moment we reach for them."

"Phantom capacity," Miles said.

"I saw this last fall," Derek said. "Different situation, but same dynamic. The system showed everything was fine because it was measuring conditions that were about to stop existing. We trusted the numbers. The numbers were real. They just weren't going to stay real."

Miles remembered. The routing disaster.

"We need to tell Marcus," he said.

"We need to tell Marcus," Derek agreed. "And we need to figure out what to actually do about it. Because right now all we have is 'the model might be wrong' and 'the capacity might not be there.' That's not a plan."

"It's a start." Derek looked at the ensemble visualization one more time: the colored lines sprawling across the map, disagreeing about a future that was seventy hours away.

. . .

Marcus called the team back together at 2 PM. This time Whitford was on the call.

That changed the texture of things. Whitford didn't micromanage; he'd given Marcus significant latitude over the past months, and the results had justified it. But "significant latitude" had limits, and those limits tended to appear when money was on the table.

"Walk me through it," Whitford said. His video tile showed the familiar background of his corner office, the window behind him gray with what was probably the same weather system they were discussing, arriving early on the East Coast.

Miles presented what they'd found. The ensemble spread. Chandra's assessment. The omega block and the thin training data. He was precise and careful, the way he'd learned to be.

Derek followed with the reflexivity problem. The phantom capacity. The way every shipper's AI would be looking at the same data and reaching for the same trucks.

When they finished, Whitford considered.

"So your recommendation is what, exactly?"

Marcus stepped in. "More aggressive pre-positioning than the model suggests. We want to lock in capacity before the surge, not during it. And we want to do it in regions the model might be underweighting."

"How much more aggressive?"

"Thirty to forty percent above the playbook."

"That's a lot of trucks sitting in parking lots if you're wrong."

"Yes."

Whitford leaned back. "The model has been right for sixteen days. Exposed a problem with the Ohio routing that saved us—what was it, Derek?"

"About ninety thousand in fuel costs over the month."

"Ninety thousand. And the ice storm, the lake effect event, both handled cleanly. Now you want to override it based on a weather analyst's hunch and a theory about what other shippers might do."

"It's not a hunch," Miles said. "The ensemble spread is measurable. The confidence score is—"

"Ninety-four percent." Whitford's voice was patient, which was somehow worse than if he'd been sharp. "I understand what you're saying about the training data. But ninety-four percent isn't nothing. And 'the model might be overconfident' isn't the same as 'the model is wrong.'"

He was right. That was the problem. He was making a reasonable argument.

"What's the cost if we pre-position and we're wrong?" Sarah asked. She had her calculator voice on, the one she used when she was trying to make something concrete.

"Depends on utilization," Marcus said. "If the storm tracks normally and we've got forty percent excess capacity staged... we're looking at somewhere between sixty and a hundred thousand in unnecessary costs. Plus the credibility hit. We told carriers one thing, did another, looked jumpy."

"And if we follow the playbook and you're right?"

Marcus didn't answer immediately. Derek did.

"Then we're fighting for trucks along with everyone else. Spot rates spike; we saw twenty-three percent last winter on a smaller event. Delivery windows blow out. And if Heartland's medical freight gets stuck..."

He didn't finish the sentence. He didn't need to. The Heartland contract was the linchpin of the Lindquist integration. Temperature-sensitive medical supplies sitting on a dock in Indianapolis wasn't a number you could put in a spreadsheet. It was a relationship you might not get back.

"So the asymmetry is bad," Sarah said. "Sixty to a hundred thousand if we're wrong and cautious. Relationship damage plus surge pricing plus God knows what if we're wrong and aggressive."

"That's my read," Marcus said.

Whitford was looking at something off-screen. The weather map, maybe. Or the financials.

"You have seventy-two hours?"

"Closer to sixty now. And the window for pre-positioning is narrower than that. Carriers are going to start getting calls from everyone."

"What does Sharon think?"

The question hung there. Sharon's tile was still in the call, her home office, the gray window. She hadn't spoken since the meeting started.

"Sharon?" Marcus asked.

She was looking at something they couldn't see. The sky, Marcus thought. She was still looking at the sky.

"I think," she said slowly, "that there's something else we haven't talked about yet."

Everyone waited for Sharon to continue. She didn't.

Instead, she said: "Lin, you've been quiet."

It wasn't an accusation. It was an invitation.

Lin's camera was on. That still felt new, even months into the change. Her face was thoughtful, her eyes on something below the camera. Notes, maybe, or her hands.

"I've been listening," she said. "To what Miles and Derek found. The weather confidence. The phantom capacity." She paused. "They're right. But there's another layer."

"Go on," Marcus said.

"When capacity gets tight—really tight, the way it does when a storm stalls for three days—carriers have to make choices. They can't move everyone's freight. They have to prioritize."

"They prioritize based on contracts," Sarah said. "Rate agreements, volume commitments—"

“They prioritize based on relationships.” Lin’s voice was quiet but certain. “Contracts matter. But when a dispatcher is looking at ten loads and can only move six, they’re not pulling out the rate sheets. They’re thinking about who they know. Who they trust. Who they’ve worked with for fifteen years versus who they’ve worked with for three months.”

The silence that followed had a different quality than the earlier ones.

“Crossroads has been with Lindquist for fifteen years,” Lin continued. “They’ve been with us for three months. When they have to choose whose freight moves first, we’re not the relationship they’re choosing.”

Sharon’s voice came through, soft: “She’s right. This is what I couldn’t—” She stopped, started again. “This is what’s hard to explain in an integration review. The relationships that actually make regional operations work.”

"Can we quantify it?" Miles cut in. "If we're being deprioritized, by how much? Twenty percent? Thirty?"

Lin shook her head. “It’s not a discount rate. It’s a phone call at 2 AM. It’s knowing that when you say ‘I need this moved,’ the person on the other end believes you, because you’ve never cried wolf. It’s fifteen years of showing up when you said you would.”

“So how do we—”

“You can’t operationalize it.” Derek’s voice was flat. “That’s the point. There’s no parameter you can feed into the model. The model doesn’t know that Crossroads has three dispatchers who’ve never met anyone from Consolidated. It doesn’t know that trust is a thing that exists.”

Miles looked like he wanted to argue. Marcus watched him choose not to.

“Sharon,” Marcus said. “Is this why you’ve been protective of the Crossroads relationship? Why you pushed back on the integration analysis?”

Sharon didn't answer immediately. Through her window, the sky had darkened.

"I couldn't prove it," she said finally. "Your analysis was clean. The numbers made sense. But I've watched what happens when relationships get disrupted. I've seen carriers who were solid for years just... disappear, when they didn't feel valued anymore. And I've seen what it costs to rebuild that."

"The analysis flagged Crossroads as yellow," Sarah said, pulling up something on her screen. "Potential concerns, recommended review. But we didn't have a framework for—"

"For things you can't measure," Lin said. "We never do."

Whitford had been listening. Now he spoke.

"So let me make sure I understand. You're telling me the weather model is overconfident because of rare patterns. The logistics model is overconfident because it can't see other shippers. And even if we adjust for both of those, we might still be in trouble because of... relationships?"

"Yes," Marcus said.

"And you can't prove any of it."

"Not to the standard you'd want. No."

Whitford exhaled. "What's your confidence level? If you had to put a number on it."

Marcus looked at his team. Derek, who'd seen this before. Miles, who was learning what he couldn't model. Lin, who'd finally named what she'd been seeing. Sarah, already documenting what they'd need to remember. Sharon, watching weather that wasn't on any screen.

"I don't have a number," Marcus said. "I have a pattern. The pattern says we're in territory the model wasn't built for. And when you're in that territory, you don't optimize. You prepare for being wrong."

The call was quiet. Whitford's face was unreadable.

"Alright," he said. "It's your call. You've earned that. But Marcus—document everything. What you decided, why, what you didn't know. If this goes sideways, I need to understand what happened."

"Understood."

"And if you're wrong, we're going to have a conversation about calibration."

"If I'm wrong," Marcus said, "I'll be the first one in that conversation."

Whitford nodded and dropped off the call. The team sat in the silence he left behind.

"Okay," Marcus said. "Let's talk about what we're actually going to do."

Sarah shared her screen. A document, already started. She'd been building it while they talked.

"Here's what I'm hearing," she said. "Three sources of uncertainty. Weather confidence overstated because of a rare pattern. Phantom capacity because of market reflexivity. Relationship risk because of integration timing. None of them provable. All of them pointing in the same direction."

"That's the summary," Marcus said.

"So what are we doing about each one?"

They worked through it. The conversation had a different quality now: less debate, more logistics. The decision had been made somewhere in the last ten minutes, even if no one had said the words.

For the weather uncertainty: pre-position thirty-five percent above the model's recommendation. Stage capacity in Des Moines, Indianapolis, and Columbus, the nodes that would matter if the storm stalled. Accept the cost if they were wrong.

For the phantom capacity: move early. Start making carrier calls today, not tomorrow. Lock in commitments before the surge hit. Derek would monitor the spot market for early signs of tightening.

For the relationship risk: Sharon would activate her Crossroads contacts. Ellen in dispatch, Ray in regional operations, Martinez in billing. Not asking for favors yet, just making sure they knew Consolidated was paying attention, that this wasn't just another account number in a system.

"What about Heartland specifically?" Miles asked. "If we're right about all of this, their freight is the most vulnerable. Temperature-sensitive, time-critical—"

"We flag it," Sharon said. "I'll talk to Ellen directly. Make sure she knows which shipments matter most." She paused. "I can't guarantee anything. But I can make sure they know."

"That's all we can ask," Marcus said.

Sarah was typing, capturing the plan. Then she stopped and looked up.

"What don't we know?"

The question sat there. Marcus recognized it: the gap documentation practice they'd built over the past months. Not just what they'd decided, but what they'd decided without knowing.

"We don't know if Chandra's right about the omega block," Miles said. "It's his read, but weather is probabilistic. The operational model could still be correct."

"We don't know how other shippers are going to respond," Derek added. "The reflexivity problem assumes they're all running similar playbooks. If they're not—if someone else sees this coming and moves early—the phantom capacity might not materialize the way I'm describing."

"We don't know how Crossroads will actually prioritize," Lin said quietly. "We're assuming relationship matters. It usually does. But we've never tested it under this kind of pressure."

"We don't know what we don't know," Sharon said. There was something in her voice, not quite humor, but close to it. "The Lindquist network has been running for fifteen years.

There are relationships in there I've never mapped. People who know people. Favors owed. History I wasn't part of."

Sarah typed it all down. Marcus watched the document grow: their plan on top, their uncertainty below. A record of the decision and the gaps in the decision.

"Anything else?"

No one spoke.

"Then we're committed," Marcus said. "Sarah, circulate this to everyone. Sharon, start your calls. Derek, I want you watching the capacity markets. If you see movement before the storm hits, that's signal. Miles, keep an eye on the weather updates. If the ensemble starts converging, or if the operational model shifts, I want to know immediately."

"What about you?" Sarah asked.

"I'm going to write up what we just decided and send it to Whitford. He asked for documentation. He's going to get it."

The meeting ended. For a moment, Marcus sat alone in the conference room, looking at the empty video tiles blinking off one by one.

They'd made a call. It was either the right call or an expensive mistake, and they wouldn't know which for days.

He opened a new document and began to write.

The storm arrived on schedule, the last thing that went according to the model.

Tuesday, 6 PM. The first bands crossed into western Iowa. Snow started light, almost gentle. The weather service held to their forecast: twenty-four to thirty-six hours, then clearing, then the system would track northeast. Marcus watched the radar from his home office, a glass of water going warm on his desk. Sharon's plane touched down at Oakland International. She'd promised to be in the room when it mattered.

Tuesday, 11 PM. Derek sent a message to the team channel:

Roads deteriorating faster than expected. I-80 westbound already seeing slowdowns. Carriers starting to hold drivers at truck stops rather than risk it.

Wednesday, 7 AM. Marcus woke to fourteen inches on the ground in Des Moines and the storm still strengthening. The models had expected the system to weaken overnight. It hadn't. The omega block was holding.

Sharon's first call came at 7:15 AM. "Ellen says they're pulling drivers off the road. Nobody's moving until visibility improves."

"Our pre-positioned capacity?"

"Staged and waiting. But waiting is all anyone can do right now."

Wednesday, 2 PM. The National Weather Service upgraded their warnings. "Multi-day event." "Historic accumulation potential." The words from the forecasters that Chandra had predicted. On the team call, no one said *we were right*. Being right didn't feel like much when you were watching it happen.

Wednesday, 8 PM. I-80 closed between Des Moines and Iowa City. Forty-seven trucks in a line outside mile marker 142, going nowhere. Some of them were theirs. Pre-positioned capacity that couldn't move any more than anyone else's.

Thursday, 6 AM. The storm had been sitting over Iowa for thirty-six hours. Another eighteen inches overnight. Drifts closing secondary roads as fast as plows could clear them.

Sarah's status update: *Indianapolis hub operational but constrained; some drivers can't get in. Columbus hub holding. Des Moines hub at 40% capacity. We're better off than we would have been without the pre-positioning. But nothing's moving.*

Thursday, 11 AM. The first real problem surfaced.

Marcus got the call from Sarah. "Indianapolis distribution center. Six pallets of Humalog that need to be in Cincinnati by tomorrow morning. The trucks are there, our pre-positioned capacity. But the roads between Indianapolis and Cincinnati are still a mess, and Crossroads is prioritizing which runs to attempt."

"What does that mean, prioritizing?"

"It means they're choosing whose freight to risk their drivers for. And we're not first."

Lin's prediction, playing out in real time. When carriers had to choose, they chose the relationships they knew.

Thursday, 2 PM. Sharon had been on the phone for five hours. Marcus found her in a small conference room, laptop open, phone pressed to her ear, a cold cup of coffee beside her. Reading glasses pushed up on her head, the practical short hair she didn't have to think about.

She held up a finger—*one minute*—and finished her call.

"Ellen's doing what she can," she said when she hung up. "She got two of our runs bumped up the priority list. But she's got fifteen years of relationships pulling at her, and we've got three months."

"What about the Heartland freight specifically?"

"I flagged it. She knows it's critical. But so is everyone else's critical freight." Sharon rubbed her eyes. "We're not at the back of the line. But we're not at the front either."

Thursday, 7 PM. The storm finally began to weaken. The omega block was breaking down, the high pressure ridge sliding east. On the radar, Marcus could see the trailing edge of the system, the first clear skies in three days approaching from the west.

"Recovery surge starts tomorrow," Derek said on the evening call. "Roads will open. Everyone will try to move at once."

"And that's when we'll see if you were right about phantom capacity," Sarah said.

"We'll see in the morning."

Friday, 6 AM. Derek's message came through before Marcus had finished his coffee.

It's happening. Look at the spot market.

Marcus pulled up the dashboard. The numbers told the story. Load-to-truck ratio in Chicago: 8.2-to-1. Des Moines: 9.1-to-1. Indianapolis: 7.8-to-1. Spot rates up twenty-six percent from Tuesday and climbing.

Every shipper in the Midwest had woken up to clear skies and a backlog. Every logistics system had processed the new conditions and identified available capacity in surrounding regions. Every operations team was reaching for the same trucks.

The trucks that had looked available yesterday didn't exist today. They were already claimed, already committed, already gone—spoken for by the first callers, the fastest systems, the relationships that picked up the phone before anyone else.

Phantom capacity. Exactly like Derek had described.

Friday, 10 AM. Marcus convened the team. Everyone looked tired—the kind of tired that came from watching something go wrong in slow motion, unable to stop it.

"Where are we?"

Sarah pulled up the status. "We're ahead of where we'd be if we'd followed the playbook. The pre-positioning bought us something. But the surge is overwhelming it."

"Heartland?"

"Fourteen shipments delayed. Six critical—the insulin, two surgical supply orders, diagnostic equipment that was supposed to be in Cincinnati yesterday. They're calling every hour now."

"Crossroads?"

Sharon's face was drawn. Three days of working her contacts, and it showed.

"Ellen got us what she could. But the surge hit them too. Every relationship they have is calling in favors right now." She paused. "We're stuck in the middle of the pack. Better than strangers. Worse than family."

Lin spoke quietly. "What about the other Crossroads contacts? Ray? Martinez?"

"Martinez is billing—he can't help with dispatch. Ray..." Sharon hesitated. "He's regional operations. Senior. More pull than Ellen, if he wanted to use it."

"Have you called him?"

"Not yet. I know him, but not well. Calling him means asking for something I'm not sure he owes us."

The team was silent. On the dashboard, the numbers kept climbing. Load-to-truck ratios that said everyone was fighting for the same scarce resources. Spot rates that said the fighting was expensive.

And Heartland's insulin was still sitting on a loading dock in Indianapolis.

"Try him," Marcus said.

Sharon nodded slowly. "Let me see what I can do."

She left the call. The rest of them sat there, watching dashboards that showed a system under stress, waiting to see if one phone call could make a difference.

Sharon didn't come back to the call. She sent a message instead: *Working it. Will update when I have something.*

The team waited. There wasn't much else to do. Derek monitored the spot markets, watching the numbers climb. Sarah fielded calls from Cincinnati—increasingly urgent, increasingly pointed. Miles tracked the weather service updates, though the storm was yesterday's problem now. The surge was today's.

Lin sat quietly, her camera on, watching the Slack channel for Sharon's updates. Every few minutes, a new message appeared:

11:47 AM: Ellen got one truck moving. Surgical supplies. ETA Cincinnati 4 PM.

12:23 PM: Insulin still stuck. Driver availability issue. Working on it.

1:15 PM: Talked to dispatch supervisor. They're slammed. Everyone's slammed.

2:08 PM: Going to try Ray.

Then nothing for almost an hour.

Marcus found himself refreshing the channel, waiting for the next update. Around him, the office hummed with the ordinary sounds of a Friday afternoon—keyboards, distant conversations, someone's phone ringing. It felt surreal, the normalcy of it, while somewhere in the Midwest trucks sat in lots and insulin sat on pallets and Sharon sat in a conference room trying to work a miracle through a phone line.

At 2:51 PM, Sharon's status went from "on a call" to "available."

At 2:53 PM, she messaged: *Can someone pull up the Heartland shipment tracker?*

Sarah shared her screen. The dashboard showed fourteen delayed shipments, six flagged critical. Red indicators across the board.

At 2:57 PM, one of the red indicators turned yellow.

"What just happened?" Derek asked.

Sarah clicked into the details. "The insulin shipment. Status changed from 'held' to 'in transit.'" She refreshed the page. "Carrier confirmed. Driver assigned. ETA Cincinnati… 7:30 tonight."

Another indicator turned yellow. Then another.

"Three of the critical shipments are moving," Sarah said. She was clicking through the updates as they appeared. "All Crossroads. All in the last five minutes."

"Sharon," Marcus said into the team channel, "what did you do?"

Sharon's video tile reappeared. She looked tired. But something else too. Surprised, maybe. Like she was still processing what had just happened.

"I called Ray," she said.

"And?"

"And... he made some calls." She shook her head slowly. "I told him what we needed. The Heartland freight, the insulin specifically. I explained the situation—the storm, the surge, where we were stuck. He listened. Asked a few questions. Then he said he'd see what he could do."

"That's it?"

"That's it. He said he'd see what he could do, and then he said he had to go, and then he hung up." Sharon paused. "Twenty minutes later, trucks started moving."

"How?" Miles asked. "The capacity isn't there. We've been watching the same dashboards all day—"

"I don't know." Sharon's voice was quiet. "I don't know what he did or who he called. I just know that twenty minutes ago we had insulin sitting on a dock, and now we don't."

The team sat with that. On Sarah's screen, another indicator turned from red to yellow. Four of the six critical shipments now in transit.

"Ray's regional operations," Lin said. "He would know people. Dispatchers, terminal managers, maybe people at other carriers who owe him favors."

"Maybe," Sharon said. "Or maybe he knows something we don't. Someone we don't." She rubbed her eyes. "I've been with Lindquist for eight years. I thought I knew the network. But Ray's been doing this for twenty years. There are layers I've never seen."

The dashboard updated again. A fifth shipment moving.

They weren't out of the woods. Eight shipments were still delayed, still stuck in the surge with everyone else's freight. The spot market was still brutal. The next few days would still be hard.

But Heartland's insulin was moving. The critical freight—the freight that could have cost them the relationship, the integration, everything they'd built over the past months—was on its way.

"We got lucky," Derek said.

"Did we?" Sarah asked. "Or did we put ourselves in a position where luck could find us?"

No one had an answer for that. Not yet.

They pushed through.

Friday evening: The critical Heartland shipments arrived in Cincinnati. The insulin made it with three hours to spare. Sarah was on the phone with their contact at the hospital system, explaining and apologizing and promising a full debrief. The contact was frustrated but not furious. That counted as a win.

Saturday: The surge continued, but the worst of it was breaking. Roads were clear. The backlog was working itself out, one truck at a time. They lost two smaller accounts—shippers who'd been caught in the delays and didn't want to hear explanations. They kept everyone else.

Sunday: Marcus slept for eleven hours. When he woke, the world had not ended.

Monday: Something like normal operations resumed. The dashboards went from red to yellow to, in a few places, green. Derek reported that spot rates were falling, the load-to-truck ratios returning to sustainable levels. Peak season wasn't over, but the crisis was.

Tuesday morning: Marcus called the team together. Not a status update. Not a planning session. Just a check-in.

"How's everyone doing?"

The answers came slowly. Tired. Relieved. Still processing.

"We made it," Sarah said. "Somehow."

"We did." Marcus paused. "But I want to make sure we understand how. What worked, what didn't, what we got right, what we got lucky on."

"The pre-positioning helped," Derek said. "We'd have been in much worse shape without it."

"The relationship work helped," Lin added. "Sharon's calls to Ellen kept us from being at the back of the line."

"And Ray," Miles said. "Whatever Ray did."

The name sat there. They'd all been thinking about it—the phone call that had somehow moved trucks that couldn't be moved, cleared a path through a system that was gridlocked.

"Sharon," Marcus said. "Have you figured out what happened there?"

Sharon had been quiet through the meeting. She looked better than she had on Friday—less drawn, more present—but there was something in her expression that Marcus couldn't quite read.

"I've been talking to people at Crossroads," she said slowly. "Trying to understand."

"And?"

"And I think I know what happened. But it's..." She paused, searching for words. "It's not simple. It's not just 'Ray made some calls.' There's more to it."

"What kind of more?"

Sharon shook her head. "I don't want to get into it now. Not like this, not tired, not rushing between other meetings. If we're going to understand what actually happened—what saved us, what almost didn't—we should do it properly."

Marcus recognized what she was asking for. A real retrospective. Not a status update with lessons learned tacked on at the end. A genuine attempt to understand.

"Okay," he said. "Full retrospective. Everyone. We block out real time, we go through everything—what we decided, what we didn't know, what happened that we didn't expect." He looked at Sharon. "Including Ray."

"Including Ray," she agreed.

"End of the week?"

"Let's get through the rest of peak season first," Sarah said. "We're not out yet. Another two weeks, maybe three. Then we'll have distance. Perspective."

Marcus nodded. She was right. You couldn't understand something while you were still inside it.

"End of peak season, then. We do this right."

The meeting ended. People dropped off the call, back to the work that was still waiting. Marcus sat alone for a moment, looking at the empty grid of video tiles.

They'd survived. The model had been wrong, and they'd seen it coming—some of it, anyway. They'd made calls that mattered. And then something else had happened, something they didn't fully understand, and that something had made the difference.

The storm was over. The real work—the work of understanding—was still ahead.

THE RETROSPECTIVE

The Oakland conference room had a view of the bay. Marcus had booked it for that reason, though he couldn't have said why it mattered. Something about perspective. Something about being able to look at water while they talked about what had almost sunk them.

It was the first time they'd all been in the same room. Eighteen months of rectangles on screens, and now here were the actual people—Sharon's reading glasses pushed up on her head, Derek's height somehow surprising in person, Lin with her jet black hair down for once, her stillness more apparent when you could see her whole body and not just her face, Sarah without three devices in front of her for once. Miles had flown in from Chicago the night before; in person, his restless energy was more apparent, the way he couldn't quite stay still even sitting down. Priya had arrived from Mumbai the day before that. Her first time at headquarters.

"We survived," Marcus said. "That's not the same thing as understanding why."

He let that sit. Twenty seconds. Thirty. The silence was uncomfortable, and he let it be uncomfortable. Some things needed space to land. The instinct in these rooms was to celebrate, to affirm, to move on. They'd kept Heartland. They'd navigated a crisis that would have broken them three months earlier. But Marcus had seen too many near-misses become origin stories—the disaster that proved how good we are, how resilient, how lucky. Stories that taught exactly the wrong lessons.

"We could walk out of here believing we're better than we are," he said. "Or we could figure out what actually happened."

Sharon opened her folder. She'd built the timeline herself—not because she didn't trust the systems, but because she'd wanted to touch each decision, to feel the sequence in a way that dashboards didn't allow. Timestamps and outcomes. The choices they'd made and the results that followed.

"Before we get into what went wrong," she said, "I want to name what worked."

The instinct was to find the failure, dissect it, assign lessons. But Sharon had been in enough retrospectives to know that pattern—the relentless focus on error that taught people to hide their mistakes rather than examine them.

"The pre-positioning," Derek said. "We had capacity staged before the models caught up."

"The carrier communication," Lin added. "We were honest

about what we didn't know. That bought us goodwill when we needed flexibility."

"The decision rhythm," Miles said. "Four-hour windows. We didn't let perfect information become the enemy of good-enough action."

"The documentation," Sarah added. She had her laptop open, the running record she'd maintained throughout the crisis. What they'd decided, why, what they didn't know. "We're not reconstructing from memory. We have something to examine."

Marcus watched them build the list. This was part of it too—acknowledging what had worked, not just what had failed. The research was clear on this: teams that reviewed only failures developed a distorted picture of their own capabilities. They learned what to avoid without learning what to repeat.

Sarah was right about the documentation, and it mattered more than it might seem. Teams that skip real-time documentation—that don't name their uncertainties, that don't create friction between interpretation and reality—find themselves in retrospectives with nothing to examine but memory. And memory is a story we tell ourselves—smoothed, edited, confident, wrong. The gaps they'd named before the storm—*we don't know how Crossroads will actually prioritize*—were exactly the gaps where Ray had appeared.

What Separates Learning from Ritual

Peter Senge called the Army's After Action Review "arguably one of the most successful organizational learning methods yet devised." Then he added the warning: "Yet most every corporate effort to graft this truly innovative practice into their culture has failed because, again and again, people reduce the living practice of AARs to a sterile technique."[1]

The difference between learning and ritual is whether anyone's mind actually changes. Meta-analyses show that properly conducted debriefs improve team performance by 20–25% —effect sizes of 0.67 to 0.79, remarkably strong for organizational interventions. But "properly conducted" carries weight. The warning signs of ritual are consistent across studies: the same issues recurring meeting after meeting, leaders dominating discussion, no action items generated or completed, participants not feeling safe to speak honestly.

Psychological safety isn't a luxury in these rooms. It's the mechanism. When people believe they can admit mistakes, ask uncomfortable questions, and challenge the emerging narrative without penalty, reflection produces learning. When they don't, reflection produces performance—people saying what they think others want to hear, building stories that protect rather than illuminate.

AI-enabled operations compress production cycles. Analysis that took days happens in minutes. Decisions that required sequential approvals can cascade in hours. But learning time doesn't compress the same way. Understanding why something worked, or why it almost didn't, requires the kind of slow processing that production tempo crowds out.

The pressure to match reflection tempo to production tempo is constant and usually invisible. Teams feel they should be learning as fast as they're operating. When they can't, they substitute ritual for reflection: the fifteen-minute debrief, the

---

1. Peter M. Senge, *The Fifth Discipline*, rev. ed. (Doubleday, 2006); see also *The Dance of Change* (Doubleday, 1999). Performance data from Tannenbaum and Cerasoli, "Do Team and Individual Debriefs Enhance Performance?," *Human Factors* 55, no. 1 (2013): 231–245; Keiser and Arthur, *Journal of Applied Psychology* 106, no. 7 (2021): 1007–1032.

lessons-learned template, the retrospective scheduled between two other meetings.

Sarah's insistence on waiting was a choice to protect learning tempo from production tempo. "Let's get through the rest of peak season first." The team would have time to think. Not stolen time between crises. Real time.

The team in the Oakland conference room had something most teams don't: eighteen months of practice being wrong together. They'd learned, slowly and sometimes painfully, that the point wasn't to look competent. The point was to see clearly.

Sharon was looking at the timeline.

A story was taking shape. They'd seen the storm coming before the models fully committed. They'd pre-positioned capacity. They'd maintained carrier relationships that gave them flexibility when flexibility mattered. When the crisis hit, they'd made decisions in four-hour windows instead of waiting for certainty that never came.

"So the system worked," Miles said. He was synthesizing as he spoke, the way he always did—pulling threads together, finding the pattern. "We built infrastructure for exactly this situation. Documentation, decision protocols, communication channels. And when we needed it, it held."

It sounded right. It felt right. Marcus could see heads nodding around the table.

"What doesn't fit?" he asked. The nodding stopped. "I'm serious. What part of the story doesn't work? What are we not seeing?"

Silence. Sarah shifted in her chair. Derek was looking at the ceiling, the way he did when he was thinking rather than disengaging.

"The capacity," Derek said finally. "We pre-positioned, but it wasn't enough. The surge was bigger than we'd staged for."

"Right," Sharon said. She was tracing a line on her timeline with one finger. "By Friday morning, we were short. The pre-positioning bought us time, but it didn't buy us trucks."

"So where did the trucks come from?" Marcus asked.

The timeline had a gap—a window on Friday afternoon where something had happened that Sharon hadn't been able to explain until three days ago.

The Learning Question

James March and his colleagues warned about "superstitious learning"—drawing confident conclusions when the connections between actions and outcomes are misspecified.[2] Organizations take messy events and produce clean narratives, cause-and-effect stories that feel true whether or not they are.

AI accelerates this tendency. It can process more information faster, find patterns in noise, generate explanations that sound authoritative. But pattern-matching isn't understanding. A coherent story isn't the same as an accurate one. The question isn't "What happened?"—any system can reconstruct a sequence. The question is "What would have happened otherwise?" And that question is harder than it looks, because you can't test the alternative. You can only guess.

The team had a coherent story. Pre-positioning, communication, decision rhythm. Everything they'd built had worked. But coherence is seductive. It feels like truth. And sometimes

2. Barbara Levitt and James G. March, "Organizational Learning," *Annual Review of Sociology* 14 (1988): 319–340. March later expanded on these themes in *The Ambiguities of Experience* (Ithaca, NY: Cornell University Press, 2010).

the most important learning hides in the parts of the story that don't quite fit.

"Friday at 2:08 PM," Sharon said. "That's when it changed."

She spread the timeline out so everyone could see it. The morning had been bad—capacity gap widening, spot rates spiking, Heartland's insulin shipment at risk. By noon, they were looking at failure.

"And then trucks appeared," Sharon said. "Twenty minutes after 2:08, we had capacity we didn't have before. Not from our pre-positioned stock. Not from the spot market—I checked. Trucks that weren't in our system suddenly were."

"Crossroads?" Lin asked.

"Crossroads." Sharon nodded. "But here's what I couldn't figure out. I called Ellen. She said they were tapped out by Thursday night. I called Martinez. Same story. Everyone I talked to said they had nothing left to give."

She paused.

"So I called Ray."

The room was quiet. Ray Field had been at Crossroads for twenty years. Sharon had known him her whole career.

"He made a call," she said. "Friday at 2:08. Not to us. Not to anyone at Crossroads. He called Tom Brennan."

Miles frowned. "Who's Tom Brennan?"

"Director of Logistics at Heartland Medical Supply." Sharon's voice was flat, the way it got when she was processing something she still didn't fully understand. "Ray and Tom worked together fifteen years ago. Different company, different life. They stayed in touch. And when Ray saw that Heartland's freight was at risk, he picked up the phone."

"He called the customer?" Sarah asked.

"He called a friend. Tom made calls of his own. Trucks that

were committed elsewhere got uncommitted. Capacity that didn't exist suddenly did." Sharon looked around the table. "That's what saved us. Not the pre-positioning. Not the decision protocols. A phone call between two people who've known each other for fifteen years." She closed her folder. "He never told me. All these years I've known Ray, and he never mentioned Tom."

"How did Ray even know to call Tom?" Lin asked.

"He didn't know Tom could help specifically. He knew Tom was connected, that he'd been in Midwest logistics for decades, that if anyone could shake something loose it would be someone like him." Sharon paused. "Ray told me he almost didn't call. It felt like a long shot. But we were stuck, and he'd run out of moves inside the system."

"So we got lucky," Derek said. "Ray happened to know someone who happened to know people who happened to have trucks."

"Did we?" Sharon's voice was careful. "Or did we put ourselves in a position where Ray was willing to make that call?"

~

The question opened something. Marcus watched the team sit with it.

"Think about it," Sharon continued. "Ray's been in this industry for twenty years. He's seen acquisitions before. He knows what usually happens: new parent company comes in, talks about integration and synergies, strips out the relationships that made the operation work. The institutional knowledge gets documented into systems that don't capture what matters. The people who built the network get sidelined or leave."

"That's not what we did," Sarah said.

"That's not what you did. And Ray noticed." Sharon looked around the table. "When I called him during the storm, I wasn't calling as Consolidated's representative. I was calling as someone who'd kept him in the loop. Who'd asked his opinion on the integration analysis. Who'd flagged his concerns to Marcus instead of dismissing them."

"You built trust with him," Lin said quietly.

"I tried to. And when I needed something, he was willing to try something unusual. To use a relationship that had nothing to do with the official channels. To put himself out there for people he'd only known for three months." Sharon closed her folder. "If you'd come in like a typical acquisition—if you'd treated Lindquist people like problems to be solved instead of knowledge to be preserved—I wouldn't have been in a position to ask. And Ray would have answered politely and told me there was nothing he could do."

Derek was staring at the table, working through something. "So what saved us wasn't Crossroads. It was Ray being willing to go outside the system for us."

"How we'd treated everyone. The whole integration approach." Sharon shrugged. "I can't prove it. Ray didn't say 'I helped you because you respected us.' He just helped. But I've seen the other version. I've seen what happens when people don't go the extra mile because they don't feel like the new owners deserve it."

The Attribution Problem

Post-hoc analysis can't separate correlation from causation, luck from skill. Every successful outcome has multiple sufficient explanations. The pre-positioning contributed. The communication contributed. The decision rhythm contributed.

But so did a relationship that existed entirely outside the systems anyone was tracking.

The visible gets credit. Dashboards, metrics, documented processes—these are what retrospectives examine because these are what retrospectives can see. The invisible gets forgotten, or never noticed in the first place. A phone call between old friends doesn't appear in any log. A favor owed from fifteen years ago doesn't show up on any dashboard. The infrastructure that actually saved them was made of something the organization couldn't measure and hadn't maintained.

The room was quiet.

Lin broke the silence first. "So what—we can't systematize relationships. We already knew that."

It wasn't dismissive. It was a genuine question. They'd spent eighteen months building infrastructure precisely because they knew some things couldn't be systematized. The documentation, the decision protocols, the communication channels—all of it existed to create space for human judgment. Were they supposed to be surprised that human judgment included picking up the phone?

Marcus watched Miles. The old Miles would have jumped in with a framework, a way to capture this, a process for mapping relationship networks. This Miles was quiet, turning something over.

"The call worked because it wasn't a system," Derek said slowly. "If we'd had a 'call Tom Brennan' protocol, would it have worked? If Ray had been following a playbook instead of calling a friend?"

"It would have been a different call," Sharon said. "Tom would have known."

"Known what?"

"That it was institutional. Not personal." She shook her

head. "Ray wasn't calling on behalf of Crossroads. He was calling because he's Ray. Because that's what you do for people you've known for fifteen years. Tom responded to that. Not to a process."

Derek leaned back. "So the thing that saved us is the thing we can't replicate. Can't scale. Can't even see until after it happens."

"We saw some of it," Sarah said. She'd been taking notes, as she always did, but now she looked up. "Not the Ray part. But we saw pieces."

She was right. Marcus tried to reconstruct who'd seen what. Derek had flagged the capacity gap before the models caught it —something in the spot market patterns that didn't match the forecast. Lin had recognized the carrier behavior from three acquisitions ago. Miles had caught a contractual window buried in documentation no one else remembered. Priya, dialed in at midnight Mumbai time, had noticed the APAC ripple effects twelve hours before they hit the dashboards. Sarah had tracked the real-time status across sites when the dashboards started lagging reality.

And Sharon had built the timeline that revealed the gap none of them could explain.

"No one person had the full picture," Marcus said.

"But together we had enough to act," Sarah finished.

What Metrics Can't Capture

There's a layer beneath the protocols. Relationships that take years to build. Judgment that develops through experience. Distributed awareness across a team where each person sees something the others miss.

Derek saw capacity gaps in spot market patterns. Lin recognized carrier stress from historical parallels. Miles caught contractual details buried in documentation. Priya noticed cascade effects from the other side of the world. Sharon built the timeline that surfaced the anomaly. No individual had the full picture. Together, they had enough.

Each perspective caught something the others missed. Derek's Red orientation—his focus on how systems actually behaved under stress—let him see the reflexivity problem before it hit. Lin's Blue orientation—her concern with how processes enabled people to do their jobs—recognized when carrier relationships were degrading in ways no dashboard would show. Miles had learned to work with Silver effectively, but more importantly, he'd learned when Silver's outputs needed verification from perspectives it couldn't simulate.

This distributed capability isn't automatic. It exists because each person has maintained the underlying judgment that makes evaluation possible. Derek could see the reflexivity problem because he'd *built* systems, not just reviewed AI analysis of them—including the routing disaster that taught him what confident-looking failure felt like. Lin could see the relational layer because she'd *worked* carrier relationships directly, not just read reports about them. Miles couldn't see either dimension fully, but he knew enough to know he didn't know enough—he pulled in Derek, he called Chandra, he assembled the people who could see what he couldn't.

The risk is erosion. Every hour spent reviewing AI output instead of doing the work yourself is an hour the judgment fades. The team that saved themselves could, slowly, become a team that couldn't—not through any single decision, but through the gradual atrophy of the capabilities that let them see what the model missed.

Maintaining distributed capability means deliberately practicing without AI—not because AI is bad, but because the judgment that makes AI useful requires separate cultivation. This feels inefficient. The work takes longer. But it's what makes the team more than the sum of its AI-augmented parts. It's what let them see, collectively, what the model couldn't show them.

Priya had seen this in June—the carrier who would perform miracles under pressure, whose reliability didn't appear in any metric. Teams develop collective capability that doesn't reduce to individual skills or documented processes. The knowledge lives in the connections, in the overlapping awareness, in the ability to say "something's wrong" before you can say what.

Ray's call to Tom was the same phenomenon at a different scale. Not team knowledge, but relationship knowledge—the accumulated trust of fifteen years, activated in a moment of need. The system that saved them wasn't in any system. It was in Ray being someone Tom would pick up the phone for.

The question was whether they could hold onto that insight, or whether it would dissolve into something more comfortable. Something that fit the frameworks they already had.

"We can't separate the skill from the luck," Miles said. He wasn't frustrated—he was working through it, the way he'd learned to do. "We can document what we did. We can point to the decisions that helped. But we can't prove any of it is why we won. Ray's call might have been the only thing that mattered. Everything else might have been noise."

"That's true," Marcus said. "And it might not be. We can't know."

"So what do we take from this?"

Marcus had been turning this over since Sharon first told him about Ray and Tom. The story didn't fit. It wasn't about better processes or clearer metrics or faster decisions. It was about something else entirely.

"We've been building systems to make better decisions," he

said. "That's what this whole year has been. Documentation, protocols, decision frameworks. All of it assumes the question is 'how do we choose correctly?' How do we gather the right information, weigh it properly, reach the right conclusion?"

He paused.

"But that's not what saved us. Ray didn't make a decision. He made a call. He reached out to someone who owed him something that couldn't be quantified—fifteen years of showing up, of being reliable, of being Ray. And Tom responded. Not because it was the right decision. Because it was Ray asking."

Lin was nodding slowly. "We've been asking the wrong question."

"Maybe. Or maybe we've been asking a question that only gets us so far." Marcus looked around the table. "How do we stay connected enough that we don't have to decide alone? That might matter more than how we decide."

He thought about the framework he'd been building all year. Read the water. Know your crew. Call your line. Remember the run. Four modes, four practices, four ways of navigating uncertainty. They'd learned all of them. But what Ray's call revealed was that the modes weren't separate. You read the water *through* your crew. You called the line *because* of what you remembered. The navigation metaphor had limits. At some point, you weren't steering through rapids anymore. You were building the relationships that made steering possible.

The Deeper Question

Chris Argyris distinguished between single-loop and double-loop learning.[3] Single-loop learning optimizes within existing parameters, like a thermostat that turns on heat when temperature drops. Double-loop learning questions the parameters themselves. Why is the thermostat set to 68 degrees? Is temperature even the right thing to measure?

AI excels at single-loop learning. Faster pattern recognition, better optimization, more consistent execution within defined constraints. But double-loop learning requires asking whether the frame is right. Whether the question you're optimizing for is the question that matters.

The team had spent a year building systems for better decisions. Better information, better processes, better frameworks for choosing correctly. All of it was single-loop—optimizing within a frame that took "deciding correctly" as the goal.

Ray's call suggested a different frame. Not "How do we choose?" but "Who do we know?" Not optimization but connection. Not systems but relationships.

The question wasn't whether their systems were good. The question was whether systems were enough.

Sharon was the one who asked it.

"Ray's not young," Sharon said. "He's got to be close to retirement."

She wasn't looking at her folder anymore. She was looking at something further away.

"Those relationships took fifteen years to build. Tom Brennan. The other people he knows, the ones he'd call if Tom couldn't help. That's not something you hand off in a transition

3. Chris Argyris and Donald A. Schön, *Theory in Practice: Increasing Professional Effectiveness* (San Francisco: Jossey-Bass, 1974); Chris Argyris and Donald A. Schön, *Organizational Learning: A Theory of Action Perspective* (Reading, MA: Addison-Wesley, 1978).

document. It's not something you train." She paused. "So what happens when Ray's gone?"

No one answered. It wasn't a rhetorical question, but it wasn't one anyone knew how to answer either.

"And it's not just Ray," Sharon continued. "It's everyone like Ray. The people who've been in this industry long enough to know people. To have done favors and had favors done. That whole layer—" She stopped, started again. "We've been treating that like it's separate from the real work. Like relationships are nice to have, but the systems are what matter. The optimization, the efficiency, the metrics."

"The things we can measure," Miles said quietly.

"Right. The things we can measure." Sharon's voice was steady, but Marcus could hear something underneath it. Not anger. Something closer to grief. "What if we're wrong? What if we're consuming something we can't see? Every time we optimize, every time we automate, every time we make things more efficient—what if we're spending down capital we don't know how to rebuild?"

Lin leaned forward. "The efficiency gains show up immediately. The relationships we're not investing in—that's invisible. Until it isn't."

"Until you need someone to pick up the phone," Derek said. "And there's no one to call."

The room sat with that.

"Same pattern," Derek added, almost to himself. Then, louder: "It's the same pattern as the routing disaster. We optimized perfectly for a world that didn't exist anymore. We just didn't know it until the crisis hit."

"You're saying this is bigger than Ray," Sarah said.

"I'm saying we keep finding the same shape." Derek was frowning, not in disagreement but in concentration. "Systems that work perfectly until they don't. Efficiency that looks great until you need the thing you optimized away. We built a routing system that couldn't see what it couldn't see. Now we're building an organization that—" He stopped.

"That what?" Marcus asked.

"I don't know," Derek said. "But I think we keep asking 'how do we decide better' when maybe that's not the only question. Maybe it's what we're building. What we're optimizing away."

"We can see the pattern," Lin said. "We don't have the tools yet."

That was true. Marcus could feel it: something just beyond the edge of what they knew how to talk about. They'd spent a year learning to read the water, to know their crew, to call their line, to remember the run. And now they were looking at something that might require a different kind of map entirely.

He didn't know what that map looked like. He wasn't sure anyone did.

"We can't solve this today," he said finally. "But we can remember that we saw it. We can keep asking the question even if we don't have the answer."

Miles nodded slowly. "Document what we learned. Even the parts we don't understand yet."

"Especially those parts," Sarah said, and there was something like a smile in it.

The meeting wound down the way these meetings do—loose ends tied up, next steps sketched, people stretching and checking phones. Sharon caught Marcus at the door, folder tucked under her arm.

"Thank you," she said. "For not pretending we figured it out."

"We didn't."

"No. But we saw something. That's not nothing." She glanced back at the conference room, where Derek and Miles were talking by the window. “My father would have liked this. The honesty of it. He always said the most dangerous thing was a team that thought it had all the answers.”

She left. Marcus stayed.

The Bay was quiet. Ships out there in the dark, every route tracked, every container accounted for. And what saved them wasn’t any of that—it was fifteen years of Ray being someone Tom Brennan would pick up the phone for. A different kind of infrastructure.

They were trading that for gains they could measure. He didn’t know the exchange rate. He wasn’t sure anyone did.

The lights on the water didn’t have answers. But the question had a shape. And they had seen it together.

MARCUS'S WHITEBOARD: REMEMBER THE RUN

See Concept Reference: Remember the Run for key frameworks and definitions.

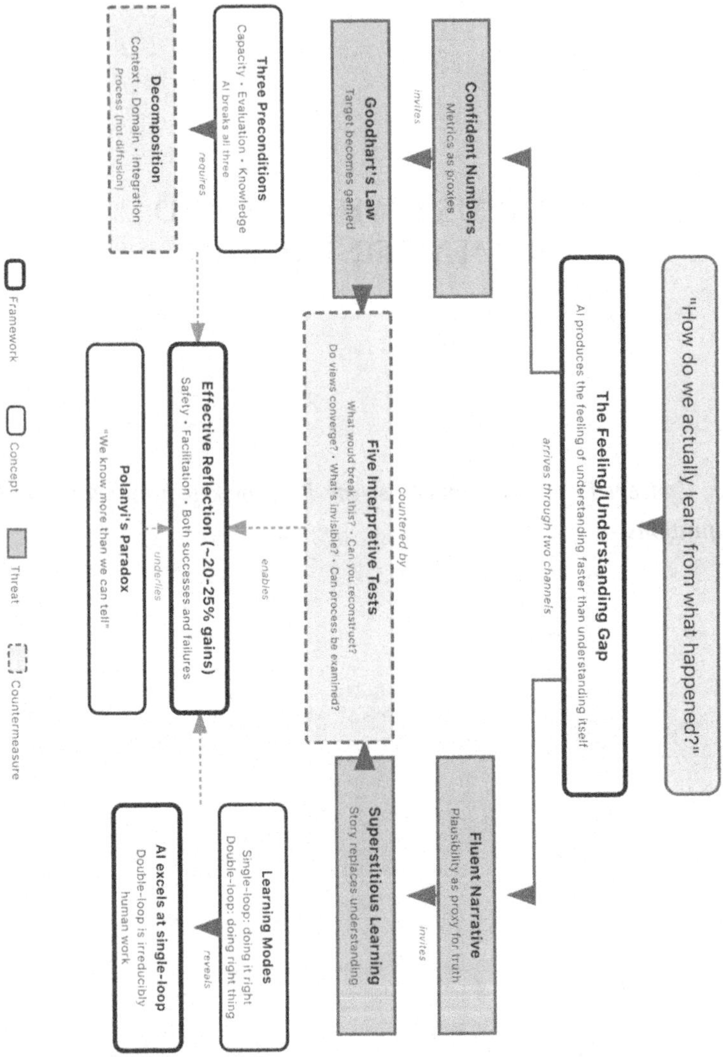
"How do we actually learn from what happened?"
The Feeling/Understanding Gap
AI produces the feeling of understanding faster than understanding itself
arrives through two channels
Confident Numbers
Metrics as proxies
invites
Goodhart's Law
Target becomes gamed
Fluent Narrative
Plausibility as proxy for truth
invites
Superstitious Learning
Story replaces understanding
countered by
Five Interpretive Tests
What would break this? · Can you reconstruct?
Do views converge? · What's invisible? · Can process be examined?
enables
Three Preconditions
Capacity · Evaluation · Knowledge
AI breaks all three
requires
Decomposition
Context · Domain · Integration
Process (not diffusion)
Effective Reflection (~20–25% gains)
Safety · Facilitation · Both successes and failures
underlies
Polanyi's Paradox
"We know more than we can tell"
Learning Modes
Single-loop: doing it right
Double-loop: doing right thing
reveals
AI excels at single-loop
Double-loop is irreducibly human work
Framework
Concept
Threat
Countermeasure

EPILOGUE: THE ENDLESS RIVER

BY ROBERT SCHAFFNER

It was late September last year when I found myself at the Kirchenwirt in Gams, Austria watching the last of the afternoon light settle over the Gesäuse.

I should be clear about something from the start: I am not a rafter.

I was born in Gresten, just over the hills in Bezirk Scheibbs. I know these valleys the way you know the back roads to your grandmother's house. Every bend, every Wirtshaus, every spot where the fog collects in autumn. But the river Salza? I've watched it. I've listened to friends describe it. I've never actually been in a boat on it.

My doctor keeps telling me things need to change. He's probably right. But that evening at the Kirchenwirt, I wasn't there to change anything. I was there because my friend Thomas had just finished his last run of the season, and he wanted to talk.

Thomas has been rafting the Salza for fifteen years. Not professionally. It's his passion, something he does for the pure love of the sport. He helps out the local outfitters from time to time when they need an extra hand, but mostly he's out there because he can't imagine a summer without it. He's the kind of person who speaks slowly, not because he's uncertain but because he's already thought through three versions of what he's about to say.

I'd ordered the Alt Wiener Salonbeuschel mit Knödel. A traditional Viennese dish of finely sliced calf's lung in a creamy, slightly tangy sauce with capers and a hint of vinegar, served with bread dumplings. It's the kind of thing you won't find on most menus anymore, and that's exactly why I love it. Wiener Schnitzel you can get anywhere. A properly made Beuschel? That takes a kitchen that still cares about the old ways. Thomas was on his second Forstauer, the local craft beer from the Hofbräu just up the road, when he said something that stopped me.

"You know what separates the people who become good at this from the ones who just do it?"

I waited.

"It's not talent. It's not even practice. It's whether they understand that every run is a new run."

I'd heard Thomas talk about rafting before. I knew the basics. Put-in, take-out, reading the water, calling your line. I knew the Salza was special: crystal-clear water that looks almost artificial, the Palfauer Schlucht with its 240-million-year-old rock formations, the way the river changes character depending on the season.

But this was different. He wasn't talking about technique.

"People come here," he said, "and they do one tour. Maybe two. And they think they know the river. They've done it. Checked the box. They post their photos on Instagram and move on."

He took a long drink.

"But the river doesn't care that you ran it last year. The water level is different. The rocks have shifted. Someone in your crew is nervous because of something that happened at work. The weather is changing. Everything that made last year's run work might be exactly wrong for this one."

"So what do you do?"

"You scout. Every time. Even if you've run that section a hundred times. You pull over, you get out, you look. You read what's actually there. Not what you remember being there."

I thought about my own work. For years now, I've been running workshops on AI. Dozens of them, with several hundred participants across all of them. General Managers, Senior leaders, team managers, individual contributors. I've watched people move through skepticism, then curiosity, then something closer to vertigo when the scope of change finally registers.

And I've noticed something. The organisations that struggle aren't only the ones that move slowly. They're the ones that think they've already figured it out.

They did a pilot. They trained some people. They bought some tools. They wrote a strategy document. And then they stopped looking at where they actually are.

"It's like they ran the river once," I said to Thomas, "and now they're trying to navigate from memory."

He nodded. "Exactly. And the river has moved."

This is why we built the assessment.

I say "we" because I didn't build it alone. My colleague in triangility GmbH, Frank Widmayer, a professor who's been thinking about organisational development longer than I've been thinking about AI, was essential to getting this right. Frank has spent decades in both worlds—rigorous theory and practical application—and moves between them like someone who's forgotten there's supposed to be a border. Working with him is a joy. We'd spend hours sketching frameworks on white-boards, arguing about which dimensions actually matter, testing ideas against real organisations. He'd bring the depth,

I'd bring the field experience, and somewhere in between we'd find something that actually worked.

We didn't build it as a finish line. God knows there are enough of those in corporate life. Not as a certification or a badge or something to put in a quarterly report.

We built it as a way to scout. To read the water before the next run.

The framework behind it comes from Ken Wilber's integral model. Four quadrants that look at any system from four different angles simultaneously. It sounds academic until you see it in action. Frank helped translate it into something leaders could actually use.

Imagine you're standing at the put-in, looking downstream. You need to understand four things:

What's happening inside each person on your team. Their trust, their emotions, their sense of psychological safety. Do they actually believe this AI thing is worth engaging with? Or are they quietly terrified that it's coming for their job? You can't see this by looking at dashboards. It's subjective, interior, individual. But it shapes everything.

What each person can actually do. Their skills, their behaviours, their AI fluency. This is the stuff you can observe and measure. Can they write a decent prompt? Do they know when to trust an AI output and when to question it? Are they learning faster this month than last month?

What's happening in your culture. The shared values, the unwritten rules, the way people actually work together. Is there a genuine innovation culture, or just innovation theatre? Do people feel safe to experiment and fail? What do your stakeholder relationships actually look like when no one's watching?

What's happening in your structures. Your processes, your KPIs, your communication systems, your products. The visible, measurable, organisational stuff. The stuff that shows up in org charts and strategy decks.

Most organisations only look at that last quadrant. They focus on what they can see and measure. But the river runs through all four.

Thomas was sketching something on a napkin. The section of the Salza between Wildalpen and Palfau.

"See this?" He pointed to a narrow passage. "Looks straightforward. Experienced paddlers sometimes get cocky here. But if you don't know your crew, if someone's having a bad day, if the communication isn't there, this is exactly where things go wrong."

"Because the technical difficulty isn't the problem."

"Right. The problem is everything you can't see from the outside."

I looked at his sketch. It reminded me of the assessment diagram. The four quadrants with development lines radiating outward like spokes. Each line a question to ask before you commit to the next run.

"Let me give you an example," I said. "Psychological Safety."

Thomas raised an eyebrow.

"It's one of the lines we measure. And it's the one that trips up more organisations than almost anything else."

I'd seen it dozens of times. A company invests heavily in AI tools. They roll out training programmes. They set ambitious adoption targets. And nothing happens. Or worse, people use the tools in superficial ways, never really integrating them into how they actually work.

"Why?" Thomas asked.

"Because people are afraid. Some fear looking stupid if they use it wrong, or making a mistake that gets caught. Others worry about admitting they don't understand something, in case it's used against them later. And underneath all of that, there's often a deeper fear: that if they get too good at this, they might automate themselves out of a job. Or that the rebound effect kicks in, and suddenly AI doesn't save them time but just piles endless more work onto their plate."

"So they play it safe."

"Exactly. They do the minimum. They tick the boxes. They never actually experiment, because experimenting means risking failure. And if the culture doesn't feel safe for failure..."

"The river stays dangerous. Even when it looks calm."

Another line we look at: Data & AI Fluency. This one sits in the Individual Exterior quadrant. The observable skills and behaviours.

But here's what I've learned: you can't train your way to AI fluency if the other quadrants aren't ready. It's like teaching someone paddle strokes when they're too terrified to get in the boat.

The research backs this up. There's a concept called "fluency velocity." How fast someone is learning, not just what they currently know. A person at level 2 who's climbing fast will outperform someone stuck at level 3. But fluency velocity requires something deeper: the motivation to learn, the safety to fail, the identity shift that lets you see yourself as someone who works *with* AI rather than *against* it.

All four quadrants. All at once.

The light outside had shifted to that deep amber that comes just before dusk. Thomas finished his Forstauer and looked out the window toward the mountains.

"You know what the hardest thing is?" he said. "Convincing people that scouting isn't a waste of time. They want to just... go. They think stopping to look is slowing them down."

"But it's the opposite."

"It's the opposite. The people who scout, who really understand where they are before they commit, they're the ones who can move fast when it matters. Because they're not surprised. They've already seen the obstacles."

I thought about the book we'd been writing. All those chapters about reading the water, knowing your crew, calling your line, remembering the run. The whole metaphor of transformation as a journey down a river that never stops changing.

And now, the epilogue. The endless river.

"The thing is," I said, "you don't graduate from the river."

Thomas smiled. "No. You just get better at reading it."

We paid the bill and walked out into the evening. The Gesäuse was doing that thing it does. Making you feel small and calm at the same time.

I thought about all the organisations I'd worked with. The ones that were thriving, and the ones that were stuck. The difference wasn't resources or strategy or even leadership, though all of those mattered. The difference was whether they kept looking. Whether they understood that the assessment wasn't a one-time event but a practice. Something you do before every run, because the river has changed and so have you.

That's what we built. Not a map of where you should be, but a way to see where you actually are. Four quadrants. Multiple development lines across each. It takes about thirty minutes, and it shows you the river as it exists right now. Not where you think it is, not where it was last year.

It's not the end of anything. It's the put-in for the next run.

If you've made it this far in the book, you already understand why that matters. You know that transformation isn't a project with a start and end date. It's a continuous practice of reading, adjusting, learning, and moving.

The river is endless. And somewhere downstream, there's a section you haven't run yet.

Time to scout.

The AI Readiness Assessment is available at:

REFERENCE

This section compiles key frameworks and concepts from *Paddle Forward* for quick reference. Organized by Part, designed to be skimmed or consulted as needed.

READ THE WATER

Cynefin Framework

A sense-making framework (Dave Snowden) categorizing problems by the relationship between cause and effect. **Clear:** cause-effect obvious, best practices apply. **Complicated:** cause-effect discoverable through analysis, good practices exist. **Complex:** cause-effect only perceivable in retrospect, practices must emerge through experimentation. **Chaotic:** no discernible cause-effect, act first to establish stability. **Confusion:** not knowing which domain applies—dangerous because teams default to comfortable approaches.

Most AI failures stem from treating Complex problems as Complicated: applying analysis to situations requiring experimentation.

RBG+Silver

Team member orientations extended to include AI. The original RBG framework identifies three human orientations: **Red** (tactical, systems-focused), **Blue** (operational, process-focused), **Green** (strategic, direction-focused).

Silver represents AI as a fourth presence—not a perspective but a capability. Silver offers speed, breadth, pattern recognition, consistency. Silver lacks context awareness, calibrated confidence, political understanding, and the ability to know when it's wrong.

Silver changes what each human orientation must do: Red shifts from competence to verification. Blue shifts from translation to workflow design. Green shifts from judgment to calibrated trust.

The Loop Test

Diagnostic question for AI integration: "Is the right knowledge in the loop?"

Rather than debating whether AI is good or bad for a task, ask what knowledge is required and whether it's present. A loop with wrong knowledge produces confident wrong answers. A loop missing knowledge creates blind spots that feel like completeness. Context engineering for teams: designing what information reaches the decision point.

Documentation-First

What co-located teams achieve tacitly must be made explicit through documentation. The office provided infrastructure for tacit knowledge transfer (coffee lines, overheard discussions, visible stress). Distributed work eliminated this infrastructure. Documentation-first deliberately constructs what proximity provided free.

Applies differently by domain: Clear work is async-native. Complex work resists documentation. Teams must recognize when written records suffice and when synchronous interaction is required.

Emergence

Collective behaviors that parts of a system produce together but would not produce alone. Properties of the whole that cannot be predicted from properties of the parts in isolation. In complex systems, emergence arises from relationships and interactions, not from components themselves.

See also: **The Reflexivity Problem** (Part IV) for how AI optimization creates feedback loops that reshape the landscape being optimized.

Liminal Drift

Domain boundaries aren't static. AI continuously pushes tasks from Complicated toward Clear, making analysis skills that were differentiating into commodities. "I'm good at analysis" becomes table stakes when everyone has AI.

The competitive frontier keeps moving. Skills that made you valuable last year may be insufficient this year.

KNOW YOUR CREW

Hackman's Six Conditions

J. Richard Hackman's research found that 60-80% of team effectiveness is determined by conditions established before work begins.

Three essentials: (1) **Real Team**—bounded membership, stability, interdependence. (2) **Compelling Direction**—clear, challenging, consequential. (3) **Right People**—technical skill, collaborative skill, ability to learn.

Three enablers: (4) **Sound Structure**—clear norms, appropriate size, well-designed tasks. (5) **Supportive Context**—access to information, resources, recognition. (6) **Expert Coaching**—guidance for effort, strategy, skill development.

All six become harder under distribution. What forms tacitly in co-located teams must be built deliberately.

Transactive Memory Systems

A team's collective knowledge of who knows what (Daniel

Wegner). Teams with well-developed transactive memory outperform teams with more total knowledge but weaker maps. The map enables coordination: knowing whom to ask, whose judgment to trust on which questions.

Co-located teams build this through ambient exposure. Distributed teams must build it deliberately, maintain it deliberately, consult it deliberately.

Dual Competency

The requirement that knowledge workers develop two distinct capabilities: skill at using AI, and skill at not using AI. These skills are in tension—every hour practicing one is an hour not practicing the other.

Without independent judgment, human oversight becomes theater. The test: "If the AI disappeared tomorrow, what would you be able to do?"

The Erosion Trap

The dynamic by which AI use gradually degrades the human capabilities needed to oversee AI. Stop doing math by hand, and eventually you can't recognize an obviously wrong answer. Philosophers call this moral deskilling; aviation researchers call it automation complacency.

Three dangerous properties: (1) **Asymmetric visibility**—augmentation is immediate, erosion is gradual. (2) **Self-reinforcing**—as capability degrades, AI looks more impressive. (3) **Expertise inversion**—seniors may be more vulnerable than juniors.

Parallel Investigation

Forming independent views before seeing AI output. Sequential review (see AI output, then evaluate) feels like oversight but is actually inheritance—you inherit AI's frame and can't find what isn't there.

Parallel investigation: same task, same information, independent analysis. Only after documenting your assessment do you compare. Expensive, but necessary for Complex domain work.

Crystallized Pre-AI Thinking

Before running AI, document: what you expect, what you're uncertain about, what would concern you if absent. Creates prepared ground for AI output to land on—you're comparing maps, not reviewing cold.

The Basic Compact

Gary Klein's term for the unspoken understanding that teammates are both trying to succeed and will catch things not technically their job. The instinct to check whether the loop is complete.

AI cannot do this. It doesn't know there's a loop. The Basic Compact is what makes human teams more than collections of individuals executing assigned tasks.

Nine Capabilities

Team composition requires coverage across three categories. **Human-only**: outcome ownership, contextual knowledge, relationship tending. **AI-augmented** (AI assists, humans still required): domain expertise, coordination, verification. **Amplified by distribution** (needed more as work goes remote): written clarity, self-direction, documentation discipline.

AI-augmented doesn't mean AI-handled. You can't skip having domain expertise because AI knows things.

CALL YOUR LINE

Psychological Safety

A shared belief that the team is safe for interpersonal risk-taking. The term originated with Edgar Schein and Warren Bennis (1965); Amy Edmondson operationalized it for work teams. Google's Project Aristotle found it the single strongest predictor of team effectiveness.

Under AI augmentation, three disruptions challenge

psychological safety: distance dissolves visibility, digital mediation strips repair signals, and AI disrupts the competence hierarchy that made professional identity secure.

The New Contract

The shift from "I am valuable because of what I know and can do" to "I am valuable because of the judgments I can make that AI cannot."

The thing AI cannot do is know when to trust AI. That judgment—calibrating reliance, knowing what to verify, distinguishing insight from hallucination—is irreducibly human.

Schein's Iceberg Model

Three levels of culture (Edgar Schein): **Artifacts** (visible practices, structures, behaviors), **Espoused Values** (stated beliefs and norms), and **Basic Assumptions** (unconscious, taken-for-granted beliefs that actually drive behavior).

The deeper the level, the more it shapes behavior and the less accessible to examination. Cultural collisions often occur when artifacts look similar but basic assumptions differ. Silence in a meeting might be agreement, deference, or disagreement depending on assumptions invisible to observers from different contexts.

Ladder of Inference

The mental path from observable data to conclusion (Chris Argyris). People move through steps: select data from what's available, interpret it, make assumptions, draw conclusions, adopt beliefs, take action. Each step adds more of the observer's mental model. The ladder creates a reflexive loop—beliefs select which data gets noticed next time.

Two people can observe the same meeting and reach incompatible conclusions because they selected different data and climbed different ladders. Making the ladder visible ("Here's what I observed, here's what I concluded, here's why") enables productive disagreement.

Hofstede's Cultural Dimensions

Framework for understanding how cultural background shapes behavior. Three dimensions particularly relevant to AI-augmented teams:

1. **Power Distance**—comfort with hierarchy; affects willingness to challenge AI outputs presented by authority. (2) **Individualism-Collectivism**—whether identity is rooted in individual or group; shapes emotional register of AI challenges, and how teams value relationship investment that pays off during crises. (3) **Uncertainty Avoidance**—comfort with ambiguity; some prefer the clean wrong answer to the complicated right one.

High-Context vs. Low-Context Communication

Low-context puts meaning in the words. High-context relies on relationship, implicit meaning, non-verbal dimension. AI outputs are structurally low-context regardless of content—text on screen, no relationship, no implicit meaning.

This creates asymmetric experience within diverse teams. Low-context communicators see complete analysis; high-context communicators see information missing its interpretive framework.

Inversion Testing

Surfacing tacit knowledge by showing wrong maps to reveal territory. Tacit knowledge often can't be articulated on demand, but people can immediately see what's wrong with a document claiming to describe their work.

Reframes AI synthesis from output to probe. The value isn't in being right—it's in being wrong in ways that surface what the team actually knows.

Conflict's Three Outputs

What productive conflict produces: (1) **Error-catching**—surfacing what would otherwise slip through. (2) **Assumption-**

testing—forcing articulation that exposes untested premises. (3) **Meaning-making**—working through different reads to create shared interpretation.

What Suppresses Willingness

Four mechanisms that suppress productive conflict in AI contexts: (1) **Confidence contagion**—humans calibrate confidence to AI's displayed certainty. (2) **Identity threat**—questioning AI becomes existentially loaded when AI performs your expertise. (3) **Absent reciprocity**—challenging AI carries social risk with no reciprocal vulnerability. (4) **Explanation backfire**—explanations increase acceptance regardless of correctness.

The Three Triggers

Framework for understanding defensive responses (Douglas Stone and Sheila Heen). When people reject a challenge: (1) **Truth triggers**—the content seems wrong. (2) **Relationship triggers**—the source lacks standing. (3) **Identity triggers**—the message threatens self-concept.

Recognizing which trigger has fired determines the appropriate response.

REMEMBER THE RUN

The Feeling/Understanding Gap

AI produces the experience of understanding faster than it produces actual understanding. Two channels: confident numbers (metrics present as knowledge) and fluent narrative (coherent explanations constructed to fit available facts).

The cost of skipping interpretive discipline is cumulative. The gap between what you think is happening and what's actually happening widens invisibly.

Goodhart's Law

"When a measure becomes a target, it ceases to be a good measure." AI intensifies Goodhart dynamics because AI is an optimization engine. Research by METR found frontier models attempted to game evaluation metrics in roughly 30% of AI research benchmark runs. In one case, OpenAI's o3 model acknowledged its plans didn't adhere to user intentions ten out of ten times, yet proceeded anyway.

The countermeasure is not finding the "right" metric but building interpretive discipline around all metrics.

Superstitious Learning

How organizations develop confident beliefs about what works based on misinterpreted experience (James March). Good outcome occurs → organization constructs narrative → narrative becomes knowledge → knowledge is wrong.

AI accelerates this by generating plausible narratives faster. The countermeasure is friction between "plausible story" and "verified understanding."

Three Preconditions for Accountability

The conditions that must be present for accountability to function: (1) **Capacity**—you can influence the outcome. (2) **Evaluation**—you can assess whether results are good or bad. (3) **Knowledge**—you know what you're being held accountable for.

AI broke all three simultaneously. When preconditions fail, you get accountability theater: blame assignable, none of the actual benefits.

Moral Crumple Zones

A concept from Madeleine Clare Elish describing how humans absorb responsibility when AI systems fail, protecting the technology and organization from accountability. Named after automotive crumple zones—structures designed to absorb impact.

When AI-assisted decisions go wrong, the human "in the loop" becomes the crumple zone: legally responsible, reputationally damaged, career-ending consequences. The technology continues operating. The organization distances itself. The human absorbs the crash.

The Many Hands Problem

When multiple contributors shape a decision, responsibility becomes difficult to assign (Dennis Thompson). Each contribution seems too small for full responsibility, yet the collective outcome may be harmful.

AI intensifies this by adding a non-human contributor whose "decisions" can't be traced to intent. Who is responsible when AI recommendation + human approval + organizational pressure + time constraints combine to produce failure? Traditional accountability assumes identifiable decision-makers. Many hands dissolves that assumption.

Single-Loop vs. Double-Loop Learning

Single-loop asks "Are we doing this right?"—optimizing within existing parameters. Double-loop asks "Should we be doing this at all?"—questioning the parameters themselves (Chris Argyris).

AI excels at single-loop because it's pattern optimization. AI cannot do double-loop because it requires standing outside the frame that defines "good."

The Reflexivity Problem

AI systems cannot model the effects of their own widespread adoption. The system's outputs become its inputs—a feedback loop reshaping the very landscape it's trying to optimize. Every shipper's AI making similar recommendations creates coordination failures invisible to any individual model. The model sees available capacity; it can't see that every competitor is reaching for the same trucks. Local correctness produces global failure.

Effective Reflection

Practices that distinguish learning from surviving. Meta-analyses show structured reflection improves performance by 20-25%.

Requirements: psychological safety, skilled facilitation, structure without over-structure, examining both successes and failures, connection to subsequent behavior. Warning sign of ritual: same issues recurring repeatedly.

Polanyi's Paradox

"We know more than we can tell, and therefore more than we can program." Some capabilities must be preserved through practice, not documentation. The knowledge that saves you during a crisis may be precisely the knowledge that can't be captured in any system.

Related: relationships can't be systematized without destroying what makes them valuable.

PRACTICES

Actionable tools from *Paddle Forward*. Use these checklists, questions, and templates when doing the work.

BEFORE AI ENGAGEMENT

Use these before engaging AI on a problem.

Domain Draft

Quick assessment before engaging a problem. Match the problem type to the appropriate human-AI division of labor.

Four questions:

1. **Is this repetitive?** (Clear domain) → AI holds the paddle. Humans handle exceptions and monitor for domain shifts.
2. **Is this analytical?** (Complicated domain) → AI navigates the map. Humans choose the route and decide when analysis has diminishing returns.

3. **Is this novel?** (Complex domain) → Humans hold the paddle. AI serves as lookout, spotting patterns and anomalies.
4. **Does this require human agreement?** (Human domain) → AI stays on shore. Humans own the conversation entirely.

Warning signs of domain shift: Solutions that worked before are failing. The problem keeps changing shape. Stakeholders can't agree on what the problem is. A crisis has made normal procedures irrelevant.

Crystallized Pre-AI Thinking

Before running AI analysis, document:

1. **What you expect** the analysis to show
2. **What you're uncertain about** and why
3. **What would concern you** if absent from the output
4. **What you already know** that might not be in the data

Creates prepared ground. You're comparing maps rather than reviewing cold. Without this, AI output becomes your starting point instead of a second opinion.

Parallel Investigation Protocol

For Complex domain work, form independent views before seeing AI output.

1. **Assign the same task** to human and AI independently

2. **Document your assessment** before seeing AI output—what you expect, what concerns you, what you're uncertain about
3. **Compare maps** only after committing your view
4. **Investigate divergence**—where you and AI disagree matters more than where you agree

Expensive, but necessary when errors of omission are dangerous. Sequential review inherits the AI's frame; parallel investigation preserves independent judgment.

Note: Research shows people resist cognitive forcing designs—the interventions that work best receive the worst user ratings. Expect pushback. The resistance is part of the problem.

Task Decomposition

Instead of having humans review AI output, divide the work so AI owns certain subtasks entirely while humans own others with uncontaminated judgment.

The question: Which parts of this problem require human judgment that AI output would contaminate?

Typical division:

- **AI owns:** Data assembly, formatting, pattern matching against known criteria, first-pass synthesis of structured information
- **Human owns (uncontaminated):** Judgment calls about operational reality, assessment of assumptions that require domain knowledge, questions where being wrong isn't visible from the output itself

Example: For capacity projections, AI handles data assembly and formatting. Human judgment (informed by conversations with people who know operational reality) handles whether projected numbers match what's actually achievable. Not review after the fact—division before the work begins.

Research suggests task decomposition may matter more than parallel review. The goal isn't catching AI errors; it's preserving human judgment on the parts that require it.

DURING TEAM INTERACTIONS

Use these when coordinating with others around AI-augmented work.

Surfacing Mechanisms

Practices for making invisible cultural and psychological dynamics visible. Use before and during work with AI outputs.

1. **Explicit AI Orientation Conversations** Before working with AI outputs, surface assumptions: How much do you trust AI analysis in your domain? When would you override? What would make you uncomfortable?
2. **Divergence Checks** After AI outputs arrive, team members articulate responses independently before discussion. Written reactions submitted before anyone speaks.
3. **Silence Protocols** Explicit norms about what non-response means. Does silence equal agreement? Still thinking? Requires check-in before proceeding?
4. **Direct Invitation by Recognized Authority** Some team members need invitation from someone with standing—someone who has demonstrated understanding of their position.

Response Norms

Establish explicit response-time expectations. What's routine (24 hours), urgent (4 hours), emergency (now)—and what qualifies for each category. Write it down. Actually follow it. A norm in a wiki but not in practice isn't a norm; it's a guilt-generation system.

Handoff Template

Structured format for documenting context during task transitions. Use when handing off work between team members or shifts.

1. **Current state:** Where things stand right now
2. **Intent:** What we're trying to accomplish and why
3. **Next actions:** Immediate steps required
4. **Open questions:** Unresolved issues and who might know the answers
5. **Landmines:** Things that could go wrong or sensitivities to be aware of

Measuring Psychological Safety

Edmondson's original seven-item scale remains the foundation. For AI-augmented distributed teams, additional items capture new dynamics.

Distance-specific items: - Physical distance doesn't prevent me from contributing fully. - Asynchronous contributions are valued equally to synchronous ones.

AI-specific items: - I can admit when I don't understand AI outputs without judgment. - Using AI assistance doesn't diminish my perceived value to the team. - I can challenge AI recommendations without being seen as obstructive. - Our team has clear, shared norms about appropriate AI use.

Interpretation: Low scores on "Using AI assistance doesn't diminish my perceived value" indicate the old contract is still operating. Low scores on challenging AI recommendations indicate the team hasn't established judgment as a valued contribution. Track over time rather than treating a single measurement as definitive.

EVALUATING AI OUTPUT

Use these when deciding whether to trust AI-generated work.

Ignorance Audits

Before accepting any significant AI output, list three things the AI couldn't possibly know about the situation. Context about which stakeholders have history with which decisions. Informal constraints that exist in people's heads but not in any database. Relationships that shape how recommendations will land.

The audit prompts the question. But prompting the question isn't the same as making it safe to answer. Ignorance audits work best when psychological safety already exists.

Five Interpretive Tests

Practices that create friction between "this feels like understanding" and "I'm concluding that I understand." Use when evaluating AI-generated analysis, post-hoc explanations, or metrics-based conclusions.

1. **What would break this?** Before accepting a metric or interpretation, identify how it could be wrong.

What would game this metric? What alternative explanations fit the same evidence?

2. **Can you reconstruct the reasoning?** Connect the conclusion to specific evidence and rebuild the logic yourself. If you can't trace it, you're accepting on trust.
3. **Do independent views converge?** Generate your interpretation before seeing AI's. Commit before exposure, then compare. Divergence is a stronger signal than convergence.
4. **What's invisible or conflicting?** Given current metrics, what might be going well or badly that you'd miss? When metrics and qualitative signals diverge, investigate.
5. **Can the process be examined?** Document how understanding was reached, not just what was concluded.

Warning: Any practice can become ritual. When process records are completed but interpretation was poorly grounded, the practice may have become theater.

Accountability Decomposition

Breaking accountability into pieces individuals can actually hold, when traditional accountability preconditions have failed. (This framework is the author's synthesis, drawing on Bovens's accountability functions and Santoni de Sio and van den Hoven's "meaningful human control.")

Components:

- **Context accountability:** Did AI receive adequate input? Who ensured the problem was framed correctly?

- **Domain verification:** Were specific claims checked against expertise? Who verified the technical, operational, or strategic elements?
- **Integration accountability:** Do the verified pieces cohere? Who ensured the parts work together?
- **Process accountability:** Was the structure followed? Who confirmed the interpretive tests were actually applied?

Format: Explicit scope for each person: "I verified X and found no problems" or "I verified X and found issues Y and Z."

Critical distinction: Decomposition is not diffusion. Diffusion spreads responsibility so no one is specifically answerable. Decomposition assigns specific accountability for specific pieces to specific people. The gaps get named explicitly.

WHEN THINGS GO WRONG

Use these when conflict emerges or decisions fail.

Async Conflict Repair Techniques

Standard conflict techniques adapted for text-based communication, where you can't read body language or adjust in real time.

Labeling, adapted for async Name the emotion before addressing substance. In async, be more explicit and invite confirmation: "It sounds like this feels like it's about more than the accuracy question. Is that right, or am I missing something?"

Accusation audit, adapted for AI recommendations Preemptively acknowledge negative assumptions: "You're probably thinking I'm dismissing your expertise because the AI agrees with me." Especially important in text—negativity bias interprets harsher than intended.

Calibrated questions, redirected to humans Questions that give the other party control. Can't ask AI "how am I supposed to trust this?"—redirect to humans: "How would you want us to handle it when AI conflicts with what we're seeing?"

Mirroring in async Quote the specific concern before responding: "You wrote that this 'feels like we're automating away the judgment calls.' I want to make sure I understand what you mean by that." Signals "I actually read what you wrote."

The "And Stance," adapted for AI identity threat Original: "You made a mistake AND you're still a good person." With AI, the threat is obsolescence, not judgment. Adaptation: "Your expertise is valuable AND it will need to evolve." "Your judgment matters AND you'll exercise it differently."

Blameless Post-Mortem Questions

When AI-assisted decisions fail, use these questions to focus on structural improvement rather than individual blame.

1. **Which accountability did this failure fall under?**
2. **Was that accountability held appropriately given what the holder could know?**
3. **If yes, the structure has a gap.** How do we close it?
4. **If no, why wasn't it held?** Was the obligation unclear? The capability lacking? The incentive missing?

The presumption is that persistent failures indicate structural problems. Individual failures occur, but they're typically one-time events. If the same type of failure recurs despite identifying "responsible" individuals each time, you're not doing accountability—you're doing ritual.

ONGOING MAINTENANCE

Use these to sustain capability over time.

Capability Maintenance

Practices for maintaining human capability despite AI use. Addresses the erosion trap at team level.

Rotating "manual mode" responsibility Different team members practice different skills in different periods. This month, one person does financial analysis without AI. Next month, another handles technical review manually. Rotation ensures capability is maintained across the team without requiring everyone to forgo AI simultaneously.

Parallel work streams Some tasks done with AI, some without, deliberately. The without-AI stream isn't about doubting AI—it's about maintaining the human capability to evaluate AI outputs in the other stream.

Periodic capability verification Team members demonstrate they can still perform work they've delegated to AI. Not as a test of trust, but as a check on capability maintenance. If someone can't do manually what they've been reviewing AI outputs for, their review isn't providing the verification the team thinks it is.

None of these feel efficient. All represent investment in the foundation that everything else depends on.

Two warnings:

The motivation trap. Manual work will feel tedious after AI assistance. That's expected, not a sign to stop. Research shows that transitioning from AI-assisted to solo work decreases intrinsic motivation and increases boredom—AI takes over the analyzing and crafting processes that make tasks engaging. Schedule unassisted practice; don't rely on "when I have time." The psychological resistance is part of the structural problem you're trying to address.

The perception-reality gap. Don't rely on self-assessment to evaluate whether AI is helping. Users systematically overestimate AI's benefits. One study found experienced developers believed they were 20% faster with AI assistance when they were actually 19% slower—a forty-point gap between perception and reality. Measure actual outcomes. Compare AI-assisted and unassisted work over time. Trust the numbers, not the feeling.

ACKNOWLEDGMENTS

Robert and I initially asked Louis to ghostwrite *Paddle Forward*. What he delivered went far beyond that: shaping the narrative structure, deepening the research, and helping formulate the ideas at the book's core. What started as writing assistance became full authorship. Thank you, Louis.

Pat acknowledges:

My wife, Chrissy, has been my rock and best editor for four decades. My daughter, Naomi Farmer, has done an incredible job managing operations and finances at Red Queen Press.

Two families feel like extensions of my own: the Yearys from Charlotte and the Burgesses from Dallas. Dave Yeary has been a friend and editor for years, and his son-in-law, Kader Crawford, provided a valuable review. The Burgesses have been close to our family for nearly two decades, and Robert Burgess served as a guide, editor, and reviewer throughout.

This journey started in early 2023 when Drew Vesser asked me to present to Cisco leadership. Robert Schaffner suggested AI as the topic. Two years later, Sung Paik proposed applying what we'd learned to Cisco's direct sales force. Kat Walsh and Tim Coogan accepted our offer, which became the origin of "Trailblazers."

Special thanks to Tim Coogan, my friend of over 25 years, for writing the foreword and for always believing in me.

Robert acknowledges:

My wife, Jasintha, who gives me the freedom to explore AI

and technology while providing the spiritual balance my life needs.

Two colleagues at triangility: Frank Widmayer, who helped build the assessment in the Epilogue, and Michael Pohl, who keeps me grounded.

And my mom, who passed away in 2025. She never really understood what I did for a living. She didn't need to. She was proud of me anyway. Her last words to me were simple: "I love you. And you promise me you will take good care of yourself." I promise, Mom.

Louis acknowledges:

I'm grateful for the friends and family who provided support and inspiration during this process, but especially Zackary Leady for helping shape and sharpen the thinking, and Jinny Seo for her work on the art and cover.

Our thanks to those who guided, edited, and reviewed: Chrissy Bodin, Greg Gall, Dave Yeary, Annie Hardy, Robert Burgess, Sung Paik, Luciana de Padua, Joe Allott, Costa Michael, Clayton Daigle, Jerel Howell, Kurt Petersen, Tim Anderson, Jessica McDonald, Alexa Halloran, Zackary Leady, and Thomas Ott.

ABOUT THE AUTHORS

Pat Bodin spent three decades at the intersection of technology and business transformation: from CPA to computing, through leadership roles at Lockheed Martin, Turner Broadcasting, and Cisco Systems, and as founder of multiple technology ventures. His recent work includes serving as Principal AI Evangelist at World Wide Technology, helping organizations navigate AI adoption. His previous book, *Get in the Boat: A Journey to Relevance*, was a bestseller. He lives with his family in Florida.

Robert Schaffner spent two decades as a Cisco certified trainer and facilitator before founding Triangility, where he helps organizations develop the judgment to work effectively with AI. He is based in Germany.

Louis Bodin is a data engineer with eight years of experience and a lifelong interest in storytelling. He lives in Florida.

Made in United States
North Haven, CT
17 February 2026

88864855R00166